Samuel Colcord Bartlett. Courtesy of Dartmouth College Library.

NEW YORK UNIVERSITY SERIES IN
EDUCATION AND SOCIALIZATION IN AMERICAN HISTORY

General Editor: Paul H. Mattingly

THE CLASSLESS PROFESSION
American Schoolmen in the Nineteenth Century
Paul H. Mattingly

THE REVOLUTIONARY COLLEGE
American Presbyterian Higher Education, 1707–1837
Howard Miller

COLLEGIATE WOMEN
Domesticity and Career in Turn-of-the-Century America
Roberta Frankfort

SCHOOLED LAWYERS
A Study in the Clash of Professional Cultures
William R. Johnson

THE ORGANIZATION OF AMERICAN CULTURE, 1700–1900
Private Institutions, Elites, and the Origins of American Nationality
Peter Dobkin Hall

AMERICAN COLLEGIATE POPULATIONS
A Test of the Traditional View
Colin B. Burke

OLD DARTMOUTH ON TRIAL
The Transformation of the Academic Community in
Nineteenth-Century America
Marilyn Tobias

OLD DARTMOUTH ON TRIAL:
The Transformation of the Academic Community in Nineteenth-Century America

Marilyn Tobias

New York *and* London   NEW YORK UNIVERSITY PRESS   1982

Library of Congress Cataloging in Publication Data

Tobias, Marilyn, 1942–
Old Dartmouth on trial.

(New York University series in education and social-
ization in American history)
Revision of thesis (Ph.D.)—New York University.
Bibliography: p.
Includes index.
1. Dartmouth College. I. Title. II. Series
LD1438.T6 1982   378.742′3   81-18779
ISBN 0-8147-8168-3   AACR2

Manufactured in the United States of America

To My Mother and Father

Contents

Contents

Contents

ACKNOWLEDGMENTS

I am indebted to a number of persons who have assisted me in various ways in the course of this study. My greatest debt is to my parents. I am happy to have this opportunity to acknowledge publicly their constant encouragement and aid. The book is gratefully dedicated to them. I owe a special debt to Paul H. Mattingly, Professor of History, New York University. Providing significant guidance from the very initial stage of this study, he has been a mentor in the very best sense of that word. His illuminating perspectives on the history of education have influenced my way of thinking about history. I also owe special thanks to Thomas Bender, Samuel Rudin Professor of the Humanities, New York University. His valuable suggestions have helped to clarify my thinking about urban and cultural history and its relationships to the history of education. I am also grateful to Floyd M. Hammack, Associate Professor of Educational Sociology, New York University, who offered important counsel during an earlier version of this study as a Ph.D. dissertation. I appreciate the suggestions of Wilson Smith, Professor of History, University of California, Davis, especially his questions regarding the changing notion of academic community. I also want to thank the Departments of Higher Education, Historical and Philosophical Foundations (now Cultural Foundations), and the History Department (Graduate Arts and Sciences) for their cooperation which enabled me to pursue the history of higher education as my area of specialization.

I also appreciate the interest and cooperation of several persons associated with Dartmouth College. I particularly want to thank Alan V. Davies, member of the board, Dartmouth Club of New York; the Dartmouth Alumni Association, particularly Herbert Swarzman and the Dartmouth Alumni Association of New York City, who appointed me Honorary Research Associate when I was a Ph.D. candidate; Robert J. Finney Jr., Director of Development, Dartmouth College; Professor Emeritus Donald Bartlett; Dennis A. Dinan, Editor of the *Dartmouth Alumni Magazine*; Frederick L. Hier, Director of Dartmouth Horizons program; Professors Marilyn Baldwin, Gregory Prince, and Jere R. Daniell II; John G. Kemeny and John Sloan Dickey, former presidents of Dartmouth College; and Edward C. Latham, Dean of Libraries.

I am especially grateful to Kenneth C. Cramer, Dartmouth College Archivist, for his cooperation, assistance, and prompt response to all my inquiries for research material. I also appreciate the assistance of the staff of several libraries, particularly the Dartmouth College Library, the New York Public Library, the Library of Congress, the Martin Luther King Library of the District of Columbia, and the New York University Libraries. I am grateful to Emma Walsh for her indispensable help in typing the tables for the final draft of the manuscript.

I would like to thank the Dartmouth College Library for granting me permission to use the photographs, manuscripts, and other Dartmouth College material quoted in the text.

CHAPTER I

Introduction

The trial is felt by all the counsel engaged to be of note and great importance, not so much for its purity in a legal aspect as for its peculiar and unprecedented character and the nature of the interests involved.

New York Times (1881)

In 1881 on complaint of the college community, the Reverend Samuel Colcord Bartlett, president of Dartmouth College, was brought to trial to justify his administration. Bartlett found himself on trial for his official theories, policies, and methods in administering the college. The trial, involving alumni, faculty, students, and trustees, elicited much public controversy. More than twenty newspapers and journals, many far from Hanover, New Hampshire, covered the conflict (from its pretrial stages to the aftermath in 1882) and advanced arguments for and against Bartlett.

The Dartmouth College alumni played a crucial role in the Bartlett controversy. The New York Association of Alumni initiated the investigation with its memorial requesting the trustees to investigate the "disquieting rumors" concerning the Bartlett administration.[1] The alumni forged alliances with groups within the college community, waged their campaign in the metropolitan press, and drew up the charges against Bartlett.[2] The New York association and their lawyers acted as the prosecution in the trial and continued to urge Bartlett's resignation or removal after the formal proceedings.

The faculty supplied much of the ammunition against Bartlett and submitted petitions damaging to his administration. Sixteen of twenty-three resident members of the faculty (the treasurer included) of the

Academical Department, the Chandler Scientific Department, the New Hampshire College of Agriculture and the Mechanic Arts, and the Medical College sent a memorial to the trustees requesting that the president resign. They served as the prime witnesses at the trial, and during the trial the faculty submitted a second memorial.

Students provided support for the anti-Bartlett movement through their petition, testimony, and open attitude of disfavor toward Bartlett (picked up and capitalized upon by the alumni and press opposing Bartlett). After commencement forty-four of sixty-one graduating seniors (academical and Chandler) submitted a document asking for the president's resignation. A few students were also called upon to testify for the prosecution.

The trustees in conducting this quasi-judicial hearing (recorded by a court stenographer) gave the alumni and faculty the opportunity to present their charges and evidence in a public trial of the college community. Two of the trustees were called upon by the prosecution to testify in reference to one of the charges, and four out of ten trustees registered an official vote of no confidence against Bartlett nine months after the formal trial. Despite all the controversy, Bartlett lingered on as president until his resignation in 1892.

Bartlett came under fire from his own people barely four years after taking office. He became president of Dartmouth in 1877, at the age of fifty-nine. A Congregational minister and professor, Bartlett had some experience in fundraising (although he indicated that he did not want to be involved in fundraising). While he did not have the urbane style of later presidents or the friendly relations with wealthy congregations in leading areas such as New York, he had contacts in northern New England, in the Middle West, and with some of the Congregational clergy. Bartlett embraced the ideals of pastoral care and the instruction of the moral conscience, and he saw the development of moral character as the prime aim of education. He conceived of the college as a closely knit paternal Christian organization with himself as pastoral head and interpreter of life and policy. The moral authority of the president was at the heart of this view. Bartlett's policies, styles, and view of the presidency were in keeping with nineteenth-century traditions, but the realities had changed on Bartlett, outstripping his conception of the college and the president's role.

Pointing to the significance of the Bartlett case, the *New York Times* of 1881 noted that the importance of the trial lay in "its peculiar and unprecedented character and the nature of the interests involved."[3] The trial represents one of the earliest instances in which a college president was brought to public account for his *educational* practice. The Bartlett controversy highlighted a significant historical change in which the basic conception of the college was transformed. The positions taken by the faculty, students, alumni, and trustees in this conflict reflected the changing perceptions of themselves and of the college held by these groups. The trial, therefore, provides a key insight into the changing character of higher learning in nineteenth-century America, while illustrating the interrelationships between the college and the larger society.

This study, then, is not a descriptive narrative of the official events of the Bartlett trial. It is, instead, an interpretive analysis of an event of historical significance—the Bartlett trial—which highlighted the transformation taking place in the conception of community, of the college, and of higher learning. Thus, for the purposes of this study, the Bartlett trial assumes the form of a vehicle from which one can view these changes. The trial illuminated such aspects of the transformation as the changing nature and interests of faculty, students, alumni, trustees, and the presidency; of collegiate service; of the organization and governance of higher education; and of the relation between the college and the larger society. The positions and behavior of the various groups in the Bartlett controversy dramatized the changing nature of the academic community and collegiate culture and reflected their transformed roles and identities. Bartlett's styles and policies, more in keeping with an older notion of the presidency and the college, came into conflict with the interests and aspirations of these various groups. His lingering on illustrated the peculiar state of the presidency during his administration when an older collegiate ideal and communal sense retained a pressure of power as a new value system impinged upon the older pattern of relationships. The controversy set the stage for a new type of liberal arts college in the so-called "age of the university."

In its broader context, the nature and implications of the transformation brought out in this case study have significant bearing upon the general transformation of the academic community and collegiate culture in nineteenth-century America. In order to frame the study and extend the base of generalization, I have used the slim literature available on the history of nineteenth-century colleges to suggest, when possible (either in the text or the notes), where the experience at Dartmouth corresponded to, and differed from, comparable nineteenth-century institutions. Although more detailed case studies are needed to test my findings, the pattern of institutional change discovered in this analysis seems representative of comparable institutions of higher education. In an important sense one may regard Dartmouth, not only as a single institution, but as a strategic moment when collegiate authority is questioned. Through the details of the Bartlett case, one can see the patterns and problems that will recur throughout all institutions of higher education that claim to be modern. The Bartlett controversy dramatizes the conflict and confusion over the various directions taken by colleges and universities in this period and highlights the competing modes of institutional change. It illuminates changing patterns of academic community and collegiate culture that go beyond Dartmouth (and continue to cast their shadows on twentieth-century higher education) and telescopes important cultural, demographic, structural, and social changes in the larger society. Its significance, thus, transcends Dartmouth, and Dartmouth becomes a problem in educational and cultural history.[4]

In order to put this study in its proper context, an explanation of its methodology, framework, perspective, and relation to past studies of nineteenth-century higher education should precede the more detailed description of the nature of the historical changes revealed in the Bartlett controversy. The traditional historiography of nineteenth-century American higher education suffers from several flaws.[5] Frequently it offers merely a descriptive chronicle of official actions, usually from the perspective of the college president. These studies suffer from a paucity of analysis. Their analysis is usually gratuitous as the process of change is neglected, and the relationship between the college and the larger community is ignored. When they consider these relationships, the college is portrayed either as isolated from the rest of society or as slavishly responding to society's needs.[6] Moreover, our knowledge and understanding of higher learning in nineteenth-century America have too frequently been the result of those who write from the perspective of the ascendancy of the university. These retrospective studies view change as inevitable, assume a uniform intellectual and social matrix, and see university "reformers" as the sole agents of change. Within the darkness-to-light framework of this historical type, nineteenth-century colleges have been used as foils to dramatize the directions of the new universities or have been dismissed as subjects for serious inquiry.

Standard accounts have provided limited insight into the nature of corporate life and collegiate culture and the idea of higher learning in the antebellum college or the significant changes the colleges were undergoing in the process of adopting an alternative collegiate route in the late nineteenth century. The traditional portrayal of American higher learning in nineteenth-century America runs something like this: The colleges of the antebellum period, petty undemocratic communities, of little consequence intellectually and of little utility, gave way in the post–Civil War period to the "age of the university." Through the academic reformers and the university movement, a revolution occurred, and higher education became truly significant. All institutions "inevitably" responded to these forces reflective of society's needs and even those institutions that did not become universities "had" to adjust to the "inevitable" or fade into obscurity.[7]

Such linear, unidimensional studies do not add to our understanding of the transformation that was taking place in an evolving concept of higher learning because they leave no room for historical context or flux, assume an inevitability between society's needs and the colleges' response, and ignore the role of groups other than university reformers in the change process. The past is considered as "simply the present writ small."[8] History is seen as moving in a straight line,[9] with change characterized simply as movement from reactionary to progressive, from traditional to modern, from sectarian to secular, from rural to urban, from amateur to professional, from community to society. The complexity of historical change remains hidden under such an interpretive framework, as does the possibility that the past may have represented a genuine alternative as opposed to a prelude to what came after—mutations rather than stages in a long evolutionary process. Such an evolutionary schema ignores the possibility that change may not have been unidirectional or a one-way process—that communal and non-communal ways may have existed side by side, that secularism may have reinforced certain new types of religious enthusiasm, or that colleges may have influenced universities (which were themselves in an experimental stage throughout much of the nineteenth and early twentieth centuries), for example. Thus, these studies do not help us to understand the nature, process, or complexity of change, its stages, why and how it occurred, and what it really represented.

This analysis provides an alternative conceptual framework and interpretive model to the presentist assumptions and unidimensional models of analysis characteristic of those standard accounts of nineteenth-century collegiate change written from the perspective of the ascendancy of the university and through the selective statements of university reformers. The study begins with a mid-nineteenth-century perspective. It considers the various groups composing the college, and it treats the college as a community within a larger community or locale. The mid-nineteenth-century perception of community envisioned a closely knit college community playing an integral role in its local and "moral" community. This perception of community changed dramatically by 1881. The notion of community within the college became less affective, more fragmented, and more competitive, and its larger community was radically redefined. One can specify and assess these changes over time, in their own terms, by tracing the changing perceptions and behavior of faculty, students, alumni, and trustees and the altering interrelationships of the college community. Since the students, alumni, and trustees came from the larger community and lived their lives in its social and economic structures, this framework enables us to better assess the crosscurrents between the college and American society.

In order to develop historical standards from which to assess the nature and process of change—its speed, its essence, its significance—this study analyzes the various groups in the Bartlett controversy and the interrelationships of the college community for the preceding generation of 1851 as well as that of 1881.[10] Acknowledging that the selection of a generation is somewhat arbitrary, the traditional thirty-year period seemed particularly appropriate in this case. Between these generations American society underwent tremendous change. The Civil War; the growth of a market economy, urbanization, industrialization, and large-scale organization; improvements in transportation; changing career patterns; and the lure of metropolitan areas—as well as the publication of Charles Darwin's *Origin of Species*—brought with them significant changes in the nature of American society and in the pattern of human relationships.[11] Higher education, too, experienced great change. Dartmouth in 1881 was an institution quite different from its antebellum counterpart of a generation before. Thus, by going back a full generation, distinct patterns of roles and identities, of aspirations, values, and beliefs emerge. The distinctions in patterns between and within the generations provide standards from which to view the nature and process of change within a clear historical context, thus providing some protection from the intrusion of a modern, normative perspective.

Separate chapters explore the background and interests of faculty, students, alumni, and trustees. Who were they? What were they experiencing in their college experience and in the larger society? Each chapter points toward the same event, the Bartlett trial, as it relates to each participant group and through the different perspectives of each group. In this context, each chapter begins with a typology of demographic characteristics relevant to the particular participant group in that chapter. Although such characteristics as age, birthplace, residence, education, and associational involvements, for example, cannot fully explain the process of change or the nature of the experience of the faculty, students, alumni, or trustees, it can provide an essential scaffold for such an explanation. The patterns that emerge, when related to the elements of historical specificity—of time, place, and context—form a foundation for understanding their ideology, aspirations, writings, activities, positions, behavior, and the pattern of social relationships. The emphasis on the detailed comparison of the faculty, students, alumni, and trustees in the 1851 and 1881 periods, on the changing structural arrangements and the values underlying these arrangements, provides an antidote to generalizations about these various groups and about changes in corporate life and collegiate culture represented in standard accounts. Such a framework offers an alternative to explanations of change built upon grand strategic theory in which we attempt to fit all data.[12] In the analysis of the problem of the Bartlett case, we move, instead, from concrete changes in the perceptions and behavior of the various groups, from altering patterns of roles and identities to larger generalizations about institutionalization, communal development, and educational and cultural change.

The concluding chapter synthesizes the preceding chapters. To assess the historical changes highlighted in the Bartlett controversy and its collegiate consequences into the twentieth century, it examines these issues in relation to the aftermath of the trial, the rest of the Bartlett period, and through the administration of Bartlett's successor. The chapter highlights the nature and significance of institutional change and communal development. It illuminates the changing conception of the college, of collegiate service, and of the administration of higher education, all as part of the general transformation of higher learning in American society. The new type of president now needed to administer and shape the "new Dartmouth" reflected the transformed communal idea and symbolized the changing character of the college and the larger society as well. Bartlett's successor, the Reverend William Jewett Tucker, represented this new type.

The changing notion of community provides the context for the transformation in the conception of the college and of higher learning revealed in the Bartlett controversy. This shifting sense of community owed much to the New England reliance on "congregation," and this notion led to expectations that Wilson Smith has characterized as "the *total* life and environment of the . . . . college."[13] The idea of community is central to both periods (1851 and 1881), but by 1881 its meaning had undergone a dramatic change. The shift in the perception of community by the various groups within the college community contributed to the historical process highlighted in the Bartlett controversy.

From the mid-nineteenth-century viewpoint, the college was an integral part of the organic community—the surrounding community or region of which it was a part. This wider, geographic community included for Dartmouth the local town, Hanover, New Hampshire; the surrounding towns of rural northern New England; and in many important ways the New England region itself. This geographic setting permits one to see the intricate, concentric yet distinct communities the college and its society represented. One might even contrast the difference between Dartmouth of 1851 and 1881 by the insistence in the antebellum period of a mutual appreciation within these communal orders. The college's physical and psychological "location" within such concentric ranges of community meant that to abstract the college from this context is to take a part for the whole. Dartmouth "served" the declining towns of rural northern New England, providing opportunities for access to the professions and to the middle class for students who were forced by a declining economy to seek their fortunes outside their hometowns. The college represented a genuine alternative to town and student alike. It diffused knowledge, shared cultural facilities, and gave economic life and opportunity to the community. The community supplied the students and the financial support. For faculty, students, alumni, and trustees, the aspirations, the audience, and the status group referent were communal. Associations were informal, tangible, and personal. The sense of community included an underlying cohesion and consensual orientation with a cultural and religious unity in fashioning a Christian nation. The organic conception of community with its localized base and pattern of social relations characterized by affective ties and mutual concern remained the predominant pattern in American society up to mid-century.

The faculty, students, alumni, and trustees shared this perception of community. In 1851 one could characterize the college as a community-oriented institution. The faculty, students, alumni, and trustees came from the community, and their associational involvements were rooted in this context. The faculty members looked to the community for their audience and status, and the community looked to them as a high-status group. Members of the faculty held leadership positions in various associations in the community and, to a more limited extent, on the state and regional levels. The primarily poor and lower-middle-class students coming from the rural towns of northern New England saw themselves as integral parts of the community. Participating in its various structures from teaching in district schools in the winter to activities in political and religious organizations, they linked their values and culture to the community. The trustees—very prominent and active in the community, state, or region—were sensitive to the community as a major source of support. Their policies were expressive of this community orientation.

In line with this belief in the cohesiveness of the organic community, higher learning stressed the unity of knowledge as well as a joining of intellect and faith in creating a Christian Zion. Most members of the faculty were ministers, and with their pastoral and community orientation, they viewed their congregation as including both the students and the surrounding community. Their aim was to insure the moral, spiritual, and intellectual progress of this moral entity. The primary mode of communication was preaching, and the aim was evangelical. The business of education was the development of moral character.

Through the development of individual character, they hoped to create a Zion. The students took their work seriously and shared, or at least accepted, the purpose of the president and faculty in the creation of a Christian nation. The alumni also shared this orientation and saw their role as repaying the institution that had given them their hard-won education. This meant living the life of a good Christian man in the organic community. The board also embodied a unity of purpose in fashioning this society, and its members saw themselves as stewards of the common good in the corporate community.

The organization of the college was on a personal, familial basis. Family or congregation provided a model of college administration. The faculty viewed the president as the "Rev. Head."[14] Students looked to him as the interpreter of life, while the community saw him as a moral leader. The president exercised his authority through his moral power as pastoral head. Even with ordinary differences of opinion over policies, the unity of purpose in creating a Christian nation and the broad cultural cohesiveness and sense of community meant that the control of the college was based on a consensual orientation rather than on the management of conflict. Along with the perception of the president as a moral leader and the central figure in the life of the college, the "virtual" representation of the trustees as guardians of the common good in the corporate community was not ordinarily questioned publicly.

By 1881 this sense of community had changed, and Dartmouth was evolving into an institution quite different from its 1851 counterpart. While neither the ideal of unity nor the older sense of responsibility to the local community were completely abandoned, Dartmouth in 1881 was no longer a closely knit communal order expressive of its local community. It served a different clientele—younger, more cosmopolitan, and from a higher socioeconomic background. And it had a different relation to the local community and region, now perceived as a special place apart. The faculty had changed: through the trial the faculty members publicized their more cosmopolitan and professional ambitions. The alumni no longer accepted the virtual representation of the trustees in the corporate community and asserted their demands for representation as alumni on the board. The organization now more clearly defined its component roles, separating personal and official duties, and the trustees increasingly began to emphasize the importance of the president in his administrative capacity. Higher learning was moving in the direction of more fragmentation, specialization within particular disciplines, and a more rationalized learning. An open pursuit of interests challenged the older ideal of organic unity. With the growing emphasis on esoteric learning, the connection between faith and knowledge was clouded and increasingly disjoined. Through the altering notion of community, one can assess the origins and significance of this transformation highlighted in the Bartlett controversy.

Although the older sense of responsibility to the local community did not completely disappear, the various services of the college to the town increasingly came into competition with a more detached, impersonal, introverted collegiate notion. There were some differences among faculty, students, alumni, and trustees, but in general their career patterns, associational involvements, and residence revealed a growing metropolitan orientation. The very definition of success had changed. Now the peer group was the primary referent, and its parameters were no longer strictly geographic. Status began to be defined according to more uniform standards that emanated from metropolitan areas instead of from the traditional local or social context. By the time of the Bartlett controversy, these groups emerged as collegiate factions. They sought to protect their interests (now extending beyond the college, locale, and region) and to influence the direction of the institution by achieving power within the college. For them, a more formal organization, differentiating personal and official roles and statuses (rather than family or congregation), provided a model of college administration. What was happening at Dartmouth was occurring in society as well. This period saw the growth of all types of interest groups and formal patterns of social organization into their modern shapes and appearances. All these changes forced the emergence of a new type of college president.

As each of the various participant groups in the college community began to define community with exclusive reference to its own peer group, the organic unity of the college obviously suffered, and the relationships between the president and these groups underwent marked change. Thus, the more diverse, cosmopolitan, professionalized faculty, with more specialized training along specific disciplinary lines, began to join associations newly created along disciplinary lines, published original research for consumption of peers, and defined the audience and status referent as the peer group. Evidencing their changing value system, communal idea, and notion of presidential authority, they asserted claims for some sense of faculty autonomy with an increasing distance between themselves and the president, for peer group evaluation, and for faculty chosen on the basis of reputation among peers in the field. They came into conflict with Bartlett over these assertions, and through the trial they asserted not only their professionalization but also the power behind this viewpoint. Bartlett's attitude toward the education given by such associated schools as the scientific department led to conflict based on the status of the education and the fields represented by these schools as well.

The alumni, and notably the New York alumni, also emerged as a collegiate faction. They acted as the sustaining agent in the Bartlett controversy and sought to transform the very scope of collegiate control (and were ultimately successful). Reflective of the changing sense of community and character of the presidency, the trial became a means for the alumni to assert their demands for representation as alumni on the board of trustees and their opposition to a president they perceived as a failure "as an administrative and executive officer."[15] To highlight alumni group power, they equated their demands with the contribution of funds. Increasingly moving to metropolitan areas and engaging in business-related positions, the alumni were competing with graduates of other colleges in these metropolitan areas. The college one attended and the club to which one belonged began to be important factors in business and social success. The alumni were concerned with the college's metropolitan reputation—a reputation defined according to national standards emanating from these leading centers—not its service to the hill country of New Hampshire.

The students also saw themselves detached from the organic community. While student protests and disciplinary incidents were not new to nineteenth-century colleges, the position and behavior of the students in the Bartlett controversy is reflective of the altered communal idea and the changing nature of the relationships between the students and the president. Most of the students, by both background and aspirations, were different from the type of student characterized as country "bumpkins" by Nathaniel Hawthorne in the antebellum period.[16] The majority of students were not quite the Dink Stover types at Yale at the turn of the century, yet by background and experiences many were moving in this direction.[17] They began to define success within the fraternities and athletics in college and in business corporations, upper-middle-class social clubs, and professional associations after college. Bartlett's older pastoral approach, his style emphasizing himself as pastoral head and interpreter of life, and his rigid policy of discipline that was linked to his conception of higher learning clashed with many of the students who were beginning to define their aims and aspirations in relation to different models. Dartmouth students now saw themselves as part of a more broadly conceived collegiate culture, and they consciously linked their ambitions to men like the New York alumni who represented the metropolitan culture and success in business.

While the ideal of shared ideology as a basis to insure cohesion was not completely abandoned at Dartmouth in the process of redefining its collegiate route, a pattern of organization and management reflective of the centrifugal effects of peer groups as community began to emerge. It was based less on a consensual orientation and a broad cultural cohesiveness, the pattern a generation before, and more on conflict management within a more formal organization, differentiating personal and official roles. As a function of this changing notion of community, the conception of the president as pastoral and paternal head, as interpreter of life and ethics, as classroom teacher and moral leader underwent significant change. In an institution choosing to remain a college, with its stress on its homogeneous nature, the primacy of teaching, and its religious spirit, the notion of the president as a moral leader was not abandoned but was transformed and redefined. Added to this altered conception was an increased emphasis on the president as an administrative officer who could insure the college's metropolitan reputation and reconcile the collegiate factions. This reconciliation was successfully accomplished in the 1890s by William Jewett Tucker. Tucker conceived of the college as an element of metropolitan culture and distinctively as a special place apart within that culture. This new collegiate idea had sufficient centripetal force to reconcile all groups *within* the college.

The trustees, especially those considered Bartlett's staunchest opponents, were a younger, more cosmopolitan group, with interests, aspirations, and status groups moving them away from the local community and linking them to peers in metropolitan areas. They were sensitive, as in 1851, to sources of support. But in the case of the Bartlett controversy, the trustees were sensitive to pressure from alumni, notably the New York alumni, a new power outside this traditional orientation. The changing sources of support, the class of students, as well as the importance of this group in terms of jobs after college and financial support, were also factors in this shift. The trustees were most conscious of the confusions of an old and a new tradition. Although they initially appeared to be in agreement with the alumni, the lingering power of an older collegiate ideal and communal sense reinforced by the college's unexpectedly favorable financial condition at the time of the trial left just enough of a question in people's minds to keep Bartlett in place. The trustees' move toward the new order, however, was already evident.

Their policies in the administration directly preceding the Bartlett period and during the Bartlett administration reflect a movement away from the older notion of community. They were creating a more insulated environment, discouraging, for example, students from teaching and faculty from holding political office. Their policies were encouraging the development of a different kind of student for the college—an upper-middle-class one, younger, more uniform in age, and from a broader geographic background. This shift, which evolved in a step-by-step process, occurred at the same time as did significant economic, cultural, and structural transformations in the larger society. The concentration of wealth and college graduates in the leading metropolises along with the emphasis in the culture upon bigness and growth—increased endowments, numbers, expansion, competition—seems to have led to a perception on the part of the trustees that if the college were to maintain its reputation as a leading institution, its future lay in an expansion of its reputation in areas such as New York and Boston. Dartmouth alumni were settling in these areas in growing numbers. And in these areas, the trustees could raise the money and attract the type of students that could bring Dartmouth into the position of prominence in late-nineteenth-century America it had held in the world of northern New England a generation before. A broadened image of the institution and an identification with developments in similar collegiate institutions accompanying the shifting structure and experience of community no doubt reinforced this perception. The trustees were also moving toward a form of governance in which the alumni, as alumni, would obtain their representation on the board. They were encouraging the development of a more professionalized and cosmopolitan faculty that could bring distinction to the college. And they began to emphasize important aspects of what would be the presidential role in modern guise.

The Bartlett controversy rooted itself in the changing notions of community and revealed the transformation of the idea in relation to the college itself that resulted in a "new Dartmouth." The conflict dramatized the reach of the city and the metropolitan culture into the college to replace the immediate local community that served Dartmouth in 1851. While not offending democratic sensibilities, the "new Dartmouth" was addressed to the ideals of an urban, aspiring upper middle class oriented to metropolitan systems of status. In keeping with the changing notion of community and its redefined boundaries, the direction of the college shifted from its central "location" in the world of rural northern New England to its "place" as a leading Ivy League college dependent upon its metropolitan reputation. The effect of this shift was a sense of exclusiveness—a privileged group of students, in a special place apart—in marked contrast to antebellum Dartmouth.

Thus, the antebellum college as a community-oriented institution with a shared sense of purpose gave way to a more fragmented conception of community, college, and higher learning. The late-nineteenth-century college emerged as a special place apart in which students would be given a broad liberal education in preparation for their special place in society as leaders whose mission would be to guide society, conserve its values, and in this way provide public or social service. Higher learning itself became more specialized, fragmented, and esoteric with divisions into separate disciplines with specific limits of study and select problems and methodologies. The emphasis on character shifted from uplifting the individual character and in this way creating a Christian

Zion, to demonstrable actions in insuring the quality of life through social service in large-scale formal organizations. At the turn of the century colleges such as Dartmouth served as models for some of the universities such as Harvard and Princeton, who shifted their emphasis back to undergraduate education. The success stories have been universities. But a number of schools succeeded by avoiding that route.

Toward the end of the century, Dartmouth still adhered to its homogeneity, its religious spirit, and the primacy of teaching; with the memory of unity and idealism still alive, President Tucker tried to bring into harmony the factions in the college community by emphasizing their unity as a privileged group, in an idyllic setting, with nevertheless a purposeful social role. This attempt to try to maintain a sense of community as an important value itself and to embody in the president the unified spirit of the college stands in marked contrast to the new universities where all elements were permitted simply to coexist as constituencies under a shared central administration. Within this altered framework of unity, however, the alumni (highlighting their rise to power) obtained their coveted seats on the board and continued to influence even more directly the direction of the institution. Faculty members considered teachers-scholars in an institution still emphasizing the primacy of teaching, assumed some sense of autonomy and encouragement to carry on research and attain distinction while maintaining their role of training the nation's leaders. The students, for their part, were now able to tout to each other the many advantages of a broader collegiate fellowship of "college life, not college work,"[18] and at the same time attain a sense of their purposeful role in society. The sense of corporate unity, however, under a rallying banner emphasizing the oneness of their position as a select or special fellowship, was no longer that of a body with a shared sense of purpose or that of one expressive of the organic community immediately outside the collegiate bounds. Other things had been gained in this transformation, but that world had been lost.

If one accepts the notion that our view of the present and future is at least in part dependent upon our understanding of the past, a historical perspective can offer important insights into current dilemmas. The decades of the 1960s and 1970s brought to the forefront the questioning of the very nature of academic institutions. Stringent financial conditions of the early 1980s have confronted educational institutions with the necessity of making complex and far-reaching choices. This process of decision making has underscored the necessity of greater introspection about historic goals and purposes, communal and institutional development, and the nature and parameters of change. Although one cannot impose a pattern of one period upon another, during an age when the question of community, of the uses and purposes of education, of responding to the needs of different types of students are such pressing questions for educators, it is important to reflect upon the transition from a college with a shared sense of purpose, an emphasis upon the social and moral uses of knowledge, and policies expressive of its community orientation. Why and how the college changed, how a college such as Dartmouth tried to maintain some sense of community as a value itself in the late nineteenth century, and what was gained and lost in this period of transformation are important questions to ponder as we confront today's problems. Such a process contributes to contemporary discussions of current problems by enriching our understanding of the nature and process of change and the past alternatives within which our present and future may be better developed and shaped.

It is also the hope of this author that the model for the historical analysis of institutions offered in this work will encourage other scholars to develop studies that will confirm or challenge my findings and modify or expand this analytical model. This will bring us one step closer to the process of theory building about institutionalization and communal development[19] and increase our understanding of the nature and significance of educational, cultural, and social change in the emergence of modern American society. With this idea in mind, I offer this historical analysis as an effort to understand the transformation of the academic community and collegiate culture evidenced in the Bartlett controversy—how it came about, what it represented, and how it sheds light upon the changing character of higher learning in nineteenth-century America.

CHAPTER II

The Faculty

What had been that [President Bartlett's] official bearing?

   A. It was this, in a word, to sum it all up, "I am the college."

That was his official manner?

   A. That was his official manner. And with that idea it was pretty difficult for anybody else to exist who did not form a spoke in the wheel of the college.

—Edward R. Ruggles (1881)

It [the Greek chair] should be filled by a man in these times who enjoyed in his own department, no matter how good a minister he was, or how good a man, the respect and confidence of Greek scholarship in this country, and I did not understand Mr. Hewitt was such a man; and if at his age he was not, I questioned the wisdom of his appointment.

—Arthur Sherburne Hardy (1881)

The conflict with the old order was most evident for the faculty who were accustomed to treat the president as the "Rev. Head of the College."[1] On 29 April 1881, sixteen of the twenty-three resident members of the Dartmouth faculty (the treasurer included) sent a memorial to the trustees requesting the resignation of the president.[2] During the trial the faculty sent a second memorial to the trustees. It stated:

> Inasmuch as it has been asserted that a paper heretofore signed by 16 resident members of the resident faculty of Dartmouth College, bearing date of April 29, 1881, does not express the sentiments at present entertained by the signers thereof, we hereby solemnly reaffirm the allegation in such paper contained, and add thereto

our convictions that the best interests of the college require that Dr. Bartlett should cease to be its head are strengthened by further consideration. While we deprecated a public investigation, and signed said paper in the hope that the desired result would be hereby accomplished, when that failed us we recognized the necessity of this investigation, and have earnestly cooperated therein.[3]

These memorials illustrate that the faculty "spokes" on Bartlett's "wheel" were loosening and that some were even becoming detached. The steps taken by these faculty members were certainly far removed from the conception of the faculty in the early days of Dartmouth when the poet Richard Hovey, in one of his verses, quipped that "Eleazar was the faculty,"[4] or even from the period around 1850 when a student described the college as a paternal organization "under the sovereign rule of President Lord."[5] And the discussion in the second memorial about the decision to go "public"—to participate in a public trial in the hopes of a presidential dismissal—raises important questions about their notion of presidential authority and about the relation of the college to society.

The introductory quotations from the trial testimony point to the faculty's changing value system and communal idea and underscore the altered nature of the relationships between the faculty and the president. The testimony of Professor Hardy regarding the appointment of the professor of Greek reveals a concern with peer evaluation and reputation being defined by peers in colleges and universities within a particular discipline or field, rather than simply with spiritual suitability or fitness. The emphasis on this concern is striking in contrast to that of a generation before when the faculty saw itself, in the words of one professor, as part of "the whole community,"[6] with status and reputation defined primarily with reference to the local community or region. Moreover in marked contrast to the relationships of the collegiate culture in mid-nineteenth-century Darmouth, Professor Ruggles's statement about President Bartlett's "official bearing" is illustrative of the beginnings of faculty demands for some sense of autonomy with an increasing separation between the faculty and the president.

How can we explain the ideas and actions of the members of the faculty? Their perceptions and behavior suggest that being a faculty member was taking on a new meaning and that the trial involved an issue that transcended both Bartlett and Dartmouth. It represents a crucial incident in the professionalization of the faculty as part of the larger question of the transformation of higher learning in late-nineteenth-century America. What were the changes in the professional experience during the second half of the nineteenth century?

There have been several recent attempts to deal with academic professionalization.[7] We know most about the colleges whose finances permitted them foresight about their archives. In his study of the Harvard
faculty in the nineteenth century, Robert McCaughey makes an important contribution in reassessing the growth of the professoriate as a
developmental process and in relation to changes within the faculty
itself instead of viewing professionalization and all academic change as
a result of presidential or social actions.[8] He offers some useful measures
with which to investigate the "pulse," that is, the values, attitudes, and
ideology of the faculty; but his emphasis on a static model of the ideal
professor is problematic. The emphasis in the study begins to center on
a replication of predetermined surface characteristics defined in relation
to the ideal professor of the late nineteenth century rather than on the
nature and process of the professorial experience over time. What
McCaughey provides, in essence, for the antebellum period are mirror
negatives of later values. And his neglect of relating the quantitative
detail to how professors, in the words of William Johnson, "related to
and operated within their social and intellectual context,"[9] obscures not
only the nature and stages of the professorial experience but also how
that experience and its significance may have differed at a Harvard or
a Dartmouth.

With this perspective in mind, one can confront several basic questions: Why did status and reputation emanating from disciplinary peers
in other colleges and universities, scholarly publications for peer consumption, peer group evaluation, and faculty autonomy become issues
of such great controversy in 1881 when they were not important in 1851?
Why were many of the 1881 faculty uncomfortable in the more personal,
informal, paternal environment they inherited from a previous generation of faculty? How is the shift in the faculty's perception of its role
in the developing academic culture and its altered notion of presidential
authority related to changing ideas of community? And how do the
answers to these questions illuminate the transformation in the nature
of the college and the evolving concept of higher learning in nineteenth-
century America?

The Dartmouth faculty in 1851[10] consisted of eight professors in the
Academical Department and five professors and one demonstrator in
the Medical College (see appendix 2). Although one must consider the
composite picture of these two faculties to get a complete view of the
college faculty during this period, one must also consider them sepa-
rately, because the professorial role of members of the medical faculty[11]
was linked to the development of their "occupation" as physicians.

The data regarding the 1851 academical faculty point to a pattern in
which the faculty role could be described as pastoral[12] and community-

oriented, in a college possessing a shared sense of purpose. It would have been very unlikely for a group of men such as these to have responded with such hostility to Bartlett's presidential policies and style.

Statistical similarity in respect to such characteristics as origins, educational background, generational affinity, community and associational involvement is striking and points to the faculty's homogeneity and its pastoral and community orientation. The structure of academic ranks was undifferentiated; all eight professors of the academical faculty of 1851 were full professors. Although the college had employed tutors in previous years, in this year there were no tutors and no associate professors. Analysis of place of birth reveals a locally rooted group. Five of the professors were born in New Hampshire, and the remaining three were born in other parts of New England (see appendix 3).

What information is available on family origins indicates that most of the faculty came from modest backgrounds, expressive perhaps of the community they represented—the declining towns of rural northern New England. The fathers' occupations were as follows: one carpenter, one farmer, one farmer and teacher, one minister (who was also the third president of Dartmouth), one merchant, and three unknown. The biographical material indicates that one of these three had to work his way through college by teaching. Other biographical information for those whose father's occupations were known indicates that at least two had to teach school while in college. One of the faculty members in the unknown category was a nephew of Daniel Webster. He and the faculty member whose father was a minister and president of Dartmouth seem to be the only two coming from prominent families.

Their educational background also points to their local roots and to their pastoral orientation. Most of the faculty were Dartmouth graduates and had ministerial training. Seven of the eight members of the academical faculty were Dartmouth graduates (see appendix 4). All of them possessed M.A. degrees, which could be obtained by graduates of three years' standing upon application and payment of a fee. Nearly all additional training consisted of attendance at a theological seminary (see appendix 5). Six of the eight members of the academical faculty had such training—four were graduates of Andover Theological Seminary, one attended, and one had other clerical training. One faculty member who also held an appointment on the medical faculty had an M.D. degree.[13]

By age the academical faculty formed a cohort group,[14] and they became full professors at a young age with little or no college teaching experience. Their age range was between twenty-nine and fifty-five; all but two were forty-three plus or minus seven years (see appendix 6). Six of the faculty became full professors between the ages of twenty-three and twenty-nine. Five of these had no college teaching experience or a few months' experience as a tutor. One of the six had a few months' experience as a tutor and two years' experience as an associate professor at Dartmouth. The other two faculty members became professors at age thirty-two and thirty-seven, respectively—one with three years' experience as a tutor at Dartmouth, during which time he was pursuing theological studies; the other with two years' experience as a tutor when he graduated from Dartmouth before spending twelve years in ministerial service (see appendixes 7 and 8).

They seemed to value their position highly. Most of them spent a substantial part of their lives at Dartmouth. Their tenures ranged from thirteen years to forty-seven years.[15] Six members of the faculty spent more than twenty-seven years at Dartmouth. The other two, who were at Dartmouth thirteen and fourteen years, respectively, died while they were professors. One professor left Dartmouth after twenty-seven years to become president of Hamilton College. One left after thirty-five years to become a diplomat. One left for four years to accept a position at another college and then came back and spent a total of forty-two years at Dartmouth.

The academical faculty was deeply involved in clerical and civic activities in the community (see appendix 9). Some of the faculty members confined their community activities to the local town, Hanover, New Hampshire. Others extended their involvement to the surrounding areas of northern New England, to the state of New Hampshire, and to the New England region generally. The faculty's participation as leaders in the community is indicative of their high status in the community as well as of the faculty members' perception of themselves as integral parts of the wider geographic and moral community. Of the eight professors, six were active in the churches in the local community or in the New England area as preachers, licentiates, or ordained ministers. They were in much demand to fill local pulpits and to act as speakers at various commemorative occasions. Their associational activities ranged from trying to beautify the town through the organization of a society to plant trees, to membership on a local school board, to participation in the cemetery association, to representation on the New Hampshire legislature. The limited number of studies available suggest a similar college-community orientation and involvement of the faculty in community activities and associations. David Potts in his study of Baptist colleges, for example, notes that faculty filled local pulpits and gave public lectures.[16]

By looking at the lives of some of the Dartmouth professors, one can assess both the specific character of their involvement in the community and the importance of the community as the audience and status referent for the faculty.[17] The activities of three professors—Edwin David Sanborn, Samuel Gilman Brown, and Charles Brickett Haddock—spanned both the local community and the New England region. Sanborn was in great demand to fill the local pulpits and to speak at various public occasions. He was an orator for Fourth of July addresses and the county fair, held most of the justice courts in Hanover for many years, and was influential in securing the cooperation of the college in the local fire company. Sanborn was a member of the New Hampshire Constitutional Convention (1850) and of the state legislature. He helped found a normal school and was president of the state teachers association.

Brown has been characterized as making his most impressive contributions "in the pulpit and on the platform."[18] In much demand in these capacities, he was a member of the White River Association, preached as a licentiate, and became an ordained minister at Woodstock, Vermont, in 1852. Influential in the formation of the Dartmouth Cemetery Association in Hanover in 1845 (which was formed under state law to care for the cemetery), he delivered the annual address before the society.[19] Brown also served as an honorary member of the American Board of Commissioners for Foreign Missions, as director of the American Tract Society, and as life director of the American Bible Society.

Haddock held numerous leadership positions in the town and the state.[20] He preached at the Hanover Village Church and at White River and organized the Ornamental Tree Society in Hanover to help beautify it by the planting of trees. Haddock served as secretary of the New Hampshire Education Society, as New Hampshire commissioner of common schools, and as a member of the New Hampshire legislature. He also was a member of the school board in Hanover and commissioner of the Grafton County Board of Education.

Four of the other professors confined their activities to a more localized level. Their activities included preaching in the local churches, speaking at public occasions, and serving as treasurer of an academy. Only one professor, Oliver Payson Hubbard, deviated from this pattern. He had an M.D. degree and a dual appointment on the academical and medical faculties. During the 1851 period he was the only member of the academical faculty involved in an association related primarily to a specific discipline. Hubbard was a founder and secretary of the American Association of Geologists and Naturalists. He was, however, active in the community and served as a member of the New Hampshire legislature.

Although the salaries of full professors were relatively low ($900 in 1847 and $1,100 in 1854) and the faculty complained about these low salaries, they were considerably higher than those of some of the ministers in the rural and small-town churches. For example, Dr. Ely, pastor of the Monson Church in Massachusetts (Bartlett served there a few years), complained that his salary of $500 was never raised and said that he was forced to take in boarders.[21] Too, the professorial position certainly offered more security in terms of duration of the position. Between 1837 and 1875 the average length of terms a minister served in a church in New Hampshire was between four and eight years.[22] Thus, when Professor Haddock said that "the clerical office seems to be naturally associated with the office of instruction,"[23] he knew that "schoolkeeping" was a viable substitute for a regular ministerial position. The educational background of the faculty and its community and associational involvement repeatedly supports this observation.[24] Certainly, as regards security, these men of modest means (as the majority of the faculty seemed to have been), and even those who may have had a more comfortable background, probably regarded it as an attractive alternative. It provided them with a home or pastorate (the college) and a congregation (the students and the wider community) in a setting that could provide for "a social extension of the pulpit."[25]

This pattern is not unusual among colleges of the period, and the ministerial background and pastoral orientation of collegiate faculty[26] are in line with developments in the religious history of the northern states that provide the general context for academic life in 1851. In a study of the New England clergy that relies upon New Hampshire as a case study, Daniel Calhoun notes a breakdown in the traditional pastorate. Terms of service in parishes were no longer measured in lifetimes; more often, they lasted only a few years. The low salaries of the clergy in rural and small-town churches meant that ministers would have to accept both low incomes and insecurity of terms of service during their lifetime, or at least at the beginning of their ministerial service. Many sought enhanced careers by building organizations such as benevolent societies and colleges. Some became college presidents and professors.[27]

Many ministers lacked regular pastorates, and ministerial bodies had to decide what to do with them. In New Hampshire, the Hopkinton Association debated whether men who did not have regular pastoral duties should be accepted as full members.[28] Although the association postponed formal decision, after 1840 it began to accept them as members.[29] Acceptance of this new ministerial role required deep psychological adjustments. The conception of the minister was changed. In the words of Sidney Mead, it "became that of a consecrated functionary, called of God, who directed the purposive activities of the visible church."[30] This work included Bible societies, tract societies, missionary and education societies, the local congregation, and denominational activities.[31] Besides parish ministers, such diverse churchmen as teachers, professors, and secretaries of benevolent societies were regarded as "equally engaged in the legitimate ministry of the one church."[32]

This view of the professoriate would account for the description by one of the students in 1851 about his education at Dartmouth:

> The dominating features of a parental supervision over personal conduct together with the religious tone given to didactic instruction whenever possible, imparted an early and continuing sense of moral responsibility to individual action. . . . They [students] were made to feel that the college was a moral training school for the conscience, as well as a gymnasium for the mind. . . . This was the trend of our education under the sovereign rule of President Lord.[33]

During the 1851 period the college was a paternal organization in which the president and the faculty watched over their congregation to insure their spiritual, moral, and intellectual progress. The pastoral and community orientation of the faculty accounts for the general lack of interest on the part of most of the faculty in original research for publication and consumption by their peers and for the pages of faculty minutes relating to discipline. As Amos N. Currier of the class of 1856 said of the faculty of this period, "There was no parade of 'original research. . . .' They gave themselves to their college work without reserve and were content to make trained and cultivated men their scholastic product."[34]

Those faculty members that made contributions as writers evidenced their community orientation. Their writings were general in nature, concerned primarily with education, religion, literature, and politics, especially of the New England region. Four of the members had no publications; one wrote a textbook. The three professors involved in writing for publication were Haddock, Sanborn, and Brown. Haddock's works included *Addresses and Miscellaneous Writings*, a volume of thirty-three addresses from speeches before the New Hampshire legislature and public occasions, such as "The Standard of Education for the Pulpit" and "The Influence of the Educated Mind." Sanborn wrote more than 1,000 articles on topics of current interest; he published lectures on education and a "Eulogy on Daniel Webster." Brown's works included published discourses, orations, addresses, and writings such as "The Spirit of a Scholar," "Eulogy on the Life and Character of Henry Clay," and *The Works of Rufus Choate, with a Memoir of His Life*. The emphasis, then, is on the region and the verbal and discursive, rather than on the original, technical, empirical research of the 1881 period. This emphasis seems in keeping with developments in institutions in other locales. In his study entitled *Church Colleges of the Old South*, Albea Godbold notes that faculty contributed sermons and numerous other writings on many subjects to various periodicals.[35]

If the faculty members' major aim as educators was to uplift the character of their congregation and to guide "the standard of thought"[36] of this moral entity, one can understand the emphasis upon student discipline. Discipline aided in character building. The faculty minutes reveal a concern for discipline over all types of offenses. But the punishments are compatible with the character-building orientation. Much of the discipline involved separation for a specified period or pastoral care in the nature of a reprimand by the president or "rustication."[37] One can see examples of these types of punishments in the faculty minutes of 30 April 1851.

> Thompson 2nd (Soph.) Voted: that Thompson 2nd be separated from College for destroying glass wantonly, drunkenness, falsehood, and tardiness and irregularity in his college duties and Exercises. No application for his return to be received till after Commencement.
>
> Thompson 1st and Strow (Soph.) Voted: That Thompson 1st and Strow be reprimanded by the President for disorder in their rooms.
>
> Dow (Freshm.) Voted that Dow be sent away (to the care of any person, the President may select, till Examination), for irregular habits and drinking spirit.[38]

And a student from this period tells us that "The chase of offenders by professors at night through buildings and over grounds, or the search of students' rooms was not an unknown occurrence."[39]

Faculty writings during the 1851 period reveal a pastoral emphasis that made instructing the moral conscience central to the conception of higher learning.[40] The writings express the basic unity of knowledge, a joining of heart and mind, and a shared sense of purpose in fashioning a Christian Zion. Brown, for example, in his discourse on "The Spirit of a Scholar," offered the view that "a high moral, a religious spirit even, . . . is essential to the highest order of scholars. . . . We use the terms here in no narrow or partial meaning."[41] Continuing along this line, he asked, "Unless men have faith in spiritual powers . . . how can his mind expand to the dimension of those themes which, as a scholar, he is bound to be conversant with?"[42] Noting the basic unity of knowledge and the aim of insuring the moral, spiritual, and intellectual progress as a step toward insuring a Zion, Brown stated that the true scholar aims "to bring a unity into the various branches of knowledge, to raise the public tastes, direct the public thought, conserve the public welfare."[43] And in concluding with the words of Milton, he highlights the significance of the evangelical aim:

> The end of learning is to repair the ruins of our first parents, by regaining to know God aright, and out of that knowledge to love

Him, to imitate Him, to be like Him, as we may the nearest by possessing our souls of true virtue, which, being united to the heavenly grace of faith makes up the highest perfection.[44]

Their writings reflect the central role of the college in the local and moral community it "served" as well as the audience, aspirations, and communal status referent of the faculty. Haddock wrote: "A New England College is a public institution—a POPULAR institution; its benefits confined to no party, no sect, no class. If there be any partiality in the distribution of its blessings, it is in favor of the middling and lower classes."[45] In a similar vein, Sanborn declared: "School-houses and churches are the true symbols of New England civilization, as temples, pyramids, and mausoleums were the symbols of ancient civilization. . . . Learning has ever been the handmaiden of religion, and on these two elements depends our prosperity as a people."[46] Sanborn's identification with New Hampshire and his pride in the reputation of the region is revealed in this statement: "The true policy of New Hampshire, therefore is intellectual culture. If she cannot raise wheat, she can raise men."[47] He also noted with pride the accomplishment of New Hampshire as "pre-eminent in all the unwritten literature of a people."[48] And Haddock, in emphasizing the role of the faculty in the community, noted:

Every well-taught man, is the property of the whole community— one of its richest treasures and highest ornaments . . . the truly educated man becomes, himself, an educator—an efficient public teacher. . . . By his influence the standard of thought is raised, and the zeal for improvement rekindled.[49]

A letter written by Sanborn after some students from Dartmouth caused a disturbance by blowing horns (a common practice) at St. Johnsbury illustrates both the pastoral emphasis on discipline for character building and the concern of the faculty about the reputation of the college in the community. He emphasized that he was ill when he heard that "15 noisy boys" from Dartmouth had gone to St. Johnsbury with tin horns.[50] "I should have gone myself," he said, "had I been well."[51] Sanborn evidently regarded this as part of his pastoral role. Asking for information about what happened and expressing his concern for the reputation of the college in rural northern New England, he queried the gentleman for his "impression of the outrage" and for his "advice as to the extent of punishment needed." Sanborn indicated that he was writing by wish of the faculty and that his views would be held confidential: "No public use is to be made of any facts or opinions we may gain from the gentlemen at St. Johnsbury, but we ask their aid in ascertaining who the offenders were & determining the degree of punishment."[52] Aberrations would be taken care of within the "family."

The faculty's notion of community is central to an explanation of its lack of identification with disciplinary peers, its lack of interest in publication of original research for consumption of peers in other institutions, and the integral role the college played in the local community and region. The college and the community it "served" exhibited a mutual appreciation, and the faculty played a key role in that wider community.[53] The *Hanover Gazette,* commenting on Sanborn's death in 1885, noted of his earlier years:

> As a citizen he was interested in village affairs, and at one time took quite an active part in them. He was the personal friend and adviser of many of our old citizens, and appreciated the mutual interests of the college and its citizens. No man in New Hampshire ever commanded more general respect, and no instructor at Dartmouth was ever more universally beloved by the students.[54]

Haddock's world has been characterized as the "world" of "New England."[55] Members of the faculty, then, came from the local community and region; their aspirations, values, and associational involvements were rooted in this context. They considered the local community and region as their audience, and their status emanated from this source. They directed their addresses and writings to this source, and with their pastoral orientation they saw their aim as insuring the moral, spiritual, and intellectual progress of their congregation. As higher learning had not evolved into the more esoteric learning common to the late nineteenth century, they did not need a special audience to communicate the results of their research.[56] The reinforcement of these values in a society emphasizing the organic notion of community[57] led to a cultural cohesiveness and organically knit organization within the college itself.

Within the communal order of the college, the fact that faculty members could become full professors with little or no college teaching experience,[58] and with little specialized training within a particular discipline, is understandable in an organization whose primary aim was uplifting the students' moral character. In fashioning this Zion, higher learning stressed a joining of heart and intellect and the basic unity of knowledge rather than its fragmentation. A grounding in the broad culture, a theological background, and purity of spirit would be more important as models for training the students than would original research in one discipline. The emphasis on spiritual and moral fitness at Dartmouth was not unique. At antebellum Amherst, qualifications for faculty members centered on their being "heartily Christian . . .

whose hearts shall be in lively sympathy with revivals . . . and whose learning . . . shall be consecrated to the cause of charity, humanity, and God."[59] This would help to insure the position of the college emphasized by President Stearns as "the most powerful engine for building up the kingdom of our Redeemer."[60]

A description of the early morning at Dartmouth illuminates further the conception of the college as a closely knit paternal Christian organization with the president at its head:

> At the dawn of the day, the community of students of God's works, summoned by the morning bell, hasten from their various quarters to the place of common prayer, to listen to a portion of God's Word, and be led by the Rev. Head of the College in a brief and fervent supplication for His paternal blessing.[61]

The president was regarded as a moral leader of this Christain community writ small. The pattern of organization and administration at Dartmouth can be found in comparable institutions of higher education during this period.[62] And while there are important differences between men's and women's colleges, in women's colleges, too, one finds a similar stress on a personal, familial organization and an emphasis on character building and the Christian religion.[63] Although the Dartmouth faculty and president experienced ordinary differences of opinion over issues, the faculty members' homogeneous background, their shared sense of pastoral purpose, and the sense of community and cultural cohesiveness led to an environment that fostered a consensual orientation and a model of organization that emphasized harmony rather than conflict. Thus, within this organically knit paternal organization, it would have been unlikely for such a faculty to demand a presidential resignation. They would also hardly participate in a public trial aimed at his dismissal.

In order to place Dartmouth historically, one might ask: How did the professorial role at Dartmouth, a country college, compare with the professorial role at Harvard, an older, coastal college?

The Dartmouth and Harvard faculties shared many characteristics, but the data indicate that a minority of the Harvard faculty possessed characteristics that the Dartmouth faculty would not evidence until a generation later.[64] The academic structure was more diversified at Harvard—60% of the faculty were full professors; 40% were assistant professors, tutors, or instructors. A majority of the faculty came from the New England area, but 27% of the faculty came from outside the United States, and 7% from the Middle Atlantic states.[65] As at Dartmouth, most of the faculty members became professors at a relatively young age, with little teaching experience. A number of them had experience as schoolmasters and seemed to value their position at Harvard, for most of them spent a substantial part of their lives there. Although a majority of the Harvard faculty did not have specialized training within a particular discipline, a minority had such training: 67% had legal, medical, and ministerial training; 27% studied in Europe (specialized training beyond the master's); and 7% had a European Ph.D.[66] Thus, the information available on the Harvard faculty indicates the beginnings of a more heterogeneous faculty. The aim of higher education may still have been, as it was at Dartmouth, the uplifting of moral character,[67] but Harvard may have had the "seeds" of a faculty that would begin to question this major aim and their role in it. Harvard's position as a coastal college probably served in part to stimulate these differences.

The professorial experience of the Dartmouth medical faculty followed a somewhat different pattern from that of the academical faculty, as it was connected directly with the members' "occupation" as physicians. The members of the medical faculty lectured for a total of fourteen weeks during the summer and fall. They maintained medical practices in Hanover and elsewhere in New England. Although the medical faculty exhibited a community orientation similar to that of the academical faculty, the collected data reveal a pattern in which members of the medical faculty viewed the college as a base from which they could enhance their status as physicians and insure the "orthodoxy" of their medical theories and practices. This pattern is suggestive of the concerns of the medical profession during the antebellum period when a wide variety of individuals considered themselves medical practitioners. Various groups of practitioners looked to the establishment of medical schools, professional societies, and legislation to define "orthodoxy," to enforce their view of medical practice, and to provide a regulatory base for their profession.[68]

The collected data on the medical faculty at Dartmouth in 1851 suggest a pattern that exhibits the concerns and interests common to physicians during this period along with a community orientation. All of the medical faculty came from northern New England. Moreover, all but one came from New Hampshire (see appendix 3). With the exception of the professor of medical jurisprudence, who was a lawyer, they all had M.D.'s (see appendix 5). Their educational background was also indicative of their local roots. Two had Dartmouth M.D.'s, and three had been undergraduates at Dartmouth (see appendix 4). One of the three who did not have a Dartmouth M.D. had studied at the Dartmouth Medical College. All had some experience as physicians; in the case of the lawyer, he had been chief justice of the New Hampshire Supreme Court. Three had experience as lecturers at Dartmouth, and they were appointed to the position of professor between the ages of twenty-eight and fifty, at an age considerably older than their counterparts on the academical faculty (see appendixes 7 and 8). In 1851 four of the five professors ranged in age between forty-eight and fifty-six,[69] seeming to form a cohort group (see appendix 6).

Only two professors made significant contributions to the literature of the period.[70] They did not focus primarily on a specialty but rather lectured on most of the branches of medicine during their professional careers. Phineas Sanborn Conner, a medical professor in the 1881 period, notes that Dr. Edmund Randolph Peaslee—who was highly regarded as a physician in the antebellum period—when tired of the labors of the anatomical department, switched to the chair of obstetrics and diseases, and then to gynecology.[71] Dixi Crosby, also a very prominent physician in the community, was characterized as "in no modern sense a 'specialist.' His professional labors concerned the whole range of medicine."[72] Later medical observers characterized the physicians as not having adopted the methods of clinical analysis or original research that would come to define progressive medical practice in the second half of the nineteenth century.[73]

The involvement of the medical faculty members in the local area and region illustrates both their community orientation (in a society in which the organic community was still the predominant pattern) and the concern over their occupation as physicians. All the professors maintained practices in Hanover, New Hampshire, and/or in the New England area. They were active in the community, especially in the local medical society, and the community considered them a high-status group. For example, Crosby and his father, also a physician in Hanover, are characterized as exercising "an immense influence throughout . . . the section."[74] Upon the completion of a bridge over the Connecticut River, it was Crosby who presided over the celebration of the townspeople.[75] He operated the first hospital in the area (near the school), and in the words of one historian of the college, "by virtue of his professional eminence and his personality he was looked upon as the head of the medical profession in the state."[76] Characterized as "a pillar of fire in the medical world of northern New England,"[77] Peaslee was also very prominent in the community. He served as president of the New Hampshire State Medical Society.[78] Another professor was a Sunday school teacher and represented his hometown of Peterborough in the legislature, in addition to being a member of the State Medical Society.

The school and those physicians affiliated with the State Medical Society worked hand in hand to give status to their theories. In 1820, at the suggestion of one of the Dartmouth medical professors, the New Hampshire State Medical Society voted to "send two delegates annually to attend the examination of the candidates for graduation."[79] The Vermont State Medical Society took a similar action in 1871. Thus, no student would be awarded a diploma from the college without the agreement of accredited members of the medical profession from these states.[80]

The faculty was comparatively independent in the administration of the medical school.[81] In the early years of the college, the president was the presiding officer at the meetings of the medical faculty, but in time the president ceased to attend meetings and the senior medical professor took over as presiding officer.[82] Part of the independence of the medical faculty stemmed from the fact that the school, from a financial standpoint, operated as a private corporation, the professors dependent on the student fees.

The information, then, points to a pattern in which the medical professors viewed the school as a means for enhancing their position as physicians in the community, as a way to insure regulation of the profession, and as a place where they could inculcate students in "proper" medical theories and procedures. The reputation of the faculty brought patients from the locale and region to Hanover, and the medical school gave the community its position of prominence as the center for medical consultation in the region.[83] Given the direct identification of the faculty with the community and the comparative independence of the faculty in running the medical school, it is unlikely that the medical faculty would have rebelled against the president during this period. But, compared with the academical faculty, if provoked, it would have been more the likely of the two to protest. The medical faculty members' concern about their status as physicians and their desire to establish orthodoxy of medical doctrine and regulation of the profession point to their special autonomy within the collegiate community.

What happened to the Dartmouth faculty in a generation? How does the movement toward a new professorial role help explain their actions aimed at Bartlett's resignation or dismissal and their active participation in a public trial?

An overall view of the 1881 faculty reveals a growth in faculty numbers, nearly half of whom became members of the faculty between 1875 and 1881; a more differentiated rank structure; and the addition of three new schools to the Academical Department and the Medical College of the antebellum period. In 1881 the faculty consisted of thirty-six members, compared with the fourteen members in 1851 (see appendix 2). Of this group, twelve became faculty members between 1868 and 1874, and seventeen between 1875 and 1881. The thirty-six faculty members were divided among the Academical Department, the Medical College, the Chandler Scientific Department,[84] the Thayer School of Civil Engineering,[85] and the New Hampshire College of Agriculture and the Mechanic Arts.[86] The more differentiated rank structure included: eight full professors, two associate professors, one instructor, one tutor, and one assistant in the Academical Department; four full professors and one tutor in the Chandler Scientific Department; one full professor and one instructor in the Thayer School of Civil Engineering; two full professors and two instructors in the New Hampshire College of Agriculture and the Mechanic Arts; and seven full professors, four lecturers, and one demonstrator in the Medical College.

Over two thirds of the resident members of the faculty signed the documents against Bartlett requesting his resignation, and most of these faculty members served as prime witnesses in the public trial regarding his administration. Of the thirty-six faculty members, twenty-three were considered to be in the category of resident members. Sixteen of these (the treasurer included) signed the documents against Bartlett. In the Chandler Scientific Department and the agricultural college, all of those in that category signed the documents, as did the resident member of the medical faculty. Of the academical faculty, six of the eleven[87] permanent members signed the documents. Of the five who did not sign it, three were supporters of Bartlett.[88] The permanent member of the Thayer School did not sign the documents and was a supporter of Bartlett.

By looking at the question that stirred the academical faculty into open opposition—the controversy over the appointment of the professor of Greek—one can gain an insight into the movement toward a new professorial role and the reasons for the actions of a majority of the faculty. In 1879 the professor of Greek died, and John Wright, the associate professor, took over the work of the department. In 1881, when that chair was to be filled, President Bartlett favored the candidacy of the Reverend John Hewitt, a teacher at Lake Forest University. The custom at this time was to discuss the qualifications of the candidates with the faculty. Bartlett had discussed the qualifications with members of the faculty who were full professors and who had been there when he became president. Bartlett did this on an informal basis. The rumor among the faculty was that the president had represented to the board that his candidate was the faculty's first choice. At first Bartlett refused to discuss the question of the appointment at faculty meetings. When the faculty forced the issue, he told the academical faculty that if they must discuss the matter that it would have no effect on the board's decision and that discussing the reputation of the proposed appointee (as they had requested) would bring into question their own reputations and endanger their positions.[89] Bartlett's position caused much controversy among the faculty, and their reactions and statements point to a change in the professorial role and the altered nature of the relationships between the faculty and the president.

In the trial testimony the faculty hinted at the importance of peer evaluation and a more formal organization separating personal and official roles and statuses. This is evident, for example, in the testimony of Arthur Sherburne Hardy, Cheney Professor of Mathematics. In describing why he asked that the question of the appointment be discussed in a faculty meeting, Hardy said:

> I brought it up because I thought it was a proper subject for discussion in faculty meeting. . . . I thought such a matter ought not to be definitely acted upon by the board without its formal discussion in some way among the faculty. . . . I thought it eminently proper that we discuss it among each other. . . . It was because all the preparations were made and I had heard nothing about it from any official source, that I brought it up in the only meeting in which we have official intercourse together.[90]

Such assertions underscore the beginnings of the transformation of an older collegial orientation. Discussion with the pastoral head and consensus *en famille* was giving way to the notion of faculty autonomy, and it was increasing the distance between the president and the faculty. Bartlett, on the other hand, explained that, whereas he did not object to faculty consultation under certain circumstances, this was not a faculty prerogative.[91] Bartlett is pressed here to defend more of a separation between the president and the faculty than his collegial values would ordinarily demand.

In their expression of concern over the president's candidate, the faculty also evidence their changing value system, away from any broad communal idea and notion of presidential primacy. In contrast to the communal referent of the 1851 faculty and the emphasis on spiritual fitness, the faculty stressed the importance of scholarly reputation and status emanating from one's peers in a particular discipline in other colleges and universities. The faculty emphasized that the Greek chair "should be filled by a man in these times who enjoyed in his own department, no matter how good a minister he was, or how good a man, the respect and confidence of Greek scholarship in this country."[92] In the same spirit, concern was expressed that "a man who had reached his 46th year . . . without becoming known at all to the persons who in the East had special acquaintance with Greek professors and Greek scholars, was perhaps not the man to appoint."[93] And John King Lord, associate professor of Latin and Evans Professor of Oratory and Belles-Lettres, noted that Hewitt "had never made his scholarship manifest by publications" and that "the college could not afford to lose" Professor Wright.[94] (Wright accepted an appointment at Johns Hopkins in 1886; in 1887 President Eliot persuaded him to accept a position at Harvard.)[95] Bartlett, for his part, told the faculty that discussion of the appointment by the faculty would not affect the board's decision and that according to the standards laid down at the last meeting (reputation in his own department and worthy publications), they all "would be found wanting."[96]

While faculty members felt that they "had been treated in an unwarrantable manner," not in keeping with their official positions, Bartlett, unable to grasp the changing order of authority, stated that he was just "putting the whole thing in the right aspect."[97] He explained that Hewitt's credentials were impressive (a fine man, minister, and teacher), and Hewitt had his recommendation. He thought he had the assent of the professors to whom he showed the recommendations. Therefore, he did not see how the discussion could influence the election.[98]

Why did these issues become increasingly important to the 1881 faculty? How are its members' changing roles and identities and ideas of presidential authority linked to their altering sense of corporate unity? What does this issue tell us about the organization of the college, the relation of the college to society, and the changing conception of higher learning?

The collected data point to a break in the 1851 pattern. They reveal a shift away from the homogeneous, pastoral, community-oriented group toward a more diverse, cosmopolitan,[99] professionalized[100] group. The trial, by bringing these issues out into the open, tended to accentuate this new professorial role and style. Since the actions of the faculty cut across school and departmental lines, one must look at both the individual schools and departments, with their separate interests and attitudes, and at the faculty as a whole. This ranking will help illuminate the overall picture and the dynamics at play. As the controversy over the appointment of the professor of Greek highlights many of the general concerns of the faculty from other schools and departments, one might begin with an assessment of the academical faculty.

In contrast to their 1851 counterparts, the data regarding such faculty characteristics as educational background, college teaching experience, age at appointment, birthplace, and associational involvements evidence the shift to a more diverse, cosmopolitan, professionalized faculty. In contrast to Dartmouth, at such eastern colleges as Princeton and Harvard the shift from college to university was under way by the 1880s. More and more faculty members were trained in Europe and joined the faculty to teach in their specialty.[101] At Harvard, by 1880, 16% of the faculty had European Ph.D.'s, 40% had specialized training in Europe, and

13% had American Ph.D.'s.[102] At Dartmouth, a country college that did not become a university, one also finds faculty members with specialized training in Europe in a particular discipline. Although in 1881 the percentages are substantially lower than at Harvard, in the 1851 period no Dartmouth faculty member had this type of training. By 1881, 23.1% of the academical faculty (all ranks included) had such postbaccalaureate training, and this figure rose to 30.8% by 1883. In addition, whereas 75% of the 1851 academical faculty had ministerial training, by 1881 only 30.8% had such training. Half of those 1881 professors had been faculty members in the 1851 period (see appendix 5).

The changes found in the pattern of the educational background and training of the Dartmouth faculty are representative of changes in comparable institutions. The faculty at Amherst and Williams, for example, exhibit a similar pattern with specialized training in Europe in a particular discipline and a decline in ministerial training.[103] At some institutions, such as Franklin and Marshall College, the movement away from a ministerial background was much slower. And although a need for faculty with some specialized training along disciplinary lines was recognized, change in this direction does not appear to have proceeded as quickly as at institutions such as Dartmouth, Amherst, and Williams.[104]

Postbellum college faculty members became full professors at an older age and with a longer period of apprenticeship. In 1851, 62.5% of the faculty had no college teaching experience or a few months' experience before appointment to the position of full professor, and another 37.5% had between one and three years' experience. By 1881, 25% of the academical faculty had more than ten years' experience before appointment to this position, 25% had between seven and ten years' experience, and 50% had between one and three years' experience (one half of this group had been faculty members in 1851) (see appendix 7). Whereas 75% of the 1851 faculty became full professors between the ages of twenty-three and twenty-nine, 87.5% of the 1881 faculty became professors between the ages of thirty-one and forty-six (see appendix 8).[105] The percentages are not dissimilar to those of the Harvard faculty during this period, although the length of apprenticeship seems to be even more accentuated at Harvard.[106]

By birthplace the 1881 faculty also evidence a movement away from the local roots of the 1851 group. In 1851, 62.5% of the faculty were born in New Hampshire, and 100% were born in New England. By 1881 only 23.1% were born in New Hampshire, and 69.2% were born in New England (see appendix 3). The percentage born in New England was comparable to that of the Harvard faculty in 1880.[107] Along with the decline in local birthplace, the percentage who had been Dartmouth undergraduates also declined slightly—from 87.5% in 1851 to 76.9% in 1881 (see appendix 4). This level was comparable to the percentage of Harvard graduates on the Harvard faculty in 1880—74%.[108]

What information is available on their socioeconomic background points to a more heterogeneous group with a number of faculty members who came from more substantial or prominent backgrounds than their 1851 counterparts. The fathers' occupations were as follows: one college professor and college president, one missionary and physician, one minister (the faculty member's grandfather was president of Dartmouth), one merchant and philanthropist, two farmers (one from the 1851 period), one schoolmaster (from the 1851 period), and six unknown. The 1880 Harvard faculty also evidence a similar type of movement toward those of a more substantial background (as compared with the 1845 Harvard faculty).[109]

Most of the faculty spent much of their professional life at Dartmouth. With the exception of the tutor and the assistant, who stayed one year each, the length of stay of the academical faculty ranged from ten years to forty-seven years.[110] Of the two who left, one became an editor and diplomat (stayed at Dartmouth nineteen years), the other became a professor at Johns Hopkins and Harvard (stayed at Dartmouth ten years). Nearly three fourths spent between twenty-five and forty-seven years at Dartmouth.[111] Thus, while members of the Dartmouth faculty evidenced their more cosmopolitan and professional ambitions, with the exception of Wright, they did not move from institution to institution to enhance their professional status. McCaughey and sociologists might classify them as professional "insiders," to use a modern term.[112] Their tenure at Dartmouth, however, should be considered within the context of the period in which they lived. While faculty began to exhibit these patterns, such career lines were not a widespread experience for many Americans until the 1890s.[113]

The associational involvements of the 1881 faculty members indicate a marked change from those of their 1851 counterparts and point toward their changing idea of community. In 1851, 75% of the academical faculty served as preachers, licentiates, or ordained ministers; 100% were involved in community activities on a local, state, or regional level. In 1881, on the other hand, the involvement of faculty members in clerical activities centered on their participation as church members and supporters. Moreover, although some of the faculty maintained an involvement in the local community, they began to evidence a translocal or cosmopolitan orientation. Associations with disciplinary peers in other institutions became increasingly important. As the faculty began to define community solely in terms of these peers, the peer group became the audience and status referent in place of the local community.[114]

Reputation among these peers was an important indicator of success. Thus, in contrast to the 1851 faculty, 1881 faculty members held leadership positions or participated in (or saw as role models those who did so) such organizations as the American Association for the Advancement of Science and the American Philological Association, while maintaining some involvement (although reduced in contrast to the 1851 faculty) in leadership positions in the local community, primarily in the small town of Hanover (see appendix 9).[115]

The faculty's interest in and the nature of their publications also point toward the sense of community underlying the new professional role. For the 1851 faculty, publication was not a high-priority item. Those contributing to the literature of the period evidenced their community orientation and contributed their addresses before various groups or wrote articles, largely journalistic in nature, on various educational, political, and literary topics with a regional identification. By the 1881 period faculty members were beginning to publish for, and identify with, scholars publishing original works in their particular discipline. They were beginning to judge others as scholars (or not) on the basis of this research, which with the development of a more rationalized, esoteric learning, scholars in the field could evaluate most easily.[116] Thus, for the scholar, the audience and status referent shifted to peers in the field. This shift is understandable, considering the beginnings of specialized training in Europe in a particular discipline, the longer period of apprenticeship, the more cosmopolitan background and metropolitan orientation, and scholars' associational involvements along disciplinary lines.

One can assess the interest in and nature of publications by looking at some of the publications of three prominent Dartmouth professors. The publications include original research in a particular discipline, and they formed a foundation for their reputation among peers in the field. In 1881 Hardy published *Elements of Quaternions* and *Imaginary Quantities*, a translation of Jean Robert Argand's French treatise. He published a number of other books in the 1880s, such as *Typographical Surveying* (1888), *Elements of Analytic Geometry* (1889), and in 1890 *Elements of the Differential and Integral Calculus*. Charles H. Hitchcock, Hall Professor of Geology and Mineralogy, published four volumes of *The Geology of New Hampshire* (1874, 1877, 1878) and contributed numerous papers to the scientific literature, especially on the glacial geology of the Champlain Valley and the fossil tracks in the Connecticut Valley. He also prepared important geological maps that appeared in United States government publications.

Wright contributed numerous articles in the 1880s, such as "The Place of Original Research in College Education" (1882), "The Greek Question" (1884), "Unpublished White Lekythoi from Athens" (1887), and "The Date of Cylon" (1888 and 1892). From 1884 to 1889 he edited the "Transactions and Proceedings" of the American Philological Association, and in 1886 he published a translation of Maxime Collignon's *Manuel d'Archéologie Greque*. In 1888 Wright served as associate editor of the *Classical Review*. From the mid-1880s onward, he contributed many pieces of original research to the periodicals of the period and served as editor of numerous journals in his field. While his peers considered him a scholar in the 1881 period, Wright revealed the true significance of his creative scholarship in 1888 with the publication of "The Date of Cylon." Through his research in Greek history, he devised a correct chronology of the economic and political disturbances in Athens at the end of the seventh century B.C. before the discovery of Aristotle's *Constitution of the Athenians*.

The interest in publication of original research in a particular discipline for consumption of one's peers also points to the changing conception of higher learning. The faculty's altered background and experiences within a transformed societal environment led to different conceptions and standards of higher learning.[117] In contrast to the unity of purpose of the 1851 faculty, the 1881 faculty exhibited a diversity of purpose and interests. The conception of the 1851 faculty of the unity of knowledge, the joining of heart and mind in creating a Christian Zion, began to give way to a more rationalized learning.[118] The development of, and emphasis on, a more esoteric learning led to a separation of the connection between faith and knowledge.[119] The conception of higher learning began to center on the specialization of knowledge, its division into separate fields of study with specific methodologies and limits of study—the fragmentation of knowledge rather than its basic unity. The emphasis began to shift to testable results[120] and intellectual analysis based on quantitative evidence in distinct areas of study, with specific methodologies related to the particular discipline.[121] This research could be communicated most efficiently by publication rather than by speeches, discourses, or orations. And one's peers, fellow specialists, could understand most easily, evaluate, and appreciate the significance of this type of information.

Since peers in the field now provided the basis for the standards of success, faculty members began to seek to regulate their profession through peer evaluation. According to the faculty members' perception, in order to insure the development of professionals, they themselves could best set standards and judge qualifications. With the erosion of a shared sense of pastoral purpose, and with an open pursuit of interests among a more diverse faculty pressing for some sense of autonomy, their professional assertions also included demands for a more formal organization differentiating personal and official roles and statuses. They saw an increasing separation between themselves and the president, and they desired to achieve power to protect their interests, which they no longer defined in reference to the organic community of the 1851 period.

In order to illuminate more clearly the movement toward the new professorial role and what it really represented, one might view this movement in relation to some of the antagonists in this controversy. The members of the faculty might be distributed along an axis representing "types." At one pole one could place those representing the new professorial role and the more cosmopolitan nature of some of the faculty. At the other, one could place those representing the older professorial style and the more traditional faculty background. Many faculty members fell into various places between these extremes, and the Bartlett trial, by raising these issues and bringing them out into the open, tended to solidify forces and alliances and intensify the scope and power of the professorial role.

Arthur Sherburne Hardy, called by Bartlett the "chief conspirator," represented the cosmopolite on the faculty. By background, experiences, and frame of reference, Hardy was far removed from the typical Dartmouth faculty member of the previous generation. The son of a merchant and philanthropist, he went to school in Switzerland, became fluent in French, traveled to Spain on one of his father's ships, and returned to the United States to study at Boston Latin School and Phillips Andover Academy. Hardy attended Amherst College, graduated from the United States Military Academy, and studied at the École des Points et Chaussées and the Conservatoire des Arts et Métiers in Paris. He taught for a brief period at West Point and served as a professor at Iowa (Grinnell) College. Hardy left Dartmouth in 1893, after nineteen years, to become editor of *Cosmopolitan* magazine and then received several diplomatic appointments. A fellow of the National Institute of Arts and Letters, his associational involvements included membership in the exclusive Century and Authors Clubs. His publications include specialized engineering and mathematical studies, poetry, novels, and an autobiography. He also lectured on art and education. A connoisseur of food and wine, an accomplished musician, a perfect horseman, the difference between this cosmopolite and Bartlett is revealed in "the contrast between the formidable Samuel Colcord Bartlett in topper and frock coat on a bicycle and the urbane Professor Hardy on his handsome gray charger."[122]

John Wright represented the pattern of the new professional, identifying his goals, aspirations, and achievements by his discipline and community of peers in other colleges and universities. Born in Persia, the son of a missionary and physician, he came to the United States at eight, studied at College Hill (Poughkeepsie), and graduated from Dartmouth. He studied classical philology and Sanskrit at the University of Leipzig[123] and served as an assistant professor of ancient languages at Ohio State. At the age of seventeen, he began attending meetings of the American Philological Association, and in 1884, while an associate professor at Dartmouth, he became secretary and treasurer of the association. In 1886 Wright became professor of classical philology at Johns Hopkins, and in 1887 President Eliot of Harvard convinced him to accept a position there as professor of Greek. He did extensive original research and edited numerous scholarly journals in his field. Wright served in such positions as president of the American Philological Association, fellow of the American Academy of Arts and Sciences, councillor of the Archaeological Institute of America, and corresponding member of the Imperial German Archaeological Institute.

Charles Henry Hitchcock represented the new professorial style, but a type for whom the presidency and the whole controversy did not assume great importance. Born in Amherst, New Hampshire, the son of Edward Hitchcock, president of Amherst, he graduated from Amherst College and then studied at Yale, Andover Theological Seminary, and the Royal School of Mines in London. Hitchcock had been state geologist of Maine and assistant geologist of Vermont before coming to Dartmouth. He also lectured at Amherst and Lafayette Colleges. Hitchcock served in a private capacity for various mining interests, and in 1868 he became state geologist of New Hampshire and Hall Professor of Geology and Mineralogy at Dartmouth. By special agreement with the trustees, he devoted part of his time to teaching and the rest to his geological studies. While at Dartmouth he carried on his geological studies, contributed various articles and papers to scholarly journals, lectured at other colleges, and in 1883 became vice president of the American Association for the Advancement of Science. Hitchcock published extensively throughout his lifetime and participated and held leadership positions in various scientific societies. He served, for example, as a founder of the Geological Society of America and of the International Congress of Geologists.

The special arrangements of his professorship through the 1881 period set him apart even from professors such as Wright. Hitchcock could look upon the institution more impersonally and concentrate more completely on his disciplinary community outside the college. He could reach these peers through his writings and associational involvements. In line with Hitchcock's concentration on his geological studies, one student said of him: "He was thoroughly absorbed in his profession, . . . but be was not quite alert enough for the human element of his audience to make a good teacher. He generally lectured with his eyes shut and often walked around the street apparently in the same way."[124] Hitchcock probably was willing to have the president, just as well as anyone else, decide the issues of internal policy as long as he was free to pursue his geological studies. He remained neutral throughout the controversy.

One could place Henry E. Parker and Charles Emerson at the other end of the scale. With the exception of Bartlett's son, they were Bartlett's firmest supporters. Parker represented the older, pastoral, community-oriented style. Born in Keene, New Hampshire, he was a Dartmouth undergraduate and a graduate of Union Theological Seminary. He served as a minister for twelve years before his appointment to the Dartmouth faculty. Parker viewed his professorial role as a pastoral one and as having an integral relationship to the wider geographic community. His associational involvements were linked to the locale and the state. He served, for example, on the school committees in Hanover and as a representative to the New Hampshire Constitutional Convention in 1876. His conception of the professorial role is reflected in this characterization: "He was not a critical scholar. [H]is classroom was not a very interesting place, he did not turn out Latin scholars; but he did impress upon his students the relative values of life, and he did give them an example of the speech and life of a Christian gentleman."[125] At sixty-one, Parker was a contemporary of Bartlett (Bartlett was sixty-three). Wright, twenty-nine; Hardy, thirty-four; and Hitchcock, forty-three, were thus separated from Parker and Bartlett not only by a different view of their role but by age as well.

The background and experiences of Charles Emerson, also a Bartlett supporter, set him apart from some of the newer types on the faculty. He did not enter Dartmouth College until he was twenty-one years old. Emerson worked on his father's farm and taught school before he entered Dartmouth. Upon graduation at twenty-five, he became a tutor of mathematics. Emerson also served as an instructor of gymnastics and astronomy, as an associate professor of natural philosophy and mathematics, and as Appleton Professor of Natural Philosophy. Emerson participated in church and civic activities of the local community. During the time of the trial he seemed to view the college as a home.

By 1890, however, Emerson could no longer be counted as a supporter of Bartlett.[126] There is no direct explanation of this shift. But in 1884 he became involved in the American Association for the Advancement of Science and visited European universities. Perhaps his frame of reference broadened through his association with other colleagues, so that the notion of the community of peers became of greater importance to his conception of his professorial role. But in 1881 he viewed the organization in more personal, familial terms, and his origins, educational background, and experiences separated him from Wright, Hardy, and Hitchcock. Although Emerson was close to them in age (thirty-eight), his background and experiences placed him apart from these new types.

Those faculty members resembling these newer types and those with aspirations along these lines asserted their professionalization during the trial and highlighted the altered notion of presidential authority. In doing this, they reflected their changed communal notion—now defined solely with reference to the distinct group of peers. In this process they pointed to the transformation in the conception of the college—its organization, its relation to society, and the evolving idea of higher learning. The trial testimony illuminates further the movement toward this new professorial role.

In their assertions for peer evaluation and some sense of faculty autonomy, they revealed a consciousness of professors having those "unique skills and functions."[127] that Robert Wiebe has argued increasingly formed the basis of social identification after 1880. One of the professors noted, for example:

> As a rule I can think of nothing that could conduce more certainly to wise decisions in matters of this kind than full, friendly and frank discussion of such a point by men who if they are fit to be at all connected with the college as professors must be especially fit to judge of the qualifications of men who are to be their colleagues.[128]

In 1851 they did not see their functions and skills as set apart from the organic community. Many of them conceived of their role as another form of the ministerial role and as an integral part of the locale and region. With the development of a more esoteric learning and with the changed idea of community, the faculty stressed that these peers could judge most effectively if a potential faculty member had the requisite qualifications for entry into their ranks. Given their changing backgrounds and experiences and their aspirations toward this new professorial role in a society itself undergoing change, this assertion is understandable[129] and is representative of what was occurring elsewhere. During the 1880s faculty members in other collegiate institutions also voiced such assertions and expressed an increasing distance between themselves and the president. At Union, for example, the faculty charged that the president hired new professors without appropriate faculty consultation and that the president moved professors from one academic field to another without faculty advice.[130] And at Wesleyan, the faculty complained that the president tried to appoint a person of his own choosing against the recommendations of the faculty.[131]

The emphasis on reputation and the definition of success being defined with exclusive reference to disciplinary peers and the development of a more specialized learning is evidenced throughout the trial testimony. For example, one professor noted:

> The point which I made most prominent in my own remarks was that it was very desirable now that in a college like this—I mean in the latter part of the nineteenth century, where expert work is so much desired and needed—we should have to fill a chair . . . [with] a man who would give character to the chair, or at any rate would not in any way impair the character and reputation of the chair in Greek. And I also thought a man who had reached his 46th year . . . without becoming known at all to persons who in the East had special acquaintance with Greek professors and Greek scholars, was perhaps not the man to appoint.[132]

The testimony seems to indicate that the faculty inquired about Hewitt's reputation among Greek scholars in other institutions. Considering Wright's deep involvement in the American Philological Association, this type of inquiry seems very likely to have taken place. The reputation of Hewitt among this group would have been of concern to a faculty aspiring to "professional" status. The individual's reputation would have been especially important when the position in question was a senior one or a special chair that would set the tone for the department.

The extent of identification with these peers to replace the communal referent for the 1851 faculty is evidenced in this testimony:

> I felt if such a man as Sylvester from John[s] Hopkins or Pierce [sic] from Harvard were called and placed over me in mathematics, I should be glad to sit at their feet, but there were some men who might be placed over me in whom I should feel insulted to have placed over me. And I thought so far as I learned . . . I asked for information about Mr. Hewitt. . . . I did not understand that he was a man to whom the Spaulding professor could go for any information in Greek. I do not think he is today.[133]

With the development of a more esoteric learning, from the faculty's perspective the specialists in the field could judge scholarly attainments that were usually evidenced by publication of original research.

With the erosion of a shared sense of purpose and with an open pursuit of interests among a more diverse faculty pressing for some sense of autonomy, their professional assertions also included demands for a more formal organization separating personal and official roles and statuses (and with a more explicit separation between themselves and the president). This difference between a more personal familial college community and the more formal model becomes evident when one compares the statements of Parker and those of some of the newer types on the faculty. Parker, regarding his relationship to Bartlett, stated:

> I perhaps should not be at liberty to speak of any ones experience except my own. So far as I am concerned, I have found him exceedingly ready to listen to suggestions and even criticisms, and I never knew him to turn a scowling look upon me in anything I offered. Whatever I said I endeavored to do it respectfully. I knew it was a somewhat delicate thing at times, but I never knew him to meet it only with the most courteous and kindly and gentlemanly manner.[134]

The stress is on approaching Bartlett on a personal basis—respectfully, these are delicate things, he never scowled at him—rather than as a professional academic on an official basis making known his viewpoints with regard to questions of policy. Parker seems to view Bartlett as the pastoral head and interpreter of policy. Bartlett also viewed the organization on a more personal basis, with expectations of a consensual orientation, if unity rather than differences were accentuated. In keeping with this viewpoint, when an instructor inquired about consultation with the faculty of the Chandler Scientific Department regarding his possible appointment to that faculty, Bartlett said, "'I suggest that you say nothing to them about it,' . . . such matters are more readily accomplished if [they are] not talked over too extensively."[135]

Some of the newer types, on the other hand, stressed the importance of separating personal and official roles, duties, and statuses within a more formal model of organization. Hardy, for example, emphasized the importance of discussing the question of the appointment to the Greek chair in an official meeting.[136] And Pollens noted the importance of "mental qualifications."[137] One could be a good man and a good person but not appropriate for a position. In emphasizing his official position on the Dartmouth faculty, Hardy stated that Bartlett's remarks regarding the faculty's scholarly reputation and lack of influence regarding appointments made him feel that he had been treated in an inappropriate manner—not in keeping with his official position. In his personal relations, however, Hardy noted: "Nothing that the President then said would prevent me from meeting him pleasantly thereafter."[138] And the theme of a document that describes the general manner in which questions relating to the trial should be answered by the faculty stressed the separation between personal and official roles and statuses:

"There had been no personal quarrel." But "the welfare of the college requires a change in the executive head."[139] As further evidence of the movement toward a more formal organization, the faculty meeting of 31 August 1881 records for the first time names of faculty members who are present.[140] Thus, the faculty began to emerge as a collegiate faction, seeing formal organization rather than the congregation as the basis of administration and seeking to protect their interests by achieving power within the college.

The faculty members of the Chandler Scientific Department and the associated schools shared the general concerns of the academical faculty and also evidenced their very strong interests in the status of the schools and the fields they represented. Members of the Chandler Scientific Department and the New Hampshire College of Agriculture and the Mechanic Arts felt themselves especially singled out by president for adverse treatment, and they viewed Bartlett's attitudes and actions as detrimental to their professional aims.

The data regarding the Chandler faculty also evidence a movement away from the homogeneous, pastoral, community-oriented faculty of the 1851 period. The Chandler faculty comprised four professors and one tutor. All of the professors were born in New England, but only one was born in New Hampshire (see appendix 3). Although four of the five members were Dartmouth undergraduates, three of these had been students in the Chandler Scientific Department and had the newer bachelor of science degrees (see appendix 4). One of the faculty members had a civil engineering degree (Thayer School of Civil Engineering); one had specialized training in his field in Europe, and one was a graduate of a theological seminary (see appendix 5).

Although they became professors at a somewhat younger age with less experience than their academical counterparts in 1881, they were older and had more college teaching experience than the academical faculty of 1851. Three of the full professors had some college teaching experience before they became full professors. One was appointed to this position at thirty with two years' college teaching experience at Dartmouth and a few years' experience as an instructor at a polytechnical institute in Dresden, Germany; one at thirty-one with two years' college teaching experience; and one at thirty with two years' college teaching experience (see appendixes 7 and 8).[141]

While the Chandler faculty members did not entirely abandon their involvement in the local community, their associational involvements evidence participation in associations of peers along disciplinary lines (see appendix 9). Their activities include membership in the American Association for the Advancement of Science, the American Society of Civil Engineers, the New England Botanical Society, and the New England Association of Colleges and Preparatory Schools, as well as participation in the local community, serving, for example, as justice for the local police court. One of the faculty members also offered expert advice to the local community and surrounding areas in his field—engineering.

From the perspective of these faculty members, Bartlett had "belittled the Chandler department,"[142] and he seemed to be determined to overhaul the school in a direction opposed to the interests of faculty, students, and alumni.[143] In a series of steps Bartlett raised the question of the status of the Chandler Scientific Department before the board. He questioned such matters as the admission requirements and the course of study (which he felt were no longer in keeping with Chandler's will, owing to their expansion by the faculty), the advisability of the academical faculty being permitted to teach in the Chandler department, the constitution of the school, and the trustees' right to accept a bequest with a provision for a board of visitors. While not agreeing completely with Bartlett's position and not adhering to the degree of change urged by the president, the board passed some measures, such as the modification of the standards for admission so that the mathematical requirements were reduced, which members of the faculty saw as debasing the school and their position.

Bartlett thought the Academical Department put the students "under vastly better moral and religious influences"[144] and objected to the portrayal of the Chandler Scientific Department as a "liberal education on a scientific basis," feeling that this might be attracting the students away from the academical course. He told Edward R. Ruggles, professor of modern languages and administrative head of the Chandler Scientific Department, that in portraying the department in this fashion, he "had furnished a statement . . . which was misleading to the public."[145] The Chandler professors were from the areas of physics, botany, French, German, civil engineering, and theoretical and applied mechanics—the fields of science, modern languages, and engineering. Bartlett was a proponent of the classical curriculum, as he felt this curriculum would aid in what he conceived was the prime aim of education—the development of moral character. In his inaugural address, he told his audience that he wanted to stimulate a culture of mental discipline with the qualities of "wakefulness, precision, fullness, equipoise, and docility."[146] His attitude toward the Chandler Scientific Department demonstrated his objections to certain developments in the field of science, essentially the fragmentation of knowledge accompanying the more esoteric learning, and especially developments in the field of applied science. "The tendency of modern science is, of necessity," he said, "steadily toward sectional lines and division of labor. It is a tendency whose cramping influence is as steadily to be resisted, even in later life, much more in early training."[147] He viewed this fragmentation of knowledge as antithetical to the unifying concept of knowledge and to the development of moral character.

The question of what constituted a liberal education was an important point for this faculty. When questioned if he considered "the primary object of the Chandler school to furnish a liberal education as college men understand the term," Ruggles said, "There is a difference of opinion . . . many of the best educators to-day, including such men as Prof. Elliot and Prof. Bain so interpret a liberal education as [that] given in the Chandler school. I have myself inclined to put it in this form, viz, liberal education on a scientific basis."[148] To the Chandler faculty, Bartlett, in effect, was questioning not only the status of the school but also the aspirations of the faculty for the fields they represented.

By questioning the authority of the Chandler faculty over admission standards and policy, Bartlett intensified the faculty's articulation of demands for some measure of faculty autonomy (with an increasing distance between itself and the president). When Ruggles asked that the president read his report to the Chandler faculty regarding the Chandler Scientific Department (Bartlett presented this report to the board), Bartlett said, "These matters do not concern the Chandler faculty; they are matters for the Board; and the Board has various matters under consideration, and will in due time arrange and settle them.[149] Ruggles said he was surprised "that this did not concern the Chandler faculty to whom the immediate interests of the school, I supposed, were entrusted."[150] In similar fashion to the academical faculty, they felt they should be advised of policy matters relating to their department as the body best able to make appropriate recommendations. And Bartlett, they felt, treated them in an inappropriate manner, not fitting their positions as faculty members. Bartlett, on the other hand, operating from his view of himself as pastoral head and viewing the college order on a more personal basis with expectations of a consensual orientation, if harmony rather than differences were accentuated, explained that he did not read the report because he thought "it would only awaken unpleasant discussion which would never have any issue."[151] When asked by the prosecution to characterize Bartlett's official manner, Ruggles said, "It was this, in a word, to sum it all up. 'I am the college.'. . . And with that idea it was pretty difficult for anybody else to exist who did not form a spoke in the wheel of the college."[152]

The growth of the engineering section in the Chandler Department, Bartlett's attempts in their eyes to discourage it, and the aspirations of some of the faculty in the area of engineering led to controversy, not only between Bartlett and the Chandler faculty, but with Robert Fletcher, professor of civil engineering in the Thayer School, as well. In 1871 the Thayer School of Civil Engineering began giving its regular course to students that was to be essentially postgraduate in nature.[153] The school was very small at this time, with usually four or fewer students each year. In the trial testimony, Bartlett revealed that the Chandler faculty had pressured Fletcher for a closer relationship between the two schools. Bartlett noted that Fletcher saw the pressure exerted upon him as "a kind of menace."[154] The engineering section in the Chandler Department was one of the most popular with the students, and some of the faculty members aspired to expand the program. Fletcher wrote in his diary that there was a "danger of having two eng[ineering] courses at Hanover."[155] Bartlett, who may have accepted the idea of "professional" courses on the postbaccalaureate level, was opposed to them on the undergraduate level. John V. Hazen, professor of theoretical and applied mechanics, complained that Bartlett made the engineering course in the Chandler catalogue appear as of "very slight importance." "He . . . makes it appear upon the catalogue," said Hazen, "as if the Engineering Course was only a set—of optional studies & not—a course at all."[156]

Fletcher, whose background placed him apart from the traditional Dartmouth faculty member of an earlier period and more toward the new professional, cosmopolitan types, supported Bartlett, no doubt in good part because of his position with respect to the Thayer School. Born in New York, a graduate of the United States Military Academy, Fletcher was a member of the American Association for the Advancement of Science and the American Society of Civil Engineers. He also was active in the local community, both as an expert in engineering, and in such groups as the school committee in Hanover and the church. The aspirations of the Chandler faculty must have seemed especially threatening to Fletcher, considering the size and recent establishment of the school.

Although engineering education had grown in the middle and late 1830s, not until the mid-nineteenth century did the great growth in industry and transportation strengthen this profession and help make engineering associations and schools a reality.[157] Engineers attempted to organize in 1837 and 1852, but they did not establish a permanent national organization, the American Society of Civil Engineers, until 1867. In the 1881 period, engineering societies such as the American Society of Civil Engineers concentrated on being learned societies, on sharing research rather than on promoting the status of engineers.[158] Dartmouth faculty members with an engineering background were active in these societies. They differed from the medical faculty, whose prime interest was with the regulation, control, and status of their occupation as physicians.

Members of the faculty of the New Hampshire College of Agriculture and the Mechanic Arts also regarded Bartlett as a prime mover against them. While colleges added separate "practical" schools to the traditional liberal arts college before the passage of the Morrill Act in 1862, this act brought a great growth of education in agriculture and the mechanic arts. The agricultural school at Dartmouth accepted its first students in 1868. Much of the concern of the agricultural faculty stemmed from Bartlett's attitude toward them as faculty members in such a school.

The data regarding the 1881 faculty of the New Hampshire College of Agriculture and the Mechanic Arts also reveal a movement away from the pattern that had been typical in 1851. The faculty consisted of two full professors and two instructors.[159] As regards birthplace, one professor was born in Ohio, one professor in New Hampshire, one instructor in Vermont, one unknown (see appendix 3). In terms of their training, the professor of mathematics had a degree in civil engineering from the Thayer School in addition to his undergraduate training at Dartmouth. The professor of chemistry was a graduate of the scientific section of Bethany College in West Virginia and had medical training at Dartmouth. One instructor was a Dartmouth graduate; no information is available for the other instructor, who stayed at Dartmouth for one year (see appendixes 4 and 5). One professor had seven years' teaching experience before appointment to the position of full professor, and the other one had one year of experience (see appendix 7). The age range of the full professors fell within the low range of the academical and Chandler professors. One professor was thirty-three, and the other was twenty-eight (see appendix 6). Their associational involvements included membership in such organizations as the American Asociation for the Advancement of Science and participation in local affairs (see appendix 9).

Bartlett made obvious his low opinion of the education offered by the school. This was of special concern to a faculty intent upon raising the status of the school and the fields they represented. At the commencement address of the agricultural school, Bartlett stressed that only the study of classics could really give a young man a "broad and rounded education."[160] According to Bartlett, the type of education offered by the agricultural school fit men "for selectmen, highway surveyors, or perhaps the legislature."[161] Bartlett said that he did not regard this remark as insulting and stood by his statement: "I stand by the remark up and down and through and through, in my intent as I meant it."[162] Benjamin T. Blanpied (professor of chemistry), expressing the view of the agricultural faculty, said that the more he thought of the address, "the worse it grew rather than better."[163]

The agricultural faculty also evidenced assertions of a sense of autonomy; within this context, however, the primary direction of their efforts centered on attaining the same status and respect one might give to professors of more traditional schools and fields. Bartlett moved to change the degree of the agricultural school from bachelor of science to bachelor of agricultural science. The faculty and students regarded this as an insult. Their aspirations centered on the acceptance of the education offered by the school as a liberal education equal in status to the scientific section. Bartlett, turning to his notion of harmony and consensus under presidential authority, noted that he was not really opposed to the B.S. degree for the school, but he thought that the Chandler faculty did not like the two schools' having the same degree. Charles H. Pettee, professor of mathematics, indicated that he thought the Chandler faculty did not object to it and "even if they should . . . as they did not, I understood . . . it would not make any difference."[164]

In 1881, as in 1851, the pattern of the medical faculty differed from the faculty pattern of the other schools and departments. And although the concerns of the medical faculty in 1881 still centered on the status of their theories and the regulation of their occupation as physicians, there were important differences from the 1851 pattern. The composition of the faculty changed from one that was local and regional to one that included physicians from other areas. Faculty members had more teaching experience, exhibited more interest in publications, were involved in organizations of peers not only on a local level but on a national level as well, and increasingly began to identify with an area of specialization to which they directed most of their efforts. Their background and experiences point to a more esoteric learning within the field of medicine and to an accentuation of the notion of peer group—fellow specialists in the field—as community.

The changes in birthplace, educational background, associational involvements, location of their medical practice, and nature of their publications evidence their more metropolitan orientation and their interest in specialization within a particular field of medicine. The medical faculty consisted of seven full professors, four lecturers, and one demonstrator.[165] In 1851, 83.3% of the faculty were born in New Hampshire, and 100% were born in New England. By 1881 only 8.3% were born in New Hampshire and 50% in New England (see appendix 3). The number of faculty members holding a Dartmouth undergraduate degree decreased from 83.3% to 41.7% (see appendix 4). As in 1851, all the members of the medical faculty except for the professor of medical jurisprudence had M.D. degrees (see appendix 5). In 1881 some faculty members maintained practices and lectured in other colleges in areas outside the local community or region (such as New York and Ohio).

They lectured at such schools as Cincinnati Medical College and New York Polyclinic. This was possible because in 1881, as in 1851, the medical faculty lectured for fourteen weeks during the summer and fall. (This period was increased to twenty weeks in 1886.)

From the information available, at least eight members of the faculty made contributions to the medical literature of the period, and most of the faculty were not only active in but held leadership positions in professional associations. These involvements included activities directed to their distinct areas of specialization and involvements on a national level. For example, on the Dartmouth medical faculty in 1881, one finds the founder of the American Laryngological Asssociation, the secretary and president of the New York Obstetrical Society, the vice president of the American Gynecological Association, a member of the National Association of Medical Superintendents of Asylums, members of the American Medical Association, and the president of the Cincinnati Academy of Medicine and of the American Surgical Society. The resident medical professor was a member of the American Medical Association, the White Mountain Society and the Connecticut River Medical Society, and served as president of the New Hampshire Medical Society and the Vermont Medical Society. He also participated in the civic affairs of Hanover, serving, for example, as precinct commissioner in 1885 (see appendix 9).

The differences between the pattern of the 1881 medical faculty and that of the 1851 faculty are in line with the developments of the medical profession during the late nineteenth century. This period marked a stage of transition for the medical profession. In the 1851 period, the physician's reputation related to his ability to modify the symptoms of the illness, such as bleeding to reduce fever. By the 1881 period, some advances had been made in medicine, such as the acceptance of the germ theory, vaccination, and anesthetics; but doctors were not successful in achieving long-range cures until around 1900. Although physicians evidenced specialization within particular fields of medicine and interest and research in these areas, not until about 1900 could they unite around a body of medical doctrine and control the medical training and practice of their colleagues.[166]

Thus, although the Dartmouth medical faculty of 1881 evidenced a decline of involvement in the locale and region, a more metropolitan orientation, and what seemed to be an accentuation of a notion of community defined with exclusive reference to their own peers, concern over the status of their theories and the regulation of their occupation remained. Owing to the financial arrangements, the medical faculty remained rather independent in running the school. Members of the medical faculty formally recommended to the board candidates for faculty positions, and it appears that the board ordinarily appointed these nominees. Whatever Bartlett's opinion of medical education, if he did not interfere with the administration of their school, why did the resident medical professor sign the memorials, and why did some others write letters to the board in support of the majority position of the faculty of the other schools and departments? Opposition to Bartlett stemmed from how his policies might reflect upon them as physicians affiliated with an associated school of Dartmouth College. As in 1851, concerns about the regulation of their profession and the status of their theories and practices were very important. During a period of transition, with scientific discoveries, specialization in particular fields, and increased identification with peers in a wider medical community, this would seem to be especially important. Highlighting these concerns, Phineas Sanborn Conner, professor of surgery, wrote a letter to the board regarding the Hewitt appointment. He stated: "I hope . . . that the college will not appoint the Rev. Dr. Stick because he is no longer able to find a flock to watch over." The man they appoint should be "a thorough Greek scholar."[167]

Thus, although differences existed between and within the various schools and departments, the emergent pattern reveals a break in the 1851 pattern. By background, experience, and aspirations they were a more heterogeneous, cosmopolitan, professionalized group. They evidenced more of a metropolitan orientation, a movement toward a more rationalized, esoteric learning, and a notion of community defined with exclusive reference to their own peer group. The audience, status, reputation, and the definition of success emanated from this source. Within the college, they emerged as a collegiate faction, desiring to achieve power to protect their interests, which they no longer defined with reference to the organic community of the 1851 period. They voiced demands for some sense of faculty autonomy with an increasing distance between themselves and the president. The faculty saw a more formal organization, separating personal and official duties and statuses as a model of administration. This pattern is striking in contrast to the pattern of the homogeneous, pastoral, community-oriented group of the 1851 period. The orientation of the 1851 faculty was a local and regional one. Higher learning emphasized the basic unity of knowledge, the joining of faith and intellect in uplifting the individual character and creating a Zion. The faculty members saw their role in the wider geographic and moral community as an integral one, with status, audience, and reputation emanating from this source. Within the college they were a cohesive, closely knit community with a shared sense of purpose and with the president as pastoral head.

If by 1881 the Dartmouth faculty members were defining community with exclusive reference to their disciplinary peers, why did some remain leaders in the local community? The population of Hanover, New Hampshire, offers a key to the answer of this question. In 1880 the population of Hanover included 2,147 persons, and the population of the village included 1,134 persons.[168] A population of this size suggests a shortage of leaders, so men of talent such as the faculty had to supply both systems.[169] The professionals combined their translocal orientation toward the community of peers with a local orientation to supply the needed services of the town. Thus, faculty members were involved both as "experts" in their area, providing, for example, advice about engineering projects to the local community and holding other local positions not related to their area of expertise, as well as being involved in associations of peers in other colleges and universities along particular disciplinary lines.

By virtue of their background, experience, and aspirations, Bartlett and some of his supporters were more typical of the 1851 period than of the 1881 period. Their ideals of pastoral care; instructing the moral conscience; a cohesive, familial order with the president as the pastoral head; and a perception of the faculty role as having an integral relationship to the wider geographic and moral community were in conflict with a faculty who by background, experience, and aspirations were beginning to define their role according to different models of success. In this grouping, both Bartlett's style and policies seem out of place. Conflict seems to have been almost inevitable. Bringing the issue of the faculty role out into the open served to highlight the difference between Bartlett and a majority of the faculty and to intensify the beginnings of this movement toward a new stage in the professionalization of the faculty.

The movement toward a new professorial role at Dartmouth was part of a more general transformation in higher education and American society, but the various colleges and universities exhibited important differences in the speed, form, nature, and impact of this movement. American society experienced a transformation in the structure and meaning of community, and this period saw the emergence of more formal patterns of social organization. Journals of wide circulation carried articles demanding that professors specialize and conduct original research.[170] At Harvard and Princeton, changes were also occurring in the faculty along these lines. With such differences as faculty patterns and location as described in this chapter, this movement toward a new professorial role appears to have begun earlier and at a more intensified pace at Harvard as compared with Dartmouth. More important, beyond that which one can illustrate by data regarding degree of specialized training in a discipline, for example, is that this movement meant different things at Harvard and Dartmouth and comparable collegiate institutions. At such institutions as Dartmouth, despite a new stage in the professionalization of the faculty, this movement did not inevitably lead to the emergence of the university model; nor, as this chapter illustrates, did it mean that because Dartmouth did not adopt this model the college was not undergoing significant change. The faculty's altered notion of community and the shift in the faculty members' perception of their role highlighted aspects of how transformed was the college and the idea and standards of higher learning within an institution remaining faithful to its commitment to the primacy of undergraduate liberal arts education.[171]

CHAPTER III

The Students

Aside from any religious sentiment, and this was general, the men enjoyed the sense the gathering [chapel] gave of the unity, fellowship, and dignity of the College body. It is certain that the presence at thirteen chapel, and one church service each week of the whole College inspired and fostered an intense College spirit, and also that the meeting of the classes here and at recitations, always by themselves and in the same order, gave a conscious compactness of organization unknown to the modern class and university. The intimacy of class association and acquaintance, and the consciousness of class entity, were enhanced by the identity of studies and the unity of each class at every exercise. Its integrating influence was definitely felt and in sum was inspiring and wholesome, and its recollection is warmly cherished and highly valued.

—Amos N. Currier (1906, Class of 1856)

They [the students] entered into the rural life of northern New England and aroused new thoughts and new purposes. They stimulated a desire for a broader education in some whose names had not otherwise honored our rolls.

—Mellen Chamberlain (1885, Class of 1844)

Students, in the words of Frederick Rudolph, are "the most neglected, least understood element of the American academic community."[1] Yet, students offer an important vehicle through which one can better assess the crosscurrents between the college and society. They come from the community, go back into it, and live their lives in its various social and economic structures.

Frederick Rudolph and David Allmendinger attempt to redress this neglect of students.[2] Rudolph contributes to our understanding of the role of students in introducing the significance of student literary societies, fraternities, and organized athletics.[3] But his prime emphasis upon the student in relation to the extracurriculum does not provide a complete picture—the interaction of the student with the larger community. Allmendinger makes a significant historical contribution in illustrating how students were agents of change in the transformation of the character of colleges and of student life. He relates the experience of the students to certain changes in the social and economic history of New England.[4] But Allmendinger's prime focus on students, without an intensive analysis of other collegiate groups as part of the process, still leads to an incomplete view.

In order to understand the transformation in the nature of the college and of higher learning in nineteenth-century America and the students' place in this process, one must look ultimately at the student in relation to the total college community and to the larger society. One might pose such questions of generations of students as: Where did they come from? What was their socioeconomic background? What were their ages? What did they learn—both within and outside the formal curriculum? What were their aspirations? What were their jobs after college? To what type of areas did they go? What value or impact did their college education seem to have on their lives?[5] With this perspective in mind, one can assess the role of the students in the Bartlett controversy.

While the antebellum period was not entirely free of disciplinary problems,[6] a generation before the Bartlett controversy the students regarded the president as the main authority figure and interpreter of life. According to this view of the president as pastoral head of the college, one student said of Dartmouth's President Lord:

They [his spectacles] furnished a "secure fence" behind which the dear old Shepherd could glance at "his sheep," without detection and watch every possible thing that happened to be going on in his vicinity, whether in chapel or recitation room or even in the solemn personal interviews with luckless students in the dreaded "Prexy's Study." I have seen him in chapel open the Bible, "repeat" a psalm (apparently reading it) and his restless eye meanwhile "over" the "edge of his glasses," searching every face in every seat and every corner. No wonder that he was credited with "semi-omniscience."[7]

For Lord, and for Bartlett a generation later, the prime aim of education centered on the development of moral character. According to this view, rules and regulations and firm discipline helped in character building. When confronted with a disturbance, Lord would say, "Disperse, young gentlemen, disperse"[8] if necessary, he would center himself in the middle of the group and strike blows with his ivory-headed cane.[9] "He was dignity itself," said one student, "and no student was brave enough to face him with anything but respect."[10]

In contrast to the mid-century students, the 1881 students did not regard the president as the authority figure, a model they could emulate but never quite reach. And although Bartlett's views and style of discipline were in the tradition of Lord's, they became an issue of great controversy for this generation of students, who openly expressed their objections through their petition, statements, and behavior. In 1881, with their diplomas safely in hand, forty-four of sixty-one students in the graduating class of the Academical and Chandler Departments of Dartmouth College sent a memorial to the trustees requesting a change in the presidency.[11] The prosecution called a few students to testify in reference to the charges that the president was graduating them "as enemies instead of friends of the college," and that the president was impairing "the prosperity of different departments."[12] With the exception of some members of the class of 1882, who said they were supporters of the president,[13] Bartlett was subject to much criticism by the students and had problems with them throughout his administration.

The seniors in 1881 said of Bartlett, "We have no personal feeling against the president, but we think that his policy is wrong, his government defective and his treatment of students, taken collectively, discourteous."[14] The students subjected Bartlett to numerous expressions of this nature, but much more bitingly. In 1882, for example, the *Aegis*, the publication of the junior class, called him "A supernatural, self-conceited piece of flesh, always ready, when he can't kick a fellow out of college, to make him apologize."[15] In 1886, in response to suggestions for a chapel window, this publication featured an illustration depicting the death of Ananias, referring to the charges in 1881, with the inscription "1817 [Bartlett's birth date], -Rev. — —— D.D., L.L.D.-?-" (fig. 1).[16] And in 1887 a student (or students) placed a "Letter from Hell" in the students' hymnbooks, which they opened during required chapel services; it was addressed to President Bartlett and signed "Satanus Diabolus."[17]

This change in students' outlook toward styles of authority and discipline relates to a fundamental shift in their background, experiences, and aspirations. It is reflective of their altered communal idea and highlights the changing nature of the relationships between the students and the president, and the shifting notion of presidential authority.

Just as the faculty of 1851 expressed a cohesiveness and shared sense of purpose, a student from this period reflecting upon his years at Dartmouth noted a unity and shared sense of purpose or "spirit" that

Students' Suggestion for Chapel Window (The *Aegis*, Class of 1887). Courtesy of Dartmouth College Library (fig. 1).

was lost in the latter part of the century.[18] Students, like the faculty, were directly involved in the localized, organic community, most obviously through their teaching in the district schools in the winter of each school year. The Dartmouth schoolmasters "stimulated a desire for a broader education in some whose names had not otherwise honored . . . [the Dartmouth] rolls."[19] Chapter 2 indicated that this type of participation assumed much less importance for the 1881 faculty members as their notion of community shifted to one defined exclusively with reference to their peers. The 1881 students, for their part, began to look down upon the "townies"[20] and to view their "world" as distinctly apart, not only from the local community, but from the interests and purposes of the president and most of the faculty.

Why were Bartlett's policies and style so objectionable to the 1881 students when a similar policy and style did not become an issue of such controversy for a previous generation of students? How is this change related to their shifting aspirations, identities, and notions of community? How does this illuminate changing conceptions of the college, of presidential authority, and of the relationship to the community? And what does this tell us about class, mobility, urbanization, and evolving concepts of higher learning in nineteenth-century America?

The class of 1851 consisted of forty-six graduates and sixteen non-graduates in the Academical Department and sixteen graduates in the Medical College.[21] For the purposes of this chapter, prime emphasis will be on the academical students, particularly graduates. Considered the undergraduate body, they offer a better picture of the general student of that period than the medical students, who were older, separated from the academical students, and engaged in a specific program of professional studies.

The homogeneity of the academical class of 1851 in respect to geographic origins and mobility, social, cultural, and economic backgrounds and aspirations is striking. All of this suggests an identification with rural northern New England and an aspiration to gain access to middle-class status and to escape the poverty of their hometowns. It points toward notions of community in which the students saw themselves as integral parts of the wider geographic community and a sense of unity and shared purpose within the communal order of the college itself.

Like comparable data for the 1851 faculty, the students' birthplace and residence point to their local roots. Of the class of 1851, 78.3% of the student body had rural northern New England birthplaces.[22] Of this number, 52.2% were born in the state of New Hampshire. And with the exception of 4.3% with Middle Atlantic birthplaces, a total of 95.7% came from New England (see appendix 10). The pattern of reported residence of the students in the academic year 1850–51 was similar to the birthplace, with even more students residing in northern New England—84.9% (see appendix 11).

A comparison of individual residences and birthplaces, however, indicates a population movement within northern New England similar to the mobility pattern typical of northern New England during this period. Upland interior New England suffered a loss of inhabitants between 1830 and 1870. Many of those remaining in northern New England moved to new and undeveloped lands in Vermont and New Hampshire.[23] At Dartmouth, 39.1% of the students indicate a different residence from birthplace, and 6.5% indicate different residences during their stay at Dartmouth. With the exception of the student who moved within upstate New York, the movement was within northern New England. In addition to those who show a different residence and birthplace and suggestive of the mobility pattern, 17.4% could not be found in the census of 1850 in either reported birthplace or residence (see appendix 12).

Although a few members of the academical class of 1851 were members of the local elite,[24] the majority of students were the sons of farmers[25] and of limited financial circumstances.[26] Most were probably close in background and characteristics to the poor and unpolished students described by Hawthorne as country "bumpkins."[27] And a member of the class of 1850 said of his fellow students:

> They were farmers' boys, brought up in the simplicity and virtuous atmosphere of rural homes. They were not born in the purple of affluence, or reared on rainbow promises of great expectations. . . . Reared on small Sabine farms they were inured to the discipline and hardships of stated labors. And better still, many of our boys knew what honest poverty meant. They had faced its hard conditions and experienced the weight of its pinching pressure. . . . Right well did they know the value of a college education that had cost them so much in labor and self denial.[28]

The data available indicate that at least 30.4% of the students were the sons of farmers, and it is likely that more than 50% could be categorized as such. A total of 17.4% of the fathers could not be identified in the area indicated as students' birthplace or residence; 2.2% had no occupation listed; and 8.7% of the students were identified as not living with the father. Considering their mobility patterns within rural northern New England and the description of students at Dartmouth during this period, it is likely that most of those not found were farmers. Another 8.7% were skilled craftsmen and workers;[29] 6.5% were lawyers, 8.7% ministers, and 4.3% doctors. In contrast to the 1881 period when business comprised over a quarter of the father's occupations, only 8.7% were businessmen[30] (see appendix 12).

Not only were most of the students of limited means, but many experienced poverty. For example, Luther Eastman Shepard did not enter Dartmouth until he was nearly twenty-seven. Lack of funds forced him to leave school before he embarked upon his collegiate studies. He worked as a mechanic, resumed his studies, and subsequently entered Dartmouth.[31] He graduated from Dartmouth in 1851 at the age of thirty years and seven months. Shepard was not unique. The age of Dartmouth's graduates suggests their economic circumstances. Nearly one third of the students were age twenty-five or over at graduation. The age range extended from twenty to thirty-one. And the median age at graduation was twenty-four years and five months—almost two years higher than it would be a generation later (see appendix 13). The college calendar was arranged to accommodate these students. In particular, they were granted leave to earn money by teaching for three months in the winter of each year while in college[32]

Observations from the antebellum period and recent quantitative analyses indicate that Dartmouth was not unique in the predominance of students who were poor or of limited financial means and from the surrounding rural areas that the college "served." The other hilltop colleges in New England (such as the College of Rhode Island [Brown], Williams, Middlebury, University of Vermont, Bowdoin, Waterville [Colby], and Amherst) faced similar situations.[33] An Amherst student of the 1850s noted, for example, "Amherst was poor. There were few students here from wealthy families—one or two perhaps upon every row of benches in the old Greek room."[34] Many of the students were sons of farmers.[35] At Amherst, as at Dartmouth, few students came from New York, Boston, or southern plantation areas,[36] accentuating further the rural orientation and homogeneous nature of the student body. And while there are some variations, the pattern for students at Mt. Holyoke—one of the few women's colleges in this period—is similar to the pattern for students at the provincial New England men's colleges.[37] Mt. Holyoke students were also from the country, from a distinct, although somewhat wider region (rural New England and New York State). If they were not as poor as the students at such institutions as Dartmouth, Amherst, and Williams, most of them were from families of modest means. We also find the same relationship between maturity and poverty, although the Mt. Holyoke students (owing to a different life cycle for women) were in general younger than the students at the men's colleges.[38]

The church colleges of the Old South and other collegiate institutions (affiliated with a variety of denominations) in the Middle Atlantic and the western states also drew students from families of small or modest means.[39] Many of the students at these institutions came from the local area or region.[40] "Little colleges," a southern writer observed in 1846, "are the means of affording liberal education to numerous youth . . . within forty miles of [their] walls, who would never go to Cambridge."[41] And statements by Professor Haddock and the Reverend John Todd that "three-fourths of the members of the country colleges are from families with small means" and that "our colleges are *chiefly* and *mainly* designed for the poor and those in moderate circumstances"[42] seem to reflect the situation in numerous colleges like Dartmouth in locations extending from the Northeast to the western states.

With the growing opportunities available in the learned professions, especially in the West, most of the students saw college as a means of entry into these fields and into the middle class. At Dartmouth, 86.9% of the class of 1851 entered the traditional learned professions—52.1% law, 8.7% the ministry, 8.7% medicine, 17.4% teaching. A small percentage of students entered other pursuits. Only 10.9% of the students went into business or business-related pursuits (see appendix 14); and although the mid-century seems to mark the beginnings of the upward trend of this pursuit, the percentage entering this area is considerably lower than in the 1881 period.[43]

Most of the students spent the major part of their professional careers either in the West or in New England. Of the class of 1851, 45.7% of the student body went to the West and 39.1% went to New England. Out of these students, 21.7% remained in northern New England (see appendix 15). But only three students went back to their hometowns, and two of these came from more prosperous areas such as Newport, Rhode Island, and Concord, New Hampshire. In contrast to the 1881 period, few of the students were attracted to more urban areas such as New York City and Boston. The "crippled state of agriculture"[44] forced them out of their homes, into college, and then to the West and to other parts of New England, where opportunities existed in the traditional learned professions. Many of those of the Yankee culture populated the western states.[45]

The students' associational activities in college reinforced their identification with rural northern New England and point toward their idea of community. Not only did the students come from northern New England, but they participated in activities in the community such as teaching; giving concerts in neighboring areas; through religious societies and political organizations; and during the commencements, which attracted people from all over the region. Students in the Handel Society gave concerts in the neighborhood and took part in conventions of sacred music in the region. In connection with this, they went to Orford in June 1847, to Windsor in June 1848, to Montpelier in May of 1850, to Lebanon in November 1853, and to Woodstock in June 1854. In September 1849 they furnished music in connection with an oration by Professor Sanborn, and in the evening they gave a concert in the chapel.[46]

When the students taught for three months during the school year, they went into the neighboring communities, lived in the homes of various people in the community, and had an opportunity to associate with different types of individuals—from the farmer to the deacon to the richest man in the community. From the reports of one of these pedagogues, one can view the place of the college student in society. One of the students, in describing his experiences of "boarding around," noted that many of the members of the community admired him. Even when he boarded with the richest man in the local community, the man was not sure of how to treat him. "I was a collegian," said the student, "and therefore must not be entirely despised—but, I had no money, and was, a country pedagogue."[47] Another student noted: "I have been vexed often at the sincere wonder of an old acquaintance, when, in answer to some question in science, I have frankly confessed, 'I don't know.' 'Don't know!—Why I thought you'd been to college!' is the usual rejoinder."[48]

The integral relationship between students and the local community is evident in the oral examination of Dartmouth students by members of the community and in the students' appeal to prominent local men to rule in a disputed election of a student society. At the end of the fall term and before commencement, an outside examining board composed of learned persons in the community conducted oral examinations of Dartmouth students. In the academic year 1850–51, for example, the examining board consisted of three ministers, one college professor, and two lawyers.[49] And in order to resolve an argument over a hotly contested election for the president of one of the literary societies, the students appealed the ruling for determination to three prominent men in the community, the Honorable Charles Marsh, Judge Coolidge, and Judge Kellogg.[50]

That the students considered themselves part of the wider geographic community is also evident in their participation and leadership in local political affairs. On 21 July 1847 the Whigs held a jubilee in Hanover in honor of the election of two members of the Whig party to Congress. Seven students took part in the speaking.[51] In the 1850s students participated in political clubs in the town. One of the students, Edward F. Noyes, became the leading debater in the Republican Club. The debate between Noyes and the Reverend Daniel F. Richardson, the Democratic postmaster, attracted much interest. Noyes made speeches on behalf of the party in the neighboring towns.[52]

Some students participated in the religious life of the community. Students in the Theological Society at the college distributed tracts in the neighborhood in 1850. At various times they undertook religious canvassing in the area, and members of the society conducted a public Saturday evening conference. Similar to the tract societies to which some of the faculty belonged, students organized the Society of Inquiry, which was concerned with encouraging missionary activities.[53]

Although some students were party to incidents of drunkenness, horn blowing, and turkey stealing, a number of the students were concerned enough with the reputation of the town and college (a sense that the two were united) that they formed a vigilance committee, held a trial, and tarred and feathered a man in the town who they thought was injurious to that reputation. After repeated warnings by the vigilance committee, the students convicted a man by the name of Parkhurst— who lived at the southwest edge of the village—for maintaining a "vile" home and forcing his daughter and wife into a "life of prostitution."[54] Parkhurst's forcing his fourteen-year-old daughter to dance naked in a student's room in the college building for five dollars was the immediate incident for the trial.[55]

The commencement created much excitement in the community. Many types of people came from all over the region. Learned men, distinguished citizens, jugglers, peddlers, and auctioneers—all participated in the festivities. The president, the faculty, and the graduating class dined with "gentlemen of a liberal education or public character"[56] from the community. The students invited the commencement speaker. Dartmouth was not unique among collegiate institutions in this period in the interest and participation by local residents and people from the region in college events and activities.[57] The local newspaper describes the great procession of people who came to hear and see Rufus Choate give the eulogy of Daniel Webster during the Dartmouth commencement of 1853:

> The procession was formed in the front of the college buildings; what a mass of squeezed, compressed, and closely wedged and moving humanity was there, stretching away from the door of the chapel, round the common two thirds of the way to the church, while the compacted crowd in front of the church, taking the best position for ingress by rush when the doors should be opened, looked in the distance like a swarm of bees clinging to the sides of a hive. Guard chains were stretched from the church door to the common fence, and a strong police force stationed to check the crowding masses. The body of the house was filled with Alumni and students—in every seat, in every aisle, on the platform, in the porch, and on the stairs,—while every inch of the galleries was densely packed with ladies—and crowds of others through the long service stood on platforms raised about the windows, or hung about the doors, while multitudes were unable to approach even within hearing distance.[58]

Thus, all this information points to a mutual appreciation between the students and the locale and region, as well as the students' values, culture, and aspirations being rooted within the communal context.

Within the college community itself, the largely poor and lower-middle-class students took their college work seriously, were going to make the most of their hard-won opportunities, and shared or at least were open to the shared sense of purpose of the president and the faculty in the creation of a Christian Zion. Articles in the *Dartmouth* expressed the desire that the continent "be peopled with enlightened and virtuous men,"[59] and "Not that intellectual powers should be prized less, but the virtues—of heart loved more."[60] Thus, they seemed to share a conception of higher learning embodying a joining of heart and mind in fashioning this Zion. And in relation to their seriousness of purpose, William Badger of the class of 1848 noted, "Recitations drive so that one cannot think of home, friends or anything else but sines & cosines, arcs & tangents, Greek & Latin roots & Campbell's Rhetoric!"[61]

The students viewed the president as the authority figure, an aspirational model they could emulate but never quite reach. One student said of President Lord, for example:

Whether in the class-room speaking to a few students, whether in the pulpit addressing a multitude, he was equally lucid, cogent and masterful in his interpretations of the prophetic Scriptures, and of our Christian Evangel. These exegetical unfoldings of spiritual laws, as applied to the moral necessities of man, were the answers of an oracle who had received new installments of illumination from a shrine of inspiration which a passionate piety led him daily to visit. No young man could have gazed upon his face at such moments without feeling that it was the face of Moses fresh descended from the Mount, with a glowing commentary on the Tables of Law. On every field, whether controversial or didactic, he was "facile princeps" in wielding the sword of the spirit and the spear of Ithuriel; everywhere exhibiting an accustomed familiarity with subjects that had long confounded the human reason, and long perplexed the human conscience, to the cleaving asunder of churches and nations.[62]

As "facile princeps" of all, the students regarded the president as the interpreter of faith, of ethics—in essence, of life. Along a related vein, another student expressed the view that the students considered the president and faculty as models "of culture, refinement, . . . mental alertness, . . . and conduct, and . . . [as] an inspiration to an earnest participation in the world's work with the highest aims."[63] One can

explain the students' view of the president as a powerful authority figure
and the interpreter of life and the cohesiveness and consensual orientation within the communal order of the college by reference to the
background and experience of the students. We should note the homogeneous nature of the student body, their rural northern New England background and identities, their class origins, the desire to make
the most of their hard-won opportunities, the shared cultural and religious values in creating a Zion, and the reinforcement of these values
in the wider community immediately outside the collegiate bounds.

The students' extracurricular activities also emphasized the unity of
the college body and served to complement the formal curriculum. Students did not engage in athletic competitions with other colleges[64] or
develop societies whose primary concern was their social nature or
exclusiveness. The two literary societies, the Social Friends and the
United Fraternity, were the main student organizations during much of
the antebellum period. The literary societies emphasized debating and
possessed libraries with larger collections than the college library.[65]
Dartmouth students taxed each other for the purchase of books, and at
the end of the sophomore year they made a donation for this purpose.[66]
The literary societies were a common feature of antebellum colleges.[67]
In addition to the literary societies that were declining in importance,[68]
the Greek letter fraternities were making their appearance. By 1851 three
fraternities had been formed—Psi Upsilon, Kappa Kappa Kappa, and
Alpha Delta Phi. But in the words of a member of the class of 1856, even
these groups seemed to include "in a modified form . . . the old-time
work of the literary societies."[69] Their programs included orations, debates, and essays.

These programs served to complement the formal curriculum, which
included the full range of subjects in the classical course of study, with
a stress on Greek, Latin, mathematics, moral philosophy, and rhetoric.[70]
The course in moral philosophy, common to the antebellum colleges,
capped the student's academic career and provided him with an interpretation of life. It included discussions of all the topics of the modern
social sciences and stressed the basic unity of knowledge[71] in fashioning
a Christian Zion. The literary societies and fraternities of this period
stressed the oratorical, while the recitation method was utilized in the
formal curriculum. And the model of the professors in their outside
activities also reinforced the emphasis on the oratorical and evangelical.
To this point, one individual said of Professor Brown's sermons:

> His sermons, whether delivered in the college chapel or on occasion
> of public interest, were always rich in thought, stimulating in their
> spiritual tone and finished in form. For a young man to have heard

his discourses at intervals during a period of four years was almost in itself a liberal education.[72]

The students found this emphasis on the evangelical or oratorical in the fields they were entering—the ministry, teaching, and the law. Many of the students who took advantage of the opportunities in law in the West found that the lawyer was judged on his performance in "oratorical contests" in the courtroom, and the lawyer as "courtroom advocate" became the pattern of the successful lawyer of this period.[73]

When we move forward one generation, from the students of the 1851 period to the students of the 1881 period, we find Bartlett making the following observations about the student body:

It is a peculiar community to deal with. They have a peculiar code of morals, a peculiar class of feelings [,] peculiar exciteableness, and you never know how a thing will take until you make a trial.[74]

What precisely were the changes Bartlett noticed in the next generation of students? How might these changes explain their hostility to a president whose style and policy were similar to that of President Lord? The collected data regarding the students reveal the beginnings of a shift away from the homogeneous, rural group of limited financial circumstances to a more diverse, cosmopolitan group of a higher socioeconomic status. They point toward their shifting aspirations, altered communal idea, and changing notion of presidential authority.

In 1881 the undergraduate body of the college consisted of fifty-one members of the Academical Department[75] and twelve members of the Chandler Scientific Department. There were also twenty-two academical nongraduates and three Chandler nongraduates. The associated schools consisted of twenty-nine medical graduates,[76] one Thayer graduate and three nongraduates, and fourteen graduates of the agricultural college.[77] As in the 1851 period, the emphasis here will be on the undergraduate body—the academical and Chandler graduates.[78]

Indicative of the decline in the locally rooted 1851 student body, the information regarding birthplace and residence indicates a marked decrease of those coming from rural northern New England. Whereas 78.3% of the academical students of the class of 1851 were born in northern New England, by 1881 the percentage had declined to 58.8% Now 40.8% of the students were born in places outside northern New England—15.7% in other parts of New England, 11.7% in the Middle Atlantic, 11.8% in the West, and 2% outside the United States (see appendix 10). The reported residence is similar to the birthplace and is further indicative of the decline in the locally rooted student body of the 1851 period. In 1881, 53% resided in northern New England as compared with 84.9% in 1851 (see apendix 11).

Whereas the total percentage of birthplace and residence is similar, a comparison of individual birthplace and residence indicates a mobility pattern that provides a contrast to that of 1851 and points toward their more metropolitan orientation. As in 1851, a large percentage of the students (45.1% in 1881) reported a residence different from their birthplace. In addition to these, 17.6% could not be found in the birthplace or residence in the census of 1880, and 9.8% were not living with their fathers (see appendix 12). But in 1881 one finds movement to larger towns and cities, both within northern New England and to southern New England, as well as movement to the Middle Atlantic and within the West. This was in contrast to the 1851 period when the mobility pattern of these students centered on movement from rural places to other small towns in northern New England. Thus, in northern New England, for example, students of the class of 1881 moved from Temple, New Hampshire, to Nashua, from Nashua to Concord, from Pittsfield to Concord, from Bedford to Manchester, and from Manchester to Lawrence, Massachusetts, in southern New England. The trends evidenced in the student body are similar to a more general pattern in New England. Beginning in the 1870s, the more "mobile" elements of the population were increasingly attracted to the cities, especially in such areas as southern New England.[79] The students who spent their professional lives in urban areas after college, especially in Boston and New York, culminated the mobility pattern of these families to larger towns and metropolitan areas.

Information regarding other collegiate institutions indicates that Dartmouth was not the only institution to evidence a movement away from a rural, locally rooted group. At a comparable institution such as Williams, for instance, the movement toward a different clientele seems to have begun somewhat earlier (during the latter part of the antebellum period). The influence of the urban culture was quite pronounced in the early 1870s as students (and usually well-off students) from large towns and cities such as Albany, Philadelphia, Chicago, and especially New York City replaced students from the surrounding rural villages.[80] At some other institutions, the movement away from a rural, locally rooted group meant that students now came from various areas within the particular state instead of the almost exclusive concentration of students from the neighboring rural areas forty to sixty miles from these country colleges.[81]

The data indicate an increase of students of a higher socioeconomic status and from backgrounds in which the father was engaged in business pursuits[82]—developments not dissimilar to what was happening at comparable institutions of higher education.[83] The percentage of fathers engaged in business pursuits increased nearly three times—from 8.7% in 1851 to 25.5% in 1881.[84] This upward trend in business accompanied a substantial decline of those engaged in farming. The information available indicates that 15.7% of the fathers were farmers. This was probably closer to one quarter of the class,[85] as the figure for farmers in 1851 was probably more than 50%. Those in the craftsman category increased slightly from 8.7% in 1851 to 13.7% in 1881.[86] Those in the traditional learned professions included 13.7% of the fathers. Considering the trends for the 1882–96 period and those who were not identified, this number, as with the farmers, may have been higher (see appendix 12). Similar to the trends for the 1881 group, those for the 1882–96 period indicate that 25.5% of the fathers were engaged in business, 27.7% in farming, 25.9% in the learned professions, and 11.6% were mechanics and laborers.[87]

The age of the students also indicates an increase in their socioeconomic status. A comparison of the median age at graduation evidences a drop of almost two years from 1851—from twenty-four and five months to twenty-two and seven months. In addition, in 1881 only 13.7% of the students were age twenty-five and over, and these were twenty-five and twenty-six, compared with the 32.6% in 1851 who ranged in age up through thirty-one (see appendix 13). Bartlett himself noted that the college had traditionally educated many young men of limited means, that farmers' sons from rural New England had once formed a majority, but that this group was declining because of the increased cost of a college education.[88] And although the number of scholarships had increased, the increase in the amounts the students were spending during their stay at Dartmouth,[89] the increase in tuition,[90] and the decrease in the numbers of those teaching are also indicative of the more comfortable circumstances of many of the students.

The college discouraged the practice of the students' teaching in the district schools, and while some students still taught in the 1881 period, many did not do so for economic reasons. In contrast to the situation in 1851 when the college facilitated the students' teaching in the district schools, the revised college calendar did not provide for an extended winter term; students desiring to teach had to obtain excuses from the faculty, had to plea financial need, and were obligated to make up any work they missed. Students in the 1870s themselves complained about allowing students to teach. The *Dartmouth* of 1873 noted, for example: "'Going to teach next winter?' 'I don't know; are you?' This question we hear at every street corner. Perhaps we can assist in answering it. We believe that few of those who teach are really influenced by pecuniary motives."[91] Since Hanover was cold and dull and many students were tired of the monotonous life, some students decided that they might like to teach.[92] At the same time, another issue of the *Dartmouth* from this period remarked that the new college calendar with the shorter winter vacation and with a summer vacation was "especially advantageous to those who teach winters and work during the summer, and was probably arranged with reference to this class of students."[93] This shift points to the diversity of the student body and a decline of those from lower socioeconomic backgrounds as they are singled out as "this class." By 1881 one also finds notations such as these in reference to some of those applying for scholarships: "To his surprise he found, upon inquiry that President Bartlett, through a correspondence with Arthur's parents, had learned—that they did not want a scholarship given to their son, as he was abundantly able to pay his bills."[94]

Those students engaged in business and business-related pursuits after college constituted a considerably higher proportion of the student body than those in the 1851 period. Although those engaged in law still constituted the highest percentage of students as a single category— 31.3%—many of the lawyers also had business interests, and the percentage of businessmen alone increased from 10.9% in 1851 to 19.6% in 1881 (see appendix 14). If one adds the lawyers who had business interests, the percentage of those with business involvements rises to one third of the class.[95] In addition, the legal profession underwent change. Reflective of the business orientation, the image of the successful practitioner shifted to "office counselor" with many of the lawyers representing big business and corporations.[96] For example, George Thompson Aldrich, member of the class of 1881 at Dartmouth, became counsel to the Manhattan Railway Company (1890–97).[97]

Warren W. Foster and John Willard Lanehart are two examples of members of the class of 1881 who were engaged in law and business and gained prominence in these areas. Foster graduated from Columbia Law School, went into private practice, and also served as a judge for a period of time. He was a founder of the American Light and Traction Company and of the Cities Service Company.[98] Foster served continuously as a director and member of the executive committee of that company as well as chairman of the executive committees of the American Light and Traction Company, of Buffalo Elevators Incorporated, and of the American Alcohol Company. He was a director of the Southern Light and Traction Company and served in various capacities with other corporations.[99] Lanehart went into law practice in Chicago. He was manager of the Ogden Gas Company and of the Cosmopolitan Electric Company and was vice president of the Unity Building Company.[100]

Those engaged in the education profession rose, while those in the ministry continued to decline. A little over one quarter of the class were in the education field. Most of those in this field filled supervisory and administrative positions such as high school principals and superintendents.[101] The trends at Dartmouth were similar to the general trend of the late nineteenth century—a general decline in those engaged in ministry, a leveling off of those engaged in law, and a rise of those engaged in education and business.[102]

The residential pattern of the class of 1881 during their professional careers is striking in contrast to the 1851 period and points toward their metropolitan orientation. Members of the class of 1881 evidently found urban areas attractive places in which to settle. They went to southern New England and the Middle Atlantic, especially Massachusetts and New York. Boston and New York City were areas of special attraction for these graduates. In 1851, 10.9% of the class spent the major part of their professional lives in Massachusetts. One went to Boston, another 6.5% went to New York City, for a total of 17.4% for Massachusetts and New York. In 1881, on the other hand, 27.5% went to Massachusetts and 19.6% went to New York, making a total of close to one half (47.1%) for these two areas alone. Of this number, 15.7% went to Boston and 13.7% went to New York City. Thus, close to one third (29.4%) of the class settled in these two leading urban areas alone. The Middle Atlantic region drew nearly three times as many students as in 1851 (31.3% as compared with 10.8%). Besides New York City, students settled in Washington, D.C., and Philadelphia.

The literature from the period notes the attraction of the urban areas in the last quarter of the nineteenth century. For example, an article in *Cosmopolitan* comments that "the attraction of the city"[103] with its increased economic opportunities drew the people from the New England countryside. Those going west also exhibited a conscious effort to settle in the more urban areas and growing metropolises such as Chicago or Denver. For example, in 1882 one student who settled in Bismarck, North Dakota, remarked that he went to "Bismarck, the 'to be' metropolis of the great Northwest," and that "business prospects are exceedingly favorable."[104] Those going to the West had declined considerably from the 1851 period (45.7% to 29.4%), and the percentage going to this region was lower than for the other regions (see appendix 15).

The collected data, then, reveal some significant differences between the 1881 academical students and their 1851 counterparts. They evidence the more diverse, cosmopolitan nature of the 1881 student body and point toward their shifting aspirations and notions of community. Now students came from southern New England, the Middle Atlantic, and the West in addition to those coming from northern New England. Some came from the larger towns and more urban areas in contrast to the sole concentration of those from rural areas. As opposed to the great majority of students from poor and lower-middle-class backgrounds in the 1851 period, although some students still came from limited financial circumstances, many came from business backgrounds and a higher socioeconomic status. Along with the increase in socioeconomic status the median age declined,[105] and they were a younger group than their 1851 counterparts. Their orientation shifted from the locale and the rural northern New England area to metropolitan areas such as Boston and New York, where many of the 1881 students spent their professional lives and entered the fields of big business, law, and education. The aspirations of many of these students shifted from access to middle-class status and a town-centered middle class to achieving success within the world of a metropolitan-oriented, peer-centered, middle and largely upper middle class. While the majority of these students probably were not quite the Dink Stover types at Yale in the early 1900s,[106] by background and aspirations many were moving in this direction and away from Hawthorne's country "bumpkins." And with the beginnings of their changed backgrounds and aspirations, their idea of community in which they saw themselves as an integral part of the local community experienced a dramatic change, as did their conception of the unity and shared sense of purpose within the communal order of the college.

Before developing these points more fully, one might assess the background of the Chandler students, the other undergraduates who, along with the academical students, would remain under President Tucker, the college proper. As regards birthplace and residence, these students exhibit a movement away from the sole concentration of students in the northern New England area. Fifty percent of the students were born outside the northern New England area (see appendix 10). Of this group, 33.3% were born in Massachusetts and 16.7% in the West. The pattern of residence is similar to the birthplace, with slightly more students reported living in northern New England—58.3% (see appendix 11). Students began to come from larger towns and cities such as Nashua, New Hampshire; Manchester, New Hampshire, Boston and Lynn, Massachusetts; as well as from small towns such as Norwich, Vermont, which had been common in 1851. And as with the academical students, the mobility pattern included movement within the West and New England.[107]

A striking percentage of these students came from business backgrounds and exhibit a marked lowering of the median age. In the Chandler scientific class of 1881, 41.7% of the fathers were businessmen.[108] In contrast to the academical students, however, another 41.7% of the fathers were farmers (see appendix 12). Also indicative of the more diverse nature of the Chandler students, the median age at graduation (twenty-two years and one month) was slightly lower than for the academical students. But one third of the Chandler students were age twenty-five or older at graduation. The age range of these students, however, was only twenty-five and twenty-six (see appendix 13).

Business and engineering were the predominant occupations of this group. Fifty percent of the Chandler students entered the field of engineering, and 25% went into business (see appendix 14). Some of the engineers, similar to the practice of some of the lawyers, served as consultants to business and corporate interests.

Most of the Chandler students spent the major part of their professional lives either in Massachusetts or in the West. Of this group, 41.7% went to Massachusetts and 41.7% went west (see appendix 15). The West seemed to be popular with many of the engineers.

Thus, while there were some important differences between the academical and Chandler students, the data regarding the Chandler students also reveal a break in the 1851 pattern. The collected data for the Chandler students of the class of 1881 point to the mixing of some of the older traditional Dartmouth students who viewed college as an entry into the middle class, with a growing number of students who probably enjoyed passing four years "with congenial companions."[109] Chandler students came from larger towns and cities and from business backgrounds along with some of the more traditional types of students from rural areas and more limited fianancial circumstances. One finds sons of manufacturers from Manchester and Boston, along with students such as George Hunt Hutchinson from Norwich, Vermont, who lived at home while at Dartmouth, "helped with the chores"[110] on the farm, and received aid in the form of scholarship funds. This trend toward more metropolitan-oriented, upper-middle-class students increased during the next administration.

The altered view of community, which this information regarding the academical and Chandler students points toward, illuminates changing conceptions of the college, of its relation to the community, and of higher learning, as well as providing a context for understanding the altered nature of the relationships between the students and the president. The collected data and the information revealed in what follows regarding their writings, associational involvements, activities, attitudes, and actions indicate the development of a more fragmented communal idea. Dartmouth students now viewed themselves as part of a more broadly conceived collegiate culture. They began to conceive of community as their own distinct peer group, and the peer group, rather than the organic community of the 1851 period, provided the basis for their values, culture, and aspirations. The redefined boundaries of their notion of community were indicative of the importance of metropolitan areas—the center of their career and social aspirations. The cumulative effect of these changes marked the beginnings of an exclusiveness in striking contrast to antebellum Dartmouth. And within the college community, the students also considered their "world" as distinctly apart, not only from the local community, but also from the concerns and aims of the president and most of the faculty. For these urban-oriented, aspiring, upper-middle-class students, associational involvements with peers in fraternities and athletics in college, and in professional associations, business corporations, and upper-middle-class social clubs out of college became important status symbols and indicators of success.

As early as the late 1860s and early 1870s, students began to evidence their changing attitude toward the local community. In 1867 the *Dartmouth* commented that during the summer months a few families came to the hotel in Hanover "to mingle with the native aborigines," but that in the winter "there was never anything going on; everybody knew everybody else, the town was rife with rumor and gossip."[111] A diary from the early 1870s refers to the contrast between styles in traditional rural Hanover and those of the more metropolitan areas. It notes the acknowledgment of the townspeople of this difference. A student went to the hotel for supper, and the proprietor—annoyed that the student came for just one meal—remarked, "You got to take what we got; this ain't the Parker House or the Fifth Avenoo [*sic*] Hotel."[112]

During the 1870s, student publications noted some conflict between the local community and the students; moreover, they reveal an increasing separation from the local community as a source of identification or aspiration. One finds comments such as this one:

Hanover is a town determined to see the law obeyed. Sometimes as many as six of its fearless police can be seen coursing over the common, or tearing down doors in the college building in pursuit of some "bold, bad man" who has broken the law.[113]

Other issues of the *Dartmouth* noted that strained relations between the students and the town occurred at other colleges during the 1870s:

The Yale students have no great affection for the New Haven policemen, one of whom they had placed on trial last term for an assault on an undergraduate. There seems, also, to be little love lost between Amherst students and Amherst citizens. Perhaps Town and Gown riots will be resuscitated in some of the American colleges as a means for settling difficulties between students and villagers.[114]

The freshman history of the class of 1881 assumed an attitude of derision toward the townspeople. The students attended the performance of

"Box Brown" at Carter's Opera House in the town. When they decided that it might be fun to extinguish the light jet on the lamppost corner, they noted that "the 'townies' couldn't see the point, or rather had a wild idea of preserving the light that they might see,—it being the first time of record when they preferred light to darkness."[115]

While some involvements with the local community remained in the early 1880s, their relationships to the people in the locale and region underwent marked change. For example, during Town Meeting Day, in which some of the students voted, the college excused students from recitation.[116] But various proprietors, in apparent recognition of the separateness between the students and the community, placed advertisements in the *Dartmouth* thanking the students for their patronage. A generation before, this was not necessary, as the students were an integral part of the locale and region. In the early 1880s one finds announcements such as these: "We take this occasion to thank our trade for their generous patronage and especially for patience shown while we were filling their orders."[117] The old Theological Society and the Society of Inquiry declined. First the Christian Fraternity and then the Dartmouth Young Men's Christian Association took the place of these groups. Although the old oral examinations conducted by learned members of the community were still in existence, they had declined in importance. With the introduction of written examinations in 1872, only a few of the oral examinations remained, and even in these the faculty sat with the examiners and ignored the marks the examiners gave. Thus, while some of the associations remained, the students began to look down upon the "townies" and to see themselves as a group apart.

If the Dartmouth students looked to a reference group aside from students in other colleges, it was the alumni, especially the New York alumni, who symbolized the metropolitan culture and success in business. In the 1870s the students asked a member of the New York alumni association to write an article for the *Dartmouth* based on his remarks before the New York Association of Alumni. The article commented upon the rise in the importance of business and the accompanying decline in "the relative importance of the learned professions."[118] While it did not recommend abandoning the present curriculum, it stressed the importance of adding modern history, political economy, geography, and modern languages.[119] The *Dartmouth* also published an article probably written by an alumnus criticizing the board for not granting the alumni representation on the board of trustees. The board also was criticized for its largely local composition now that many of the students came from areas other than New Hampshire.[120] And the alumni's specifications against the president in relation to the students were such that the alumni would have had to have obtained them from the students.[121] The trial testimony indicates the influence of the alumni on the students. In reference to Hewitt's appointment, one of the students stated that they had planned votes of disapprobation against him, since he was not the unanimous choice of the faculty and trustees.[122] When asked how "it became material to the class whether it was the unanimous choice of the trustees,"[123] one of the students said, "Well, being nearly graduates, and sometime some of [us] might have a chance to get on the board of trustees, and we should probably like to see into the action and see how these things are managed."[124]

The students evidenced a translocal identity independent of the local college hierarchical community. In the *Dartmouth* of the 1870s, 1880s, and 1890s, one finds notations and frequent references to what was occurring at other colleges and much interest in other students and student activities. This was probably due in part to the advent of organized athletic competitions and fraternities, which were forming more and more a part of the students' time, and to the communications transmitted by the metropolitan press. Students at other colleges and universities also evidenced a translocal orientation, and student publications at these institutions also provided much space to student activities in other institutions.[125]

In contrast to the extracurricular activities of the students in the 1851 period, the activities of the students in the 1881 period centered on intercollegiate athletics and fraternities. In 1860 Dartmouth students organized a baseball club, and Dartmouth played its first intercollegiate baseball game in 1866. By 1871 the college granted students leaves of absence to play at other colleges. Around this time, entries in the faculty minutes refer to repeated student absences explained by those who had incurred them as for athletic training and practice and in the students' words, incurred "for the good of the college."[126] In 1879 Harvard, Yale, Brown, Amherst, Princeton, and Dartmouth formed an athletic league, and Lewis J. Rundlett of the class of 1881 was the first Dartmouth pitcher to bring defeat to Yale.[127] Dartmouth students formed a college football association in 1880, and they played their first intercollegiate game in 1881. In 1886 Stevens, the Massachusetts Institute of Technology, Amherst, Trinity, and Dartmouth formed a league. In 1879 Dartmouth also began to participate in intercollegiate track, and in 1886 Dartmouth joined with Tufts, Brown, Bowdoin, Trinity, and Williams to form the New England Intercollegiate Athletic Association. Students also formed a tennis club in 1884 and a bicycle association in 1886.

Fraternities were the major student associations in the 1880s.[128] One of the fraternities, Kappa Kappa Kappa, erected its own hall in 1860, and in 1872 Alpha Delta Phi built a fraternity house with accommodations for its members at a cost of $4,000. In 1886 and 1887, respectively,

students formed the Sphinx and the Casque and Gauntlet, senior societies. Student organizations, fraternities, organized athletics, class
suppers, meetings at "Bedbug Alley" to decide such things as whom
to serenade with horns that evening, took up much of the leisure time
of students. The traditions at Dartmouth were such that besides the
social element of good fellowship, in the 1870s and early 1880s the
fraternities still retained some of their literary overtones. The strict class
divisions that developed at Harvard and the intense competition on Tap
Day at Yale were modified at Dartmouth during this period.[129] But the
idea of community of these metropolitan-oriented, aspiring, upper-middle-class students evidenced an exclusiveness of associational involvement and separateness in marked contrast to the 1851 students.

Students initiated a number of traditions during this period. In 1879
students began the tradition of carving senior canes, and in 1881 the
senior class reintroduced the custom of the senior ball, which had not
been held for much of the nineteenth century. The class of 1881 as
freshmen also tried to introduce the custom of wearing Oxford caps,
but the student body did not adopt this practice until 1891, and then
only during the commencement exercise. The *Dartmouth* of 1882 expressed the sentiment that "all the benefits of college life do not come
from a study of textbooks" and that "the senior class was cutting recitations recklessly."[130]

While cribbing was not an unknown occurrence in an earlier period, its open pursuit to pass examinations so one could devote one's
time to student activities is in marked contrast to the 1851 period. In
the "Pocket Elucidator" we find this explanation: "Cram v.t. To set up
all night previous to examinations, and to become so thoroughly conversant with the subject that it crops out on one's cuffs or leaves a visible
impression even on divers scraps of paper that may, inadvertently,
have been left in sundry apertures known as pockets."[131] The freshman
history of the class of 1881 refers to preparations for a mathematics
examination:

> The preparations for "cribbing" were simply enormous, and alas
> they amounted to nothing, as "Quibe" had fixed up a paper that
> absolutely defied the best efforts in that line. Many simply *looked*
> at the paper, and with a groan departed. Of those who remained
> to wrestle with fate "Zero" was the first to finish. There were no
> *figures* on his paper, but there was a little "Greek Prose" and a little
> "short hand" (?) exercise. He thought it a pity that after setting up
> all night inventing mechanical contrivances to regulate "cribs" that
> they should prove of no avail, yet such was the case.[132]

For class recitations many students used interlinears, and the class history notes that "there was a 'run' on the book store for these delightful texts."[133] Even the class poet and an excellent student such as Richard Hovey would delight his fellow classmates with this "supreme cheek"[134] on one occasion when he indicated to Professor Richardson that he could not translate a Greek passage because he had brought with him only the text.[135]

The students now stressed values and skills different from their 1851 counterparts, as well as exhibiting a fragmentation of the notion of community. One historian has commented that the fraternities institutionalized "new prestige values, the attributes of a successful man of the world, *this* world, at the expense of those various signs of Christian grace—humility, equality, and morality—which had long been the purpose of the college to foster."[136] While this type of characterization is a simplification of what happened, the assumption of a general change in values and identities is no doubt valid. It was not that the antebellum college did not aim to produce the "successful man of the world,"[137] but that the world that was envisioned and that operated in the antebellum period was different from that of the latter part of the century. As with the shared sense of purpose in the communal order of the college and the appreciation of the students of their integral relationship to the wider community of the locale and the region, their conception of higher learning stressed the basic unity of knowledge and the union of faith and intellect in fashioning a Zion. The students aimed at access to a town-centered middle class in which they would live the life of the good Christian man in the organic community. By 1881 the students' more fragmented communal idea separated them from the local community and from the president and faculty within the college community as well. The students' world stressed the skills and values needed for success within their separate aspirational sphere—a metropolitan-oriented, peer-centered upper middle class. Their associations with peers during and after college provided the basis for status—fraternities, athletic competitions, clubs such as the University and Chevy Chase, professional associations, and business corporations. Values, skills, and knowledge also began to be fragmented, not only with the introduction of electives and optional studies[138] in recognition of the beginnings of a more rationalized, esoteric learning, but with the conception that activities such as football competitions were "legitimate school [s] for training in leadership."[139]

Bartlett's older pastoral approach, his style emphasizing his conception of his role as the "supreme head,"[140] and his rigid policy of discipline, which was linked to his conception of higher learning, were at odds with students who were beginning to define their aims and aspirations in relation to different models. The very fact that the student body was composed of a sizable number of students of a higher socioeconomic background than their 1851 counterparts may have explained in part their outspokenness. Although they may have valued the diploma, it was not their means of entry into the middle class, since they were already there.

The trial testimony and the history of the freshman class of 1881 reveal Bartlett's problems with the students and his disciplinary policy and style. At the trial Bartlett stated:

> I have believed in severe penalty for grave offenses, such as that in the famous case of 1878, when it was a penitentiary offense, as I understand it. . . . In the general discipline my idea has been this: to enlighten and try and raise the moral tone in one way and another. I have taken the statutes of New Hampshire into the chapel twice if not three times and read to the young men to remind them of their responsibility to the laws of the land. I sometimes remonstrated in chapel, and sometimes, . . . I have treated certain indecorums or offenses by ridicule, as being the best method, or, as some men would say colloquially, by "making fun of it." In the latter part of the time I have fallen more and more intò the practice of anticipation, of private conversation, if I found young men were going wrong. . . .My policy has been to anticipate serious discipline by private conversation. . . . And when it was clear that an offender was incorrigible, to get rid of him not by formal discipline but by writing to his father.[141]

He was thus emphasizing his policy of discipline as part of character building. The action in 1878 caused much disfavor with the class of 1881, as they lost some members of their class, but they also objected to Bartlett's actions after the verdict had been rendered. "A committee was appointed, and a memorial sent to the Faculty," the class historian reported, "but it only roused the ire of 'Prexie,' who, calling the class together, delivered that remarkable lecture on the 'character' and 'bringing up' of '81. His points were 'enthusiastically' received, but he didn't seem to appreciate that kind of enthusiasm."[142] Two.of those who had been assaulted complained to the authorities in the town; warrants were issued, and one person was bound over for trial. The freshman history states that two of those involved escaped, and Bartlett posted a reward for their return. In response to this, the freshman history indicates that "Retribution was in store for the 'supreme head.'"[143] As the students went "to breakfast they were surprised (?) to see pasted on every available spot the following"[144] poster:

$2.00 REWARD

WHEREAS, SAMUEL DISCORD BLARITT has escaped from his lawful
keepers, the Medical Faculty of Illinois State Lunatic Asylum
we do offer the sum of $2.00 for the apprehension of said lunatic
and his delivery to his proper keeper.

Per Order,
ILLINOIS STATE INSANE ASYLUM
Chicago, March 22, 1878[145]

In reference to Bartlett's treatment by the students, the *Journal of
Education* commented:

[He] has been for several years the object of the most scandalous
treatment by the students, and he has been helpless to restrain or
control these expressions of disfavor. To such an extreme has this
treatment been carried that he has been made the butt of ridicule,
sarcasm, and insult, in and out of college, to such an extent as to
excite the pity even of those who did not sympathize with his
treatment of the students and members of the faculty.[146]

The article suggested that he resign.[147]

While the disturbances at Dartmouth seem to have received the most
publicity, the altered nature of the relationships between the students
and the president and the shifting view of presidential authority were
not unique to Dartmouth. This is evidenced in conflicts at several other
institutions.[148] When President Bartlett wrote to President Chadbourne
of Williams of his problems with the students, Chadbourne wrote back
that he understood from his own experience the "unfortunate disturbances" Bartlett described.[149]

If the president was no longer an aspirational model for the students,
neither were most of the faculty. The *Aegis*, in reference to the controversy and trial in 1881, portrayed Bartlett and the faculty as engaged in
a dogfight (fig. 2). There was, however, substantial respect for Hardy,
the leading "cosmopolite" on the faculty. They said of him: "He is a
man of great intelligence, of progressive ideas and of broad education
. . . young, active and abreast of the times, Professor Hardy would make
an ideal college president."[150]

The contrast between the attitude of many of the students toward
Bartlett as "a supernatural, self-conceited piece of flesh,"[151] and the
attitude of the 1851 generation toward Lord as "facile princeps"[152] in

Students' Portrayal of the Bartlett Controversy (The *Aegis*, Class of 1884). Courtesy of Dartmouth College Library (fig. 2).

everything relates to their changing backgrounds, experiences, and aspirational models and is reflective of their altered idea of community. Bartlett's conception of the college as a personal, familial, communal order with himself as pastoral head was at odds with these metropolitan-oriented, aspiring, upper-middle-class students whose sense of community and definition of success were defined with exclusive reference to their own peer group.

And the students of the Chandler Scientific Department had additional grievances against the president because of his open questioning of the course being portrayed as equal to the traditional liberal arts program. In relation to the specification that Bartlett was impairing the prosperity of different departments, Joseph Enright of the class of 1879 testified in relation to the specification that:

Upon the graduation of Enright from the Chandler Scientific Department in 1879, said Bartlett stated to him in a conversation with him relative to the training in that Department "I am glad your father is going to give your *brother* an *education*," meaning a classical course the result of which was that the brother referred to went to another college instead of Dartmouth.[153]

At the trial Enright said, "The substance of the conversation was this, that the education of the scientific department was not sufficient to carry a man into the active duties of life."[154] Thus, Bartlett's disciplinary policy reflective of his conception of higher learning and his interpretation of a "liberal education" stood in marked contrast to the aspirations and identities of many of these students.

CHAPTER IV

The Alumni

The Alumni of the college have come to its rescue. Fearing that the Trustees were too much influenced by the desire for peace and good-will, they represented to the board that an investigation was needed, and this action has aroused both the Trustees and the Faculty. . . . Their present state of mind promises to lead to the discovery of the source of the troubles at Hanover, and the application of the proper remedy. The credit of the result will belong chiefly to the New York Alumni. This is an important step toward the admission of graduates of the college to a share in its management. . . . The question of Alumni representation does not concern Dartmouth alone, but most of the other colleges in the country. . . . The close corporation system of management fails to yield the best results. The graduates of a College are its natural governing body. To exclude them from all representation in its councils alienates their affections, and no college can afford to lose the sympathy of its graduates.

—Charles R. Miller, *New York Times* (1881)

The epigraph heading this chapter regarding alumni demands for representation in governance, their position of leadership in the Bartlett controversy, and the linking of their demands to their control over potential resources highlights a trend that became increasingly important in higher education in the late nineteenth century. The alumni became much more important in supporting and influencing institutions of higher education. Despite this trend, most histories of American higher education in the nineteenth century have paid little attention to the role of the alumni. If their role in the Bartlett controversy is at all typical of the period (and it seems to be), these studies omit an important element in analyzing the changing nature of higher learning in American society.

Those studies that do offer information relating to the alumni movement provide little analysis of how and why this movement changed during the nineteenth century. Why did a voice in governance become so important to them? How does this illuminate changing conceptions of the college, of community, and of higher learning? Much of our knowledge of the role of the alumni comes from individual institutional histories that chronicle specific (official) events. Webster Stover provides a much-needed description of the general alumni movement but fails to relate it to significant historical changes.[1] Merle Curti and Roderick Nash offer an illuminating study of the role of philanthrophy in shaping higher education,[2] but this touches only one dimension of the alumni role. Publications from the American Alumni Council[3] also provide information regarding alumni. But few studies, if any, focus on how and why the alumni movement changed over time and how it illuminates changes in the college and in American society. An analysis of the role of the alumni in the Bartlett controversy provides a vehicle for redressing this imbalance and for adding to our understanding of what Daniel Boorstin has called "the peculiar American entanglement of higher education with the whole community."[4]

Ironically, the faculty's efforts to transfer power to themselves was not clearly a gain for the faculty, and the full impact of their initiatives was carried forward not by the faculty but by the alumni, the sustaining agent here. Pointing to the altered communal idea and notion of the presidency, through the trial they asserted their demands for alumni group representation on the corporate board and voiced their opposition to a president they perceived as lacking the qualities necessary to manage successfully the students and the faculty and to enhance the college's metropolitan reputation. On 7 April 1881 thirty-one members of the New York Association of Alumni sent a memorial to the board asking them to appoint a committee to investigate the "disquieting rumors concerning the state of affairs in the college, tending to impair the natural increase and growth of the College, to alienate the interest of the Alumni whose co-operation and assistance are so needful, and to reflect upon the management of the present incumbent of the presidential chair."[5] The New York alumni passed resolutions in favor of the memorial of the faculty requesting the resignation of the president.[6] When the trustees agreed to investigate and when Bartlett demanded that there be specific charges, the New York alumni drew up the charges and acted as the prosecution in the trial. Even after the trial, the New York alumni passed resolutions in support of the sentiments expressed in 1881 and urged Bartlett to resign.[7]

Various alumni groups discussed the Bartlett controversy and passed resolutions regarding the trial. The alumni of the Chandler Scientific Department wrote memorials to the board opposing the policy toward that department.[8] While not all the alumni were as adamant in their opposition to the president as the New York association, and some were supportive of the president, most of the alumni seemed to agree with the following statements regarding the president and the role of the alumni: "The Alumni of Dartmouth have no voice in the management of the college. The Board of Trust is a close corporation, and a law unto itself. . . . We are convinced that Dr. Bartlett's continuance in the Presidency will be an irreparable damage to the college."[9] One historian of the college notes that one of the most serious consequences of the Bartlett controversy was the general lack of sympathy and support among the alumni of the college as well as the permanent alienation of the New York group throughout the rest of the Bartlett administration.[10]

The actions and ideas of the alumni in 1881 are in marked contrast to those of the alumni in 1851, who had regarded the president as the interpreter of faith and intellect and accepted the "virtual" representation of the board in the corporate community. Although a member of the class of 1827 attempted to organize an association in the earlier part of the century,[11] the alumni did not form such an organization until 1854. At this time the alumni did not evidence any demands for a voice in the governance of the institution. It was not until the late 1860s and early 1870s that local associations emerged and that the alumni began to voice demands for representation as alumni on the board of trustees. These assertions and their dissatisfaction over the Bartlett presidency manifested itself in the trial and controversy surrounding it.

Why did Bartlett, whose policies were in keeping with Lord a generation before, incur the disfavor of so many of the alumni? How is the alumni movement for a direct voice in governance and their role in the Bartlett controversy related to the changing sense of community and character of the presidency? And how does this illuminate changing conceptions of the college; of the value of higher learning; and of career opportunities, growth, and patterns of social organization in the nineteenth century?

The career patterns of Dartmouth graduates underwent significant change in the nineteenth century, as did their backgrounds, residential patterns, and aspirations. This information provides a framework for assessing their changing perceptions of the alumni role, their ideas of community, and their notions of the presidency. Similar to the pattern of the class of 1881, the data regarding the alumni of the Academical Department and the Chandler Scientific Department (the undergraduate body)[12] indicate a general rise as the century progresses of those entering the nontraditional fields for college graduates, especially business. In the 1771–1820 period 90% of the Dartmouth graduates entered the traditional learned profesions, leaving only 10% for other fields. The traditional learned professions category decreased to 86% in the 1821–1870 period, leaving 14% for other pursuits. By the 1861–1910 period the number entering nontraditional pursuits rose dramatically to 50%, with 29% going into business (see appendix 22).

The information regarding individual occupations of Dartmouth graduates indicates a substantial decline in the ministry, a significant rise in business pursuits, a slight decline of those going into law (although this remains an important field for graduates), the rise of engineering, the maintenance of medicine in a comparatively constant state, and the importance of the field of education as a professional pursuit. Although there are some differences in aggregate numbers, the pattern at Dartmouth is similar to the general trend for college graduates during the nineteenth century. The ministry declined significantly, and teaching and commercial pursuits became the two most dominant professions by the end of the century.[13] In a study of thirty-seven colleges and universities, Bailey Burritt notes that the rise of graduates going into commercial pursuits "is one of the most striking facts"[14] his analysis brings out. Along a similar vein, an analysis of graduates from such prep schools as St. Paul's also confirms the rise of business pursuits for graduates.[15] While the overall rise of nontraditional fields for college alumni may have been sharpest in the 1890s (as one historian has suggested),[16] the designation of business as the first choice of the class of 1868 at Williams[17] highlights student aspirations toward this end and the general rise of this field during the last half of the nineteenth century that Burritt's study reveals. And this trend seemed to be in keeping with the general trend in the country for an increase in occupations related to commercial pursuits, especially trade and transportation.[18]

The difference in the patterns of Dartmouth alumni between one and thirty years' standing in 1851 (classes of 1821–50) and one and thirty years' standing in 1881 (classes of 1851–80) indicates the progress of the general trends for college graduates and its acceleration in the decade of the 1880s through the rest of the Bartlett administration.[19] In the 1821–50 period the average percentage of Dartmouth graduates pursuing the ministry was 28.3%. In the 1851–80 period this declined significantly to 12.9%, and from 1881–90 it declined even further, to 9%. Law along with the ministry was the dominant profession for Dartmouth graduates in the 1821–50 period, with 32.9% going into the field of law. In the 1851–80 period law still remained an important field for graduates, with 30.9% pursuing this field, but this slight decline signaled a downward trend in the latter part of the century. By the 1881–90 period the percentage in this field declined to 21.6% (see appendix 23).[20]

The data regarding the field of business reveal a marked rise of those pursuing this field in the 1851–80 period. The average percentage of those entering business pursuits in the 1821–50 period was 4.3%. By the 1851–80 period, this increased almost four times, to 16.1%; by 1881–90, this increased even further, to 20.4% (see appendix 23).[21] This same type of rise, but in a considerably smaller proportion, is evident in the field of engineering. In the 1821–50 period this field comprised only 0.6% of the graduates. In the 1851–80 period this increased to 3.8%, and by 1881–90, it rose to 8.4%. Business and engineering were especially attractive to those in the Chandler Scientific Department. Fifty percent of the class of 1881 chose engineering, and 25% chose business. This attractiveness held true for members of the New York Association of Alumni from the 1851–80 period, with 40.6% of the Chandler graduates engaged in business[22] and 18.9% in engineering (see appendix 24). It should be noted, however, that as the proportion of Chandler graduates to academical graduates was small, one cannot attribute the increasing attraction of commercial pursuits to these students alone.[23]

Teaching, always an attractive pursuit for Dartmouth graduates, continued to rise, while medicine remained constant. During the 1821–50 and the 1851–80 periods, 15.9% of the graduates went into teaching. In 1881–90 this field attracted even more graduates—21.7%. In the 1821–50 period 11.9% went into medicine. In the 1851–80 period 10.4% went into medicine, the same percentage for the 1881–90 period.

If we compare these statistics with those of the national picture in Burritt's study, we find some variations in the percentages but trends similar to that at Dartmouth. The average percentage pursuing the ministry for the 1821–50 period was 28.3%. This declined to 18.8% in the 1851–80 period and to 11.6% in the 1881–90 period. For these same periods, law declined slightly from 26.8% to 25.4% and then to 20.9%; medicine was comparatively constant, with a tendency to decrease— 10.8% to 8.6% to 8.4%; education rose from 9.5% to 12.9% to 19.1%; commercial pursuits rose considerably from 7.9% to 16.5% to 21.3%; engineering also rose (although taking a much smaller percentage of the graduates) from 1% to 2.2% to 4.1%.[24]

The trends of the Dartmouth alumni in general and those of college graduates as reported in Burritt's study were similar to those for the New York alumni, with the exception of a larger percentage of the New York group being attracted to business pursuits at an earlier period. In the 1851–80 period 20.9% were in this field[25] as compared with 16.1% of Dartmouth graduates in general (see appendixes 23 and 24). The figure for the New York alumni in the 1851–80 period is even slightly higher than for the alumni in general for the 1881–90 period, when the figure reached 20.4%. The figure for the New York alumni in the 1851–80 period is closer to the Yale and Harvard graduates of the same period, with 20.8%[26] and 24.1%,[27] respectively, of these graduates entering the field of business.

Beginning in the 1860s and accelerating greatly as the century progressed, leading metropolitan areas, especially New York and Boston, were increasingly attractive areas for Dartmouth graduates. A list of members of the New York Association of Alumni as of 1883 reveals that the members of the classes between 1860 and 1880 (those who would have been alumni in 1881) made up 52.8% of the members. Those in the classes between 1870 and 1880 made up 37.9% of the membership; and if one includes the classes of 1881 and 1882 as of 1883, those in the classes between 1870 and 1882 made up 41.8% of the members (see appendix 25).[28] On the other hand, the data regarding the class of 1851 indicate that few settled in metropolitan areas, while graduates of the class of 1881 found these areas, especially New York City and Boston, increasingly attractive places in which to spend their professional lives. This trend seemed to hold true for other college graduates as the century progressed. A study of the Yale alumni, for example, notes "a crowding of the college graduates into that section [Middle Atlantic], especially into the neighborhood of New York City. . . . where the growth of population and concentration of industries offer . . . the greatest opportunity for usefulness and success.[29]

The career patterns, backgrounds, and aspirations of the 1851 Dartmouth alumni and the nature of the society in which they lived help us to understand their view of the presidency and why the question of alumni representation did not become an issue for this generation of graduates. And, reflective of the shared sense of community, the alumni's perception of their role was in keeping with the college's expectation of them. The collected data, then, reveal a pattern in which the 1851 alumni (classes of 1821–50) chose the traditional learned professions, especially law, the ministry, and also teaching and medicine. They were not particularly attracted to more urban areas (as would be the case in 1881). And judging from the information regarding the class of 1851, they were a more homogeneous group, from northern New England, and from limited financial circumstances. They aspired to middle-class status and to opportunities in the traditional learned professions in areas outside their declining hometowns and farms. Graduates settled in other parts of northern New England and the West. They shared the sense of purpose of the faculty and the president in fashioning a Christian nation. The alumni saw their role as repaying the institution that had given them the education they had struggled so hard to get by being an example of the good Christian man in the organic community.

Along this vein, the president of the Association of Alumni of Dartmouth College in 1855 stated that although the graduates were not successful in forming an association before this period, this was not due to a lack of feeling for their alma mater, because wherever her graduates went, "the world has been made better because they have lived in it."[30] He called upon President Lord to explain how the graduates could help their alma mater. Although Lord hoped for additional funds for the college, he saw their efforts to make it a Christian Zion of critical importance. Lord stated that the most important thing they could do was to stay true to the principles for which the college stands as they would be carrying out "the common good" and in so doing "the favor of Him who ruleth over all."[31] And a member of the class of 1850, in observing the influence of Dartmouth on the lives of his classmates, said: "Throughout them all, there runs an iron thread of stern, assiduous labor; of unflagging industry; of hope that yields to no discouragement; and of uplifting Faith that seeks its aid in a higher power than self, on every battlefield of Christian endeavor. . . . [These] seeds of firmness, self-reliance and virtue once planted there, have borne fruit to make the vintage rich in justified promises of secular and spiritual advancement."[32] Thus, the emphasis on the part of the college and the alumni centered on their fashioning a Christian Zion. And the basis of loyalty evidenced by the alumni seems to have been based both on the practical or utilitarian grounds[33] of giving them access to the middle class and an opportunity to escape the poverty of their hometowns and on religious grounds—not in a narrow sectarian sense but, in the words of President Lord, in fashioning a Christian "kingdom of God."[34]

Consistent with the shared sense of purpose for this generation of alumni, their conception of higher learning pointed to a joining of intellect and faith. In 1844 a member of the class of 1834 told the literary societies of Dartmouth, "I cannot here separate our mental from our moral attitudes, because—Deity never intended a separation—Nor can I conceive of any well directed intellectual effort, which shall be disconnected with a well regulated moral sense."[35] Another alumnus expressed the fusing of heart and mind and its influence upon the lives of the alumni this way: "Dr. Lord . . . while . . . [holding] us to our tasks in the grinding mills of his Academic Athens, still kept our windows open towards Jerusalem, it was this training that had woven its iron threads into each day's work."[36] Through his college experience, then, the student was provided with an interpretation of life to better fashion a Zion.[37]

The sense of community with its underlying cohesion and consensual orientation helps to explain their view of the president and their lack of demands for a voice in governance. Given their backgrounds, aspirations, and shared sense of purpose, that they regarded the president as the interpreter of faith and intellect does not seem unusual. And that the alumni did not question the board of trustees' exercising their stewardship through individuals acting as guardians of the common good,[38] rather than through interest group representation (namely, the alumni), seems in keeping with this orientation. In addition, viewing this within the context of the society in which they lived, until mid-century the organic sense of community (locality based and with a network of social relations characterized by affective bonds and mutual concern)[39] remained the predominant pattern. Organization on a large-scale level, the shift to metropolitan areas, and the growth and influence of interest groups[40] had not yet become the forces they would later in the century.

In contrast to this sense of community in 1851, by 1881 the alumni saw themselves as the "natural governing body"[41] of the college and observed that excluding them from "its councils" results in the alienation of "their affections."[42] This perception points to the assertion of the alumni as a collegiate faction desiring to gain power to secure their interests and determine the course of the institution. And one finds the same type of allusion to "affections,"[43] with its implications of support, financially and otherwise, in the memorial of the New York association regarding their request for an investigation of the Bartlett administration.

In 1881 Bartlett, in similar fashion to Lord, looked to the graduates to permeate the society "with Christianity" and to be "examples in a great Republic."[44] At the same time, under the pressure of competition of other institutions, he intensified requests (which Lord had hoped for) for alumni support in the form of financial aid. Bartlett noted that Dartmouth should be "the great Northern New England College," but that it needed the alumni of the college to "come to the rescue" with financial support.[45] The New York Association of Alumni answered this request, in effect, by expressing its dissatisfaction with the Bartlett presidency (which other alumni groups seemed to share), initiating an investigation, acting as the prosecution in the trial, and equating financial support of the institution with a greater share in its governance. (It should be noted that the trustees were sensitive to pressure from the alumni before the Bartlett controversy. In 1876, upon the request of the New York alumni, they granted the alumni a limited measure of representation on the board.)

What happened to the alumni in a generation to make them oppose a president who held views similar to Lord's? Why did the movement for representation as alumni on the board of trustees become so important? Their changing backgrounds, career and residential patterns, and aspirations suggest answers and point toward their changing ideas of community and notions of the presidency.

An analysis of the information presented in the previous pages reveals a marked shift in career and residential patterns for these two generations of alumni and the progress of these trends in the decade of the 1880s. More and more students entered fields other than the traditional learned professions, especially that of business. At Dartmouth this trend was accentuated in the New York group (who had percentages similar to those from Harvard and Yale)[46] and the Chandler alumni. Reflective of this trend, in 1872 a member of the New York Association of Alumni described the growing importance of this field, the importance of a college education for preparation for a career in business, and how the curriculum might be modified in light of this. He said:

> There is no denying that in the progress of the world, the relative importance of the learned professions has steadily diminished; not because the minister, the lawyer, the doctor and the teacher are less useful to society than formerly, but because men of other pursuits have become more useful. Other occupations have been found to require as wide a range of information, and as well trained intellectual powers, as either of the professions; and some of them afford a much broader field of activity and influence. . . . These men require the highest intellectual training and the largest amount of actual knowledge which can be given by any college or university in any country. . . .
> . . . The chief thing wanting in college courses for the training of business men are more of political economy, modern history, (political and social,) *geography* (physical, ethnological and commercial,) and the modern languages.[47]

Alumni such as this one were attracted to the growing opportunities in business as the country moved from an agrarian and rural society to an industrial and urban one. Law, teaching, the ministry, and medicine had been the traditional professions for college graduates: this period saw the rise of "new professions" such as business and engineering.

Arthur Comey, in his study of the New England colleges, finds that students increasingly pursued scientific studies such as those offered at the Chandler school.[48] Increased opportunities in engineering, accompanying the growth in transportation and industry from mid-century onward, attracted many students to this field.[49] Growth of scientific schools, such as the Sheffield Scientific School at Yale and the Massachusetts Institute of Technology, occurred during this period.[50]

Within the traditional learned professions, what is outstanding for the 1881 generation of alumni as compared with the generation in 1851 is the marked decline in the ministry, the importance of the education field,[51] and the change in the nature of the law profession, more and more related to the field of business.[52] Many in this field had business interests or represented corporations. For example, the treasurer of the New York Association of Alumni in 1881 (Sanford H. Steele, class of 1870) who drew up the charges against Bartlett and acted as counsel for the prosecution, was a lawyer and organizer and president of the General Chemical Company of New York.

Not only did their occupations shift, but so, too, did their choice of residence, bringing them more and more into metropolitan areas. Like the Amherst students who were attracted to opportunities in industrial corporations such as Standard Oil of New York and distinguished law firms in New York City and Boston,[53] the leading urban areas of New York City and Boston began to be especially popular with, and lucrative for, Dartmouth graduates. The lure of these metropolitan centers was not unique to Dartmouth graduates and other college graduates. Frederick Law Olmstead, writing in the late 1870s, observed, "Millions of people have been concentrating at New York, Philadelphia, Boston, Baltimore, Cincinnati, Chicago, St. Louis, and San Francisco, while rural neighborhoods in New England, Virginia, the Carolinas and Georgia have been rapidly losing population and still more rapidly losing various forms of wealth and worth."[54]

Not only did their career and residential patterns change, but judging from the students from the 1870s onward, so did the alumni's socioeconomic background, birthplace, and residential patterns before college. Like the influx at Williams of more well off students from such areas as New York City,[55] Dartmouth students began to come from areas outside the rural towns of northern New England. Some came from the larger towns and cities, from the Middle Atlantic, other parts of New England, and the West. Many of these alumni did not see a college education as a means of entry into the middle class via the traditional learned professions.

Their background, career patterns, and aspirations drew them to leading metropolitan areas, and they evidenced a changed notion of community. Dartmouth alumni were competing with other college graduates in these areas, and the college one attended or the club to which one belonged began to be important factors in selection for a position and for business and social success. The emphasis upon the rank of the institution eventually translated into a concern with its exclusiveness and the associational status it could confer.[56] The status referent here is associational as opposed to the traditional local or social context. No doubt this was one reason why the alumni, especially the alumni from New York, a leading urban area and the center of upper-class life by 1880, were so concerned with the college's metropolitan reputation—a reputation defined according to national standards emanating from these leading centers—not its services to the hill country of New Hampshire. This was of great importance to a group who now began to define success within the select community of peers. Given this framework, the alumni emerged as a collegiate faction at the time of the Bartlett trial.

In contrast to a collegiate domain that can be dominated by personality and the work of one man, the alumni sought to transform the very scope of collegiate control. The members of the New York association perceived themselves as leaders in the alumni movement for a greater voice in the governance of the institution. (It was through a resolution presented by the New York alumni in 1876 that the alumni gained their first limited measure of representation.)[57] In 1881, Charles R. Miller, the youthful secretary of the New York Association of Alumni who acted as spokesman for this group through his editorship of the *New York Times*, referred to the board as a "close corporation."[58] He remarked that the initiation of the investigation of the state of affairs of the college would lead to the discovery of the source of the problem, that "the credit of the result will belong chiefly to the New York Alumni," and that "this is an important step toward the admission of graduates of the college to a share in its management."[59] The New York alumni seemed to be saying that had they been on the board, Dartmouth would not be in danger of "ruin" or "impending disaster" through Bartlett's "deplorable management."[60] These statements stand in contrast to the ideas and behavior of the 1851 alumni and point to their altered communal sense and idea of the presidency.

The "impending disaster," as the alumni called it, referred to the college's status and potential as to growth, numbers and types of students, rank, sources of support, and its ability to attract and keep faculty of distinction—in essence, to its metropolitan reputation as a leading eastern college. The alumni complained, for example, that Dartmouth was not growing at the rate of other New England institutions and that Dartmouth had sunk in rank and would continue to do so if Bartlett remained as president. Along this vein, one alumnus remarked: "The college catalogues are not yet out, but from such statistics as are obtainable it is apparent that the year opens prosperously with most of the New England institutions. . . . In unpleasant contrast with these

Charles Ransom Miller. Courtesy of Dartmouth College Library.

favorable exhibits are the statistics from Dartmouth."[61] Other alumni declared that Bartlett was a failure "as an administrative and executive officer,"[62] that the college had "sunk from her place beside Amherst and Brown University, in the second rank of New England colleges, to the level of Wesleyan,"[63] and that she would go "lower still if the Trustees . . . did not take the millstone from her neck."[64]

In addition to these concerns, the Chandler alumni had other reasons for opposing Bartlett. They regarded his attitude and actions as degrading both their preparation for a professional life and the fields they were choosing, many of which were the new professions such as engineering and business. For example, Bartlett said of the Chandler course, "there is no intellectual nor moral science and almost nothing in the wide circle of English & general literature. It is too one-sided and too deficient in the great and fundamental branches to fit him [the student] for the best and widest uses. The academic department puts him under vastly better moral and religious influences."[65] Bartlett's recommendations to the board such as lowering the standard of admission to the scientific school and the subsequent actions of the board (some of which were later modified) led to much opposition against Bartlett and a series of memorials from graduates of the school.[66]

However valid from the perspective of the alumni who opposed Bartlett was their criticism of him and their feeling that for the good of the college he should resign or be removed, one must also view the Bartlett controversy within the context of the aspirations of the alumni for a greater voice in the governance of the institution. Similar to the sentiments expressed in the statements of the New York alumni, Ernest Martin Hopkins, secretary of the college under Tucker and afterward president, concluded from his conversations with some of those involved that "whatever else this trial was it was an extraordinary manifestation of the existent discontent with the established College government represented in the Board of Trustees."[67] And within this context, the *Boston Post*, in reporting that forty Boston alumni had signed a petition asking for Bartlett's resignation, stated:

> The alumni of Dartmouth college have doubtless felt themselves called upon to express their views upon the matter now under serious consideration by the friends of that institution, all the more unequivocally because denied representation on the board of trustees.[68]

Through achieving power on the board, these aspiring upper-middle-class graduates sought to represent their interests and guide the development of the institution, including the selection of a president who possessed the qualities necessary to administer and shape the college so as to enhance its metropolitan reputation. And judging from their relationship to the students in the 1870s and 1880s, they probably saw themselves as role models or surrogate parents to these younger students and thus desired to chart the course of the institution to what would be in their minds the students' benefit as well.

Aspirations of alumni for a greater voice in the governance of colleges and universities was not unique to Dartmouth graduates. Writing at the turn of the century, Samuel Ranck observed:

> During the last third of the nineteenth century a new interest has come to be recognized in the government of many of our colleges— the alumni, and the interest of the alumni is being more and more counted on as a source of moral and financial strength. The alumni as alumni are directly represented in the government of the col- lege.[69]

While graduates themselves formed alumni associations (primarily lit- erary and social in nature) during the antebellum period, college pres- idents, in the hopes of raising funds, encouraged their formation toward the end of the antebellum period and through the latter part of the century.[70] In the post–Civil War period, the alumni perceived boards of trustees without their representation and election as a group—as alumni, elected by them and representing them—as "close corpora- tions."[71] Before 1865, although individual alumni may have served on boards, no alumni were elected as alumni representatives.[72] In many institutions alumni obtained their representation only after controversy and struggle. In the 1860s two institutions gave alumni a voice in gov- ernance. In the 1870s eleven more followed this path, as did six more in the 1880s and twelve more in the 1890s.[73]

If one views the specific manifestation of the alumni movement at Dartmouth, one finds that the developments at Dartmouth were similar to the more general trends. After the president encouraged the for- mation of the general association in 1854, and perhaps highlighting the growing importance of metropolitan areas and the settlement of Dart- mouth alumni in these areas, the early local alumni associations were formed in urban areas. The alumni formed associations in New York in 1863 (first informal meeting); in Boston in 1864; in Cincinnati in 1875; in Washington, D.C., in 1876; in Chicago in 1876; in the Northwest in 1880; in the Pacific in 1881; and in Manchester, New Hampshire, in 1881. In 1868 one finds the first hint of a shift in the perception of the alumni of their role. The New York association called a meeting and invited all the graduates to participate, to submit their opinions on the curriculum, and to indicate whether they approved or disapproved of the currciulum.[74]

In 1869 the Association of Alumni of Dartmouth College organized a committee[75] to formulate a list of resolutions regarding alumni rep- resentation that they would submit to the board. The plan called for a minority of the board to be elected upon nomination of the alumni and for these board members to hold office for a definite number of years, for the other trustees to hold their office for a limited term, and for the consideration of a proposal to the legislature for reducing the number of trustees required by the charter to be residents of New Hampshire. The plan also proposed that a committee of alumni examine annually the accounts of the treasurer and make reports of their findings. The alumni linked their financial support, such as a special subscription, to the board's acceptance of their plan. The board did not accept the alumni's resolutions. They proposed, instead, the formation of an annual alumni examining committee (but not with the power to examine financial reports). As regards the number of trustees who were New Hampshire residents, the trustees indicated that they would not elect more than the number required by the charter. At the same time, the trustees told the alumni of their importance to the college and expressed their enthusiasm for the alumni's proposal to raise funds.[76]

In 1875 the New York association passed a resolution calling for alumni representation, and they presented it to the board in 1876. The alumni gained their first limited measure of representation from this resolution. The trustees agreed that the next three vacancies on the board should be filled on the nomination of the alumni of the Academical and the Chandler Scientific Departments. When a vacancy occurred, graduates of at least four years' standing were to vote for four candidates for the vacancy. The trustees agreed that from the four receiving the most votes they would "ordinarily, and in all probability, invariably"[77] elect one to the vacant place. At an election in 1878 they elected three alumni to the board.

But the alumni were still dissatisfied with the extent of their voice in governance and considered the board, in the words of the secretary of the New York Association of Alumni, a "close corporation."[78] Within this context, Miller noted that in an election the previous month the board had not consulted the alumni, and that the initiation of an investigation of the president and the state of affairs of the college marked a significant step in the admission of graduates to the management of the college.[79] Thus, while many of the alumni objected to Bartlett's policies and presidential style, the Bartlett trial also was a vehicle for the alumni to voice their dissatisfaction with the form of governance of the college. Highlighting the extent of the alumni's dissatisfaction and pointing to their aspirations, the *Springfield Republican* remarked, "The Trustees are on trial here rather more than the president."[80]

To emphasize alumni group power, the alumni equated their demands—in this case, the removal or resignation of Bartlett as recognition of their influence moving toward the direct election of alumni as alumni on the board—with the contribution of funds. During the aftermath of the trial, for example, a member of the class of 1873 stated:

> The Boston Transcript says: "If there is a single prominent graduate of the college in this vicinity who does not really believe that Dr. Bartlett would promote his own welfare not less than that of the college by seeking another field of labor, we have not heard of him." The doctor [Bartlett] is very anxious to complete the foundation for the Webster professorship, which still needs a few thousand dollars, yet he cannot solicit funds with any hope of success from a great body of alumni. With the advent of another president at Hanover, the alumni of New York would be under special obligations to rally to the support of their alma mater. It would seem clear that President Bartlett can best serve the college by retiring in the interests of family harmony. The fact that the opposition to him is implacable, whether the blame is his or not, appears to make the duty of the trustees a clear one.[81]

All the alumni groups intensified their efforts for alumni representation during the rest of the Bartlett administration. In 1891 the board agreed to "the unrestricted nomination by the alumni of five members of the board,"[82] giving them the voice in governance they had pressed for.

Dartmouth was not unique among colleges and universities in the late nineteenth century in open conflicts involving the alumni and the president and in the leadership of urban alumni from leading metropolitan centers in the movement for a greater voice in the governance and direction of the institution. We find examples of such conflicts at Hamilton and Wesleyan, for example, with the alumni asking for a complete investigation of the current administration and the resignation or removal of the president.[83] And the New York and Boston groups at Williams, the Philadelphia group at Bucknell, and the New York group at Princeton, for instance, provided leadership (in varying degrees) in the alumni movement for greater influence in the management and direction of these institutions.[84] While there were important differences in the western state universities, where trustees were elected by the people, appointed by the governor, or elected by the legislature, urban alumni also seemed to have played an important role in those institutions in which alumni demanded alumni group representation on the board. It was the Chicago group, for instance, that acted as the leaders in this movement at the University of Illinois.[85]

A salient factor, then, in the nature of the change in the alumni's perception of their role and the character of the presidency was their changed sense of community. A generation before the Bartlett controversy, the alumni conceived of their role as living the life of the good

Christian man in the organic community. With their shared sense of purpose, cultural and religious cohesiveness, and consensual orientation, they did not publicly question the virtual representation of the board in the corporate community. A generation later, with their changing backgrounds, career and residential patterns, and aspirations drawing them to metropolitan areas and within a society itself undergoing tremendous change, their notion of community underwent significant change. They now had interests that extended beyond the locality, and they sought to protect these interests. As the faculty joined associations relating to their discipline, as students from the 1880s onward found fraternities in college and upper-middle-class social clubs and peer-centered professional associations after college so important to their aspirations, so the alumni saw themselves as a group apart, a collegiate faction seeking status, influence, and power. With the increasing competition of college graduates settling in large numbers in the leading metropolitan areas, the associational referent—the school they attended, for example—seemed to be an important indicator of status among their peers. Through achieving power on the Dartmouth board, these urban, aspiring, upper-middle-class graduates could represent their interests and "modernize" and "improve" the institution, including the selection of a president who could administer and shape the college so as to enhance its metropolitan reputation. This was of great importance to a group who now began to define success within their select community of peers.

Along with their altered communal idea and notion of the presidency, Bartlett's conception of higher learning also seemed out of place to many of these alumni. Like others before him, Bartlett saw as the heart of higher learning the unity of knowledge, the fusing of faith and intellect, and the development of moral character. This conception of higher learning stood in marked contrast to the development of a more rationalized, esoteric learning emphasizing specialization within disciplines, specific methodologies, and an emphasis on the empirical and quantitative in the solution of problems. While most of the alumni did not want to turn Dartmouth into a university,[86] they did look to what would occur under Tucker—a fragmentation of what had been included in the old moral philosophy into specific disciplines of specialization in the social sciences and to a parallel acceptance of the type of concentration in the "scientific" exemplified in the Chandler course. Thus, for most of the alumni, Bartlett was "the wrong man for the place,"[87] and the trial became a vehicle for them to gain greater recognition in their movement toward a voice in the governance structure.

CHAPTER V

The Trustees

The Trustees earnestly solicit the contributions of the community. . . . it is hoped that the College will be enabled, by the timely liberality it may receive to keep pace with the increasing population and intelligence of the important section of the country which it represents.

—Board of Trustees (1841)

The active interest of the board, growing more minute in its work every year, in every department and part of the college, is evidence that the alumni may safely give their confidence to its administration, their gifts to its care, their sons to its shelter. The board will assume all its own responsibilities, and all under its care must conform to its decisions.

—Investigating Committee, Board of Trustees (1881)

The trustees were most conscious of the confusions between old and new traditions. At first they appeared to be in agreement with the alumni, a new power with much potential for financial support. The decision to hold this public trial, the open challenge to the authority of the president, the desire to clear it all up once and for all and decide who was blameworthy, and the preoccupation with finances and concern with the college's metropolitan reputation were all indicative of that position. Then the trustees seemed to be acting as the moral guarantors of the college. Along this vein, they stated:

The Trustees have but one work, viz., to fulfill sacredly the trust committed them by a charter in whose faith many generous men and women have left their gifts to the cause of a high and wise education. The Trustees must do their own duty fearlessly. The active interest of the board, growing more minute in its work every year, in every department and part of the college, is evidence that the alumni may safely give their confidence to its administration, their gifts to its care, their sons to its shelter. The board will assume all its own responsibilities, and all under its care must conform to its decisions.[1]

In their own transition during the trial, the trustees seemed to be somewhat sympathetic to Bartlett's role in balancing the moral authority of the president and the college's books.

In their quandary, in the end, with all the charges lodged, the trustees did not ask for Bartlett's resignation but sought an older form of harmony that would accommodate the new realities. In a series of recommended resolutions that the board unanimously adopted, the investigating committee noted that the board needed the help of the alumni in New York and other alumni and acknowledged "gratefully" that the "success" of the New York alumni had "added so much to the reputation of the college."[2] The trustees indicated that they were awaiting "the results of its efforts for the harmony of the college, the adjustment of all its parts, the allotment of respective duties, and the procuring of a kind, forebearing and helpful spirit on all sides, with confidence that will not at present allow the possibility of failure, and with a determination to secure such results in any event."[3]

Meanwhile, a special committee of the board had met and listened to appeals from the Chandler alumni to restore the status of the Chandler school. The board restored most of the previous entrance requirements.[4] The trustee committee appointed by the board to restore harmony in the college went to Hanover. The controversy continued. Finally, in April 1882, nine months after the trial, four out of ten members of the board cast a negative vote to the following resolution:

> Resolved. That we put on record the expression of our continued confidence in him [Bartlett] as an able, efficient administrator, and an admirable instructor and we believe that the best interests of the college require that he should continue in his present position.[5]

How do we account for the trustees' actions? On the one hand, the trustees were sensitive to alumni pressure for a voice in governance and for the investigation and trial that was held; they issued a very politic report emphasizing the importance of the alumni and the trustees' active interest and watchfulness of the situation. On the other hand, although four out of ten members of the board cast a vote of no confidence regarding the Bartlett administration and opposed him on various policies, a majority stoppped short of removing him, and he lingered on for eleven years after the trial. An analysis of the sensitivity of the board to different sources of support will help to illuminate the changing nature and interests of the board and what their positions represented.

The sensitivity of the board to pressure from what they considered to be their constituency in terms of money, students, and support was not new in itself. A generation before the Bartlett controversy, during the administration of President Lord, the trustees were sensitive to the views of the local community, the surrounding region, and the Congregational clergy of New Hampshire.[6] For example, in 1841 they appealed to the community for funds, and in 1851 the President's Report to the board assured the trustees that the "irregularity" of the students in blowing horns while participating in the public celebration at St. Johnsbury, Vermont, was "corrected."[7] And the response of the board to resolutions passed by the Merrimack County Conference of Congregational Churches regarding President Lord also is indicative of their sensitivity to pressure from the locale and region. The resolutions of the Congregational clergy asked the trustees to consider a change in the presidency of the college because of what they termed the "popular prejudice" against it arising from the publication of President Lord's views on slavery.[8] The trustees passed a series of resolutions thanking the clergy and churches of New England for its "support and patronage" and trusting it would continue "in view of its past history and great service to the Church and the State."[9] In contrast to the situation in 1881, the trustees did not hold a public trial, nor did they directly ask for his resignation. But they made obvious their concern that Lord's views might be jeopardizing the college.[10] And although Lord, like Bartlett, was acting within the context of his view of himself as a moral leader, he found a solution quite different from Bartlett's. Considering the actions of the trustees as a vote of no confidence, he resigned.[11] Thus, although sensitivity to sources of support is not new in itself, the sensitivity and nature of response to different sources of support in 1881 and a generation before seem to undergo change as do the nature and interests of the board.

If one attempts to determine the changing character and concerns of the Dartmouth board of trustees in relation to that of other governing boards, one finds a paucity of such studies. Two studies that do provide some insight into the nature and interests of trustees are Thorstein Veblen's *Higher Learning in America*[12] and Richard Hofstadter and Walter P. Metzger's *Development of Academic Freedom in the United States*.[13] Veblen stresses the philosophical and cultural gap between scholars seeking the "quest for knowledge" and the business-dominated boards of the late nineteenth and early twentieth century with their utilitarian outlook and business management techniques and purposes. He terms the presidents hired by these boards as captains of erudition and emphasizes that the adaptation of bureaucratization and of a business orientation placed restraints on academic freedom. Veblen offers useful hints about the composition and interests of these boards, but he does not provide a clear picture of the larger historical shifts. Many of the ideas and practices he ascribed to business were part of the larger culture as well, and aspects of bureaucratization he attributed to business interests were adapted by the faculty themselves in the process of professionalization.

Metzger and Hofstadter offer a long-range view of the trustees within the context of their study of academic freedom. They note, for example, that the fact that businessmen were serving on boards of trustees was not new in itself. Businessmen served on boards in the antebellum period. Although they furnish important glimpses of the boards in different periods, within a historical context their portrayal is flawed in that they interpret their findings from the perspective of the triumph of the university. They depict the trustees in the antebellum period from the viewpoint of colleges perceived as backward and sectarian, whereas they portray those from the post–Civil War period from a perception of a sudden transformation with the flowering of the university, of secularization, greater knowledge, and greater usefulness.[14]

In contrast to the problems of this perspective, an analysis of the role of the trustees in the Bartlett controversy can help illuminate the changing nature and interests of the trustees and shed light on the historical shifts involved in their positions and policies. How are the nature and reaction of the trustees to different sources of support both in 1881 and a generation before indicative of the shifting nature and interests of the board? How is this related to altered notions of community? How does this highlight changing conceptions of the college—its organization and administration, the role of the president, whom it served—as well as the changing nature of culture and higher learning in nineteenth-century America? And finally, why did Bartlett remain in his position as president despite all the controversy?

The collected data regarding the board of trustees in 1851 reveal a community-oriented board of men of mature years, prominent in the locale and region, and embodying a unity of purpose in their view of the college. The charter required that eight of the twelve members be New Hampshire residents.[15] If we exclude the president of Dartmouth and the governor of New Hampshire (included in the category of New Hampshire residents), who were members of the board by virtue of their position, one finds that in keeping with this provision, 60% or six of the ten remaining members were New Hampshire residents. The local composition of the board is emphasized further in that those who were not New Hampshire residents in 1851 were born in New Hampshire or spent part of their life there. The board members who were not New Hampshire residents in 1851 were from Massachusetts and Vermont. In similar fashion to the faculty, this seems to be indicative of the influence of the college in the northern New England area and in some respects in the New England region generally as well.

Men rather mature in years served on the board. No one on the board was under fifty-two, and 50% were over sixty (see appendix 27). President Lord, at fifty-eight, although seemingly from the same generation as most of the trustees, was slightly younger than a majority of the trustees. In 1881, on the other hand, Bartlett was older than 70% of the board.

Contrary to generalizations that the clergy dominated the 1851 board, 50% of the board were lawyers[16] and 10% were businessmen (see appendix 28). The percentage of 1851 board members who were ministers is comparable to the percentage in thirteen private institutions (Dartmouth included) in 1861—39.1%. Those who were lawyers (20.6%) constituted a smaller percentage than at Dartmouth, while the percentage of businessmen (22.8% business and 4.6% bankers) was higher than at Dartmouth alone (see appendix 29). This difference no doubt reflects the lagging development of the New Hampshire economy. While most state universities in the antebellum period also seem to have had presidents who were clergymen and faculty with ministerial backgrounds,[17] information for four middle western universities in 1861 indicates that the percentage of ministers on these boards was much lower than it was at the thirteen private institutions. The trustees were primarily lawyers, businessmen, and farmers (see appendix 30).

Reflective of the integral role that they played in the wider geographic and moral community, the Dartmouth trustees were very active and prominent in the locale, the state, northern New England, and to some extent the New England region itself. From the information available,[18] the board member who was a businessman (president of a railroad and factory owner) served as governor of New Hampshire from 1846 to 1847. While most of the board seemed to have some affiliation with the Congregational church or to view them as supporters of the college, this board member had Baptist affiliations. Active in the Baptist church, he did much toward furthering the interests of the denomination in the state.

Of the five lawyers on the board, at least four were active in community affairs. One of the lawyers was a member of the New Hampshire legislature, clerk of the House, state councillor, and author of many articles in "Proceedings" of the state historical society and the *New England Historical and Genealogical Register*. One served as judge probate

(New Hampshire), as Speaker of the New Hampshire House of Representatives, and as a member of the Constitutional Convention of New Hampshire in 1850. Another served as a member of the New Hampshire legislature, as judge of the Supreme Court of New Hampshire, as a delegate to the Massachusetts Constitutional Convention, and as commissioner to revise the statutes of Massachusetts. He also was professor of medical jurisprudence at Dartmouth, Royall Professor of Law at Harvard, and authored publications on legal and historical topics. Another lawyer held the position of judge of the Supreme Court of Massachusetts and served as a member of Congress.

Of the ministers on the board, at least two were active in both clerical and secular activities in the community, state, and region. One served as pastor of a Congregational church, secretary of the General Association of New Hampshire, corporate member of the American Board of Commissioners for Foreign Missions, and member (and chaplain) of the New Hampshire legislature. He published articles, essays, and sermons in periodicals of the period and participated in many of the educational and religious movements of the period. Another held positions as pastor of a Congregational church, president of the New Hampshire Historical Society, president of the New Hampshire Missionary Society, vice president of the American Home Missionary Society, director of the New Hampshire Bible Society, and corporate member of the New England Historical and Genealogical Society. He also edited the provincial records of New Hampshire; served as state historian; and contributed numerous sermons, addresses, and articles to periodicals on educational, historical, and religious topics.

Along with this community orientation, the trustees, as well as the faculty and president, embodied a transdenominational unity of purpose in fashioning a Christian Zion—an orientation not unusual in this age of "the Christian college."[19] They were united in the faith that by somehow uplifting the character of the students the nation would be a step further on its way to being a Zion. In exemplifying this aim, Richard Fletcher, a lawyer, a judge, and a board member in 1851, was described by his biographer this way: "Mr. Fletcher was a sincere Christian. His religion was not so much of the aggressive kind, nor did he often urge his view upon others; but it pervaded his entire character, and shone out in all his actions."[20] When he died he made provision for the publication biennially of a prize essay in college that impressed "on the minds of all Christians, a solemn sense of their duty to exhibit in their godly lives and conversation the beneficent effects of the religion they profess."[21]

In producing this Christian nation, one finds a fusing of the religious with the secular and utilitarian. The Reverend Nathaniel Bouton, a board member, noted, "The sons of Dartmouth build high and enduring super-structures of personal glory and public influence. As citizens of New Hampshire we owe much to the influence of this college in elevating the character of our primary schools and academies, and in promoting education through our country."[22]

While the Congregational clergy of New Hampshire were important to the college as sources of encouragement and support, and the board regarded them as such, one should also view them within the context of the college as an integral part of the community. When appeals for funds were made to the clergy, they were usually made by way of asking them to recommend to those they knew in the community the importance of their financial support to Dartmouth as an institution of great service to all in the surrounding community and state.

The collected data regarding the trustees suggest their idea of community. They seemed to perceive themselves as integral parts of the community, with their audience, status, and aspirations derived from this source. This orientation is also reflected in their sensitivity to the community as board members and is evidenced in their policies and actions. It points to the mutual appreciation of the college and the community. The community supplied the students and money, and the board's policies are illustrative of its sensitivity to this source of support and to its community orientation. This orientation and the mutual appreciation between the college and community were typical of most antebellum institutions. To this point, President Tyler of Amherst noted that the American college with its trustees from the community was "a magnetic chain of reciprocal influences by which light flashes from the college to the community, and life streams back again from the community to the college."[23]

The board's policies regarding students' teaching in the district schools are expressive of its community orientation and suggest its conception of collegiate service. The trustees made special provision so that the largely poor and lower-middle-class students from the declining towns of rural northern New England could teach for three months in the winters to help them pay for their education.[24] They instituted enrichment courses for those staying during the short term. Students who taught did not have to make up any of the work of the short-term enrichment course.[25] Dartmouth students were in great demand in the district schools of New Hampshire, Vermont, and eastern Massachusetts. So great was this emphasis on teaching and so great were the number of students who taught during their college career that one historian of the college has commented that "for several decades Dartmouth was really a teacher's college."[26] Thus, the board's policies in facilitating and sanctioning students' teaching during the school year[27] "served" the community. The college diffused knowledge in the New England region through the students' teaching in the district schools and provided opportunities for these poor and lower-middle-class students to earn money to complete their education and thus to gain access to middle-class status and to opportunities in the learned professions.

The trustees' actions and the president's stand in relation to developing a learned society also reflect their sense of community and conceptions of collegiate service and of higher learning. In 1841 the trustees brought the Reverend William Cogswell, class of 1811,[28] into the faculty; his chief duty was the solicitation of funds and the organization of "a learned society that should be nearly related to the College, & serve to concentrate the moral and intellectual resources of the Northern part of New England upon it."[29] The trustees and president thought that the society would be beneficial to the community "in diffusing knowledge & the principles of morality & virtue among the people."[30] President Lord stated that it would be "of great importance to the College, . . . a sort of popular branch, which altho[ugh] it has no coordinate corporate powers with the Board of Trustees, yet in a measure represents public opinion at the College, & . . . may be expected to perpetuate its influence upon the people."[31] The trustees' and the president's aim, then, of diffusing knowledge and virtue throughout the community and in this way helping to establish a Christian nation, reflects their perception of the central location of the college in the wider geographic and moral community.

If the students came from the community during the Lord administration, so did much of the school's funds. In the early 1830s the college obtained funds for a $30,000 subscription, primarily from individuals in New Hampshire. The college received subscriptions from 883 individuals in 118 towns of the state; 190 individuals outside the state also subscribed. The small town of Hanover raised $4,343.25 (from forty-two subscriptions). A number of persons in Hanover also purchased a bell for the college.[32] The subscription enabled the college to pay off its debts.[33]

Raising funds, however, was a source of anxiety for the trustees throughout the Lord administration.[34] The payments from the subscription came in slowly, and in 1841 they still were short of the expected $30,000. The actual sum obtained was almost $25,000.[35] In 1834 they tried to institute another subscription and appealed to the "clergy and churches of New Hampshire and the liberal members of the public at large."[36] This subscription did not meet with success. They tried to raise funds again in 1841 and appealed to the community. And when Cogswell resigned in 1844 to become president of Gilmanton (N.H.) Theological Seminary, the trustees employed the Reverend G. N. Allen as a paid agent. By 1845 they received pledges in the amount of $32,566, but the hoped-for $50,000 was never received and actual payment was only $26,565 (the last payment coming in 1854). In 1854 the trustees hoped to institute a new subscription, and the president went to Boston with the hope of organizing an alumni association and raising funds. In 1858 the trustees called for a subscription of $100,000 and did not employ paid agents, with the expectation that the alumni would help bring in some of the funds. The subscription was not very successful. One estimate placed the total subscribed at $16,572,[37] but even this amount was not secured.

In addition to the money received from subscriptions, the college received gifts and bequests from individuals in New Hampshire and the New England region. A sample of these gifts and bequests reveals the diversity of these donations and the seeming commitment to the college as a community resource. In 1835 the trustees received $1,100 from the estate of Mrs. Mary Clark of Portsmouth, New Hampshire, for students studying for the gospel ministry. In 1838 Frederick Hall, class of 1803, gave $5,000 worth of mineral specimens (in 1844 he gave the college the balance of his collection) and $5,000 in cash, which was to be allowed to accumulate until it was large enough for the endowment of a professorship of geology and mineralogy. The Parker family (two of whom were trustees) gave $1,000 in 1846, the interest to be used for the purchase of books for the library. Dr. George Shattuck, class of 1803, gave $7,000 in 1852 for the construction and equipment of an observatory and $2,000 more for the purchase of books. In 1854, upon the death of Samuel Appleton of Boston, the trustees received $15,000 for the endowment of a professorship of natural philosophy. Through the influence of the Reverend Austin Wright, class of 1830, they received in 1857 six sculpture slabs from the excavation at Nineveh. In 1851 Abiel Chandler of Walpole, New Hampshire, bequeathed to the college $50,000 for the endowment of a scientific school. This was the largest donation the college ever received up to this time.[38]

Thus, not only did the community supply the students,[39] but they also supplied direct financial assistance to the institution in the forms of gifts, bequests, and donations through subscriptions. In 1863 the assets of the college had increased from $85,752.30 with $20,659.95 in debts in 1830 to $201,176.33 with $34,000 in debts to its own funds.[40] While these assets were not especially substantial, the funds and gifts were donated by individuals in the local community, surrounding area, and region. If one translates the assets into the amount the college would have received from tuition alone, the assets of $201,176.33 equalled tuition from 3944.6 students at the rate of $51.00 per student. While more detailed studies of contributors and contributions to antebellum institutions are needed, the information available indicates a similar pattern of broad-based support by the local community in numerous institutions in this period—of donations of money and gifts from local residents and people in the surrounding areas.[41]

The trustees' allocation of those funds that were not restricted is indicative of their community orientation and sheds light on the nature of culture and higher learning in society as well. During the 1840s and 1850s, for example, the trustees expanded their allocation of funds for certain fields of science. In 1846 they appropriated $2,300 for the purchase of geodetical, astronomical, and meteorological equipment, and when the trustees' appeal for funds was made in 1841 they listed philosophical and astronomical apparatus along with the building of an observatory as ways in which the funds would be allocated. Ira Young, professor of natural philosophy and astronomy, toured other colleges to look at their equipment and went to Europe to purchase the equipment.[42] The trustees built an observatory, and the telescope, sidereal clocks, and transit equipment were housed in it. The observatory was very popular with both students and visitors alike. The instruments were in constant use both for instruction and for "the gratification of visitors."[43] The trustees built a permanent observatory in 1854 with Shattuck's donation and their allocation of $4,800.

The interest of the trustees in allocating funds to these scientific fields, the contributions of those in the community for this purpose, and the community's interest in looking through the telescope and examining the instruments and specimens seem to indicate that science was regarded as part of the general cultural activity of the community. Science, much of it on a simple empirical level, was an integral part of the culture of local communities throughout the country and not set apart from the lives of ordinary people, as would be the case with the development by 1870 of a more professional and esoteric science.[44] The nature of the trustees' and donors' policies and actions indicates that they were willing to support improvements in science that would be part of the cultural activity of the community as well as aiding in the instruction of students.

One should view the trustees' acceptance of the Chandler bequest for the establishment of a scientific school in terms of the responsiveness of the trustees to demands in the community for a "practical"[45] education as well as their desire not to forfeit the benefits of such a large gift to the college.[46] They could, in similar fashion to the development of the Sheffield Scientific School at Yale, meet the demands for some in the community for this type of education, while leaving the academical course untouched. Thus, the trustees stated that although they considered the Chandler School of Science and the Arts (original name before its change by the trustees to the Chandler Scientific Department) as a new endeavor, "an experiment" for the college, they regarded the bequest as "the gift of God."[47] They noted that the change in the college consists "*of additions.*"[48] They emphasized that the academical "*course is left untouched, no arrangement is made or contemplated that will diminish the number, quantity or proportion of the studies* or exercises heretofore established as a foundation for the learned professions."[49] Thus, while leaving the traditional liberal arts course untouched, the college would also receive students "who contemplate, not the professional but the active pursuits of life."[50] In this way, in the words of the president and trustees, they would increase the "*usefulness of the College*"[51] and maintain its central position in the community.

And within the communal order of the college, the board's policies evidence the personal, informal organization of the college, the underlying cohesiveness and consensual orientation within the college community, and the emphasis on the role of the president as a moral leader. At the same time Cogswell was brought into the faculty and an appeal was made to the community for funds, the trustees asked "the Faculty to present the College to its friends and the friends of good learning, for their sympathies and patronage." "These gentlemen," the trustees noted, "will make the proper explanation of the views of the Trustees."[52] In 1842, during a time of financial problems, the trustees "affectionately entreat[ed] the respective members of the Faculty to unite as a band of brothers, especially in this time of unprecedented pecuniary distress and divide the burden of such labors among them without expectation of further compensation."[53] While the trustees may have considered the faculty as employees, they evidence in these statements a more personal, informal organization of the institution. Unlike a generation later, there was less of a differentiation of duties and a corresponding lack of separation between personal and official roles and statuses.[54] Their appeal to the faculty seems to assume an underlying cohesion and consensual orientation on the part of the faculty as members of the communal order of the college. The conception of the moral authority of the president is highlighted in the case involving President Lord.

Both the actions of the trustees in 1863[55] in response to the resolutions of the Merrimack County Conference of Congregational Churches [56] and those of the president in reaction to the board's response to these resolutions illustrate the sensitivity of the board to the community and the perception of the role of the president on the part of the president, the board, and the community. The trustees did not express their disapproval to the president's views on slavery while it remained on an abstract level. They acted only when these views had immediate and direct effects upon the relation of the college to the community.[57] First the publication of Lord's proslavery views (which he held on religious grounds) caused heated discussion on the platform of orators and cler-gymen. These spokesmen implied that if the president of the college held such views the college was probably an unsafe place for youth.[58] Then in November 1862 his views were printed in a letter to the editor of the *Boston Courier* and reprinted by the antiwar Democrats of Con-necticut in 1863 and used as a campaign piece. These actions then caused the Merrimack Conference to pass resolutions indicating that in their opinion popular prejudice existed against Darmouth because of the pres-ident's views. They expressed the hope that the trustees would consider a change in the presidency.[59] At this point, these community-oriented trustees acted. Although they took no dramatic action, such as a trial as in 1881, nor did they directly ask for his resignation, they did make evident their displeasure at the president's views and their concern that his views might be hurting the college.[60]

Lord's position and response highlight his view of the president as a moral leader. According to Lord's view of himself as a moral leader, a public educator, his moral duty compelled him to speak out on all types of issues wherever it might lead him. This view of the presidency was in keeping with the traditional role of antebellum college presidents. College presidents were spokesmen for social concerns, both directly by trying to influence reform, and indirectly through their students by instruction in moral philosophy.[61] In this spirit, President Lord, in his letter of resignation, protested the right of the board "to impose any religious, ethical, or political test" and regarded the action of the board on the resolutions of the Merrimack Conference as such a test.[62] In keeping with his view of himself as a public educator, he stated that he would not surrender his "moral and constitutional right and Christian liberty, . . . nor . . . submit to any censure, nor consent to any conditions such as are implied in the aforesaid action of the Board."[63] Emphasizing his view of the president as a moral leader, he resigned, "believing it to be inconsistent with Christian charity and propriety to carry on my administration, while holding and expressing opinions injurious, as they [the trustees] imagine, to the interests of the College."[64]

Thus, although Lord, like Bartlett, was trying to insure the moral integrity of the college, he found a solution different from that of Bart-lett's. While the board did not ask directly for his resignation, Lord regarded their action as a vote of no confidence. With the mid-nine-teenth-century fusion of personal and official—the lack of differentiation between the man and his actions—he felt they were calling into question his character, his moral leadership, and imposing restrictions upon what he conceived to be his role and duty as a public educator.[65] Given this framework, he resigned.

If the trustees were a community-oriented group with a unity of purpose during the Lord administration, by 1881 the trustees were very sensitive to pressure from the alumni, notably the New York alumni—a collegiate faction outside this traditional orientation. What happened to the trustees in a generation that helps explain this shift? How are their positions and behavior related to altering communal ideas and notions of the presidency? And how does this illuminate the changed character of the college and conceptions of culture and higher learning?

The collected data regarding the trustees in 1881[66] point to a younger, more cosmopolitan group with interests, aspirations, and status groups being more and more defined out of the traditional context of community and with these tendencies being accentuated among those considered Bartlett's staunchest opponents. The 1881 trustees were younger than their 1851 counterparts. Eighty percent of the 1851 board were between fifty-five and sixty-nine, whereas 70% of the 1881 board were between forty-two and fifty-four (see appendix 27). Bartlett, at sixty-three, was considerably older than 70% of the board—seemingly of a different generation—whereas Lord had been of a similar age to the 1851 board, even slightly younger than 50% of the board. The four members who were considered Bartlett's most vigorous opponents and cast votes of no confidence in 1882 ranged in age from forty-two to fifty-three, thus comprising four of the seven younger members of the board. In addition, the treasurer of the college, forty-one in 1881, also was counted among Bartlett's opponents.

The data regarding occupations indicate a slight decline in ministers on the board since 1851, but as two of Bartlett's most vigorous opponents on the board were themselves ministers, one cannot conclude that the controversy was simply one of sectarianism versus secularism.[67] The ministry itself was changing along with other segments of American society. In a related context, Baptist clergy played important roles on both sides of a conflict between the board of trustees and the board of curators (both part of the governing body) of Bucknell University. The "conflict reflected a geographical and generational split rather than a reaction against denomination or clerical control."[68] The data indicate that of the Dartmouth board members as a whole, 30% were ministers, 40% lawyers, 10% businessmen, 10% physicians, and 10% educators (see appendix 28). The figures for the Dartmouth board as regards the category of ministers are similar to the figures for fifteen private colleges and universities in 1881 (Dartmouth included).[69] Those for business were somewhat higher at other institutions; those for law were somewhat lower than at Dartmouth (see appendix 29). If we compare the figures for the private institutions with the figures for board members in five middle western state universities, we find that ministers constituted a much smaller percentage of the board (as in 1861); bankers, businessmen, and lawyers combined constituted a somewhat higher percentage. The percentage of farmers had declined considerably from the 1861 period, and the percentage of educators and physicians rose (see appendix 30).

The information regarding residence reveals that Bartlett's most vigorous opponents had more metropolitan roots. In 1881 the charter requirement that only four members could be nonresidents of New Hampshire remained. Of the four listed as nonresidents, two were Massachusetts residents (one having moved there recently from New York City) and two were Vermont residents. One of those listed as a New Hampshire resident spent most of his time in New York City, where his business was located. Of the four members that formally cast votes of no confidence, three resided outside northern New England.[70] The fourth trustee included in this category came from the more industrial and urban area of Manchester, and the treasurer had resided in New York City and Washington, D.C.

Whereas the 1851 trustees were all community-oriented with their associational involvements, status groups, and aspirations rooted in the locale and region, the information regarding the 1881 board indicates a more cosmopolitan board with involvements and identification with peers in metropolitan areas. Among Bartlett's most outspoken opponents, these changing interests, status groups, and aspirations are the most striking.

If Arthur Sherburne Hardy represented the cosmopolite on the faculty, one could regard Hiram Hitchcock as his counterpart on the board. Both were leaders among those in the faculty and board working to oust the president.[71] Although Hitchcock's residence in 1880–81 was listed as Hanover, he seems to have spent much of his time in New York. A resident of Hanover at the time and an undergraduate during this period noted: "In the village our most distinguished guests during the summer were Mr. and Mrs. Hiram Hitchcock, of New York, who had developed a beautiful summer home."[72] Forty-eight in 1881 and proprietor of the fashionable Fifth Avenue Hotel of New York City, Hitchcock had interests in Madison Square Garden, the Metropolitan Museum of Art, and at one time served as president of the Nicaragua Canal Company. In 1878 he was elected as an alumni board member and was reported to have close ties to the New York alumni.[73]

William Jewett Tucker, Bartlett's successor, also represented the alumni on the board and evidenced ties to more metropolitan areas. Barely forty-two at the time of the trial, he was the youngest member of the board and a Bartlett opponent. He served as minister of the Presbyterian church in New York City from 1875 to 1880, where he was reported to be very popular with the rather prosperous congregation.[74] In 1880 he accepted a professorship at Andover Theological Seminary. In 1876 Dr. Edmund Peaslee of New York and Governor Cheney of New Hampshire, representing the board, asked Tucker if he would consider the presidency of Dartmouth, but he declined.[75] A popular figure with many of the Boston alumni, they brought up his name as a presidential possibility during the Bartlett controversy.[76] His associational involvements include membership in the American Antiquarian Society and the Colonial Sons of Massachusetts and election to the American Academy of Arts and Sciences. He was founder and editor of the *Andover Review* and founder of Andover House in Boston, a settlement house. His involvements evidence a more metropolitan orientation, a quest for ancestral roots common to many interest groups in the late nineteenth century, and an emphasis on the urban environment and social causation. These interests were translated during the Tucker administration with the emphasis on the discipline of sociology and the further development of the collegiate service of the institution relating to the social service mission of the largely upper-middle-class student body.[77]

The Reverend Alonzo Quint, another opponent of Bartlett, served as a member of the original alumni committee in 1869 that had asked for alumni representation in governance. He was elected to the board in 1875, just before the board granted the alumni the limited measure of alumni representation. Fifty-three years of age at the time of the trial, he resided in New Bedford, Massachusetts. The testimony of Quint at the Bartlett trial reveals both a metropolitan orientation regarding status and reputation similar to that voiced by some of the faculty and alumni and a conception of higher learning moving toward a more esoteric, specialized learning along disciplinary lines. Quint explained why he did not vote regarding the Hewitt appointment:

I had never heard of that gentleman before in my life, and thought a man who had graduated as long back as that, if he was an eminent Greek scholar, ought to have been heard of generally. . . . I said that the recommendations, which were very handsome in certain particulars did not satisfy my mind that he was fit for the chair as a Greek scholar specially. Although they did certify that he was a fine minister and a fine man and a good teacher.[78]

The emphasis here is on judgment by the community of peers and on Hewitt's metropolitan reputation rather than on his pastoral role in the college community and the hill country of New Hampshire.

Clinton Washington Stanley also cast a vote of no confidence regarding the Bartlett administration. Fifty years old at the time of the trial, he resided in Manchester, one of the more industrial and urban-oriented cities in New Hampshire. He had been judge of the Circuit Court of New Hampshire and, at the time of the trial, held the position of judge of the Supreme Court of New Hampshire.

Frederick Chase, another Bartlett opponent, served as treasurer of the college. Forty-one years of age in 1881, he had practiced law in Washington, D.C., and New York before accepting the position as treasurer of the college. During this period he also served as judge probate in New Hampshire.

Of the six other board members, some were considered to be supporters of Bartlett; others were considered to be independent, voting against Bartlett on certain issues of policy but stopping short of requesting his resignation.[79] Of these six, three were lawyers, one a minister, one a doctor, and one an eduator. Of the three lawyers not voting against Bartlett, one had served as judge of the Supreme Court of New Hampshire and as a member of the Constitutional Convention of New Hampshire in 1850. At eighty years of age in 1881, he was the oldest member of the board. Another lawyer held such positions as secretary of state of New Hampshire and governor of New Hampshire. He also served as vice president of the New Hampshire Historical Society, president of the Vermont Battle Monument Association, and fellow of the Royal Historical Society of Great Britain. An alumni trustee, he filled the New Hampshire vacancy in 1878. The other lawyer had served as a member of the state senate. A trustee of Norwich University, in 1889 he became interstate commerce commissioner. The doctor on the board had been mayor of Nashua, New Hampshire, in 1864. He had served as a member of the Constitutional Convention of New Hampshire in 1876 and of the Governor's Council in 1877–78.

The member listed as an educator also had clerical and business involvements in Vermont. Ordained as an evangelist, he entered the service of the Vermont Domestic Missionary Service. In 1859 he became professor of natural philosophy and then professor of natural history. His effectiveness in the department of natural philosophy had been a subject of much criticism,[80] and in 1865 he received a new appointment as professor of natural history.[81] He resigned from this position in 1868 and became a board member in 1870. His associational involvements included serving as chairman of the state committee of the Young Men's Christian Association, as corporate member of the American Board of Commissioners for Foreign Missions, as president of the Vermont Domestic Missionary Society, and as president of the board of trustees of St. Johnsbury Academy. He also held the position of secretary of a lucrative family business.

Thus, the collected data point to a shift in the 1881 board, especially accentuated in the case of Bartlett's most vigorous opponents, of a group of men younger and more cosmopolitan than their 1851 counterparts. Although some identification with the local community remains, their aspirations, status, and interests were being defined increasingly outside this context. And their policies evidence a growing concern with the college's metropolitan reputation rather than with its services to the locale and area.

One must go back to the preceding administration before one can assess the board's position in 1881—the nature of the interests involved, and the sensitivity of opponents, independents, and supporters of Bartlett to pressure from the alumni, especially groups such as the New York alumni. Between the mid-1860s and mid-1870s, during the administration of Asa Smith, the board began to embark upon policies with ramifications relating to whom the college would serve, its relation to the community, the organization of the college, and the role of the president. Interacting with these policies were certain changes occurring in nineteenth-century America that tended to intensify the direction of these policies. This background and the collected data regarding the 1881 board offer a framework within which to assess the trustees' sensitivity to pressure from the alumni, their position in holding the trial, and their concern with the college's metropolitan reputation. The lingering power of an older ideal, on the other hand, helps to explain why Bartlett ultimately retained his position as president despite all the controversy.

In contrast to the community orientation of the 1851 board and the integral relationship in the wider geographic and moral community, between the mid-1860s and the 1870s the board embarked upon policies to create a more insulated college environment—a special place apart from the community. In this process they were developing a different clientele for the college. By the time of the Bartlett trial, the student body was younger, more uniform in age, and from a higher socioeconomic background than their 1851 counterparts. These changes occurred at the same time as did changing occupational and residential patterns among college graduates, the lure of the cities for business opportunities, the changing sense of community and culture in nineteenth-century America, as well as different sources of support for the college.

These changes involved new expectations regarding the role of the alumni, especially those in metropolitan areas such as New York and Boston, involving their recommending to students the advantages of attending the institution and aiding in job opportunities after college. The quest for bigness and growth[82] in the post–Civil War period and the emphasis on these standards in the general culture, as well as the attempts of the board to create a new college environment, increased the demands for larger and larger endowments. The alumni—especially successful alumni in metropolitan areas—both directly and indirectly through their business and personal associations could be a source of these funds. Probably in recognition of the potential resources of this group, the trustees moved toward a form of governance in which the alumni, as alumni, obtained their representation on the board. Board policies regarding the faculty also tended to separate them from the community; the beginnings of a choice of a more professionalized, cosmopolitan group interacted with this policy. The faculty members began to see themselves in terms of their own status group of peers along disciplinary lines. While many institutions in the latter part of the nineteenth century chose a route not dissimilar to Dartmouth's, some institutions sought to reinforce older aims and missions and to sacrifice financial success and a metropolitan reputation.[83]

In the board's process of fashioning a different collegiate environment and a different type of institution, some of the board members may not have understood all the ramifications of this shift that came to the fore during the Bartlett controversy: namely, the development of the faculty and alumni as self-conscious collegiate factions demanding a share in the power structure, as well as the effects of a different type of student body upon the institution. The previous administration, that of Asa Dodge Smith (1863–77), provides a backdrop for these developments.

In a step-by-step process during the Smith administration, the board discouraged and restricted students' teaching in the district schools for three months during the winter. In 1867 they dropped the short term. A six-week vacation followed Thanksgiving, and students were required to make up all work missed. In 1871 the vacation time was changed to three weeks between the end of January and the beginning of February. In 1872 the board required the students to submit written statements indicating that they needed to teach for financial reasons. During the Lord administration (1828–63), perhaps 30% of the students were in attendance during the short term.[84] By the winter of 1874–75 the opposite situation existed. Excuses were granted to only seventy-three students, or between 21.3% and 27.5% of the students.[85]

The board also raised the tuition rate. The tuition rate went from $31.50 in 1851 to $90.00 plus a $6.00 library charge in 1876. The greater part of the increase occurred between 1867 and 1876, particularly between 1872 and 1876. The tuition rose from $51.00 to $60.00 in 1867, from $60.00 to $70.00 in 1872, and from $70.00 to $90.00 plus a $6.00 library charge in 1876.

At the same time, during the early part of the Smith administration the college increased the number of its scholarship funds. This would be especially important until such time as the college grew and the nature of the student body changed. The amount of the scholarships during the Smith administration was $70.00 each for 103 scholarships, plus numerous temporary grants of support for the year to worthy students from charitable persons.[86] The amount of the scholarship equalled what the students earned in the district schools. According to figures in the student publication, the *Aegis*, students teaching in the winter of 1860–61, after deducting expenses, made an average of $81.99 for 13.2 weeks of teaching.[87] Thus, they could keep the students on campus with scholarship funds and select those they thought worthy of them. In addition, the limited funds available during the Lord administration had been restricted to students from New Hampshire and for those studying for the ministry. The new scholarships, in addition to the older funds, enabled them to finance a wider group of students according to their own selection as these funds had no geographical or professional restriction.

It should be noted, however, that toward the mid-1870s the expenses of the students began to increase considerably and that the scholarships did not meet the tuition rates. Toward the mid-1870s, when students were indicating in their publications that many of those teaching did not have to do so for financial reasons, students were spending between $300 and $900 a year at Dartmouth, with $500 being average. Although this amount was not as high as the $700 or $800 needed at Columbia, Yale, and Harvard, the amount needed at Dartmouth to support students comfortably equalled the amount at the other well-established eastern colleges such as Williams and Amherst.[88]

Thus, in line with these policies to create a more insulated college environment, a student body quite different from its 1851 counterpart was developing. Students no longer came just from the surrounding areas of rural northern New England. They began to come from more metropolitan areas and from other parts of New England, especially Massachusetts, from the Middle Atlantic, and from the West.[89] They were a younger, more well off group. Their changing choice of occupations and the lure of the cities were bringing them more and more into metropolitan areas, especially New York City and Boston. The students also began to see themselves as a group apart—both from the local community and from the faculty and president.

The trustees also implemented policies that had the effect of moving the faculty away from their integral relationship to the community. During the Lord administration, the faculty had an integral relationship to the locale and the region; they held numerous leadership positions in the wider geographic community. For example, while Charles Brickett Haddock was a professor at Dartmouth, he also served as a member of the state legislature. By 1864 the board tried to discourage practices such as these. By a resolution in 1864, for example, the board informed the faculty members that a town office (these offices involved little time on the part of the faculty) was the only type of civil office they could hold outside of the college. The resolution stated that "hereafter the acceptance of any civil office by any member of the Faculty, except the office of Justice of the Peace or any Town office, shall operate *ipso facto* as a resignation of this position as a faculty member."[90]

Concurrently, probably in an attempt to attract and keep a more cosmopolitan, professionalized faculty who could bring distinction to the college, they raised the salaries of the faculty. The salary of full professors rose from $900 in 1851 to $1,300 in 1865. A year later it rose to $1,500, and in 1869 it was set at $2,000.[91] The increase in salaries occurred at the same time as an increase in the salary of the Harvard professors. While the salary was lower at Dartmouth—$2,000 for full professors as compared with $3,000 to $4,000 for full professors at Harvard [92]—the lower expenses in Hanover may have offset some of the differences. The Dartmouth salaries were not high, but they compared favorably with those in other colleges.[93] The increase in salaries seemed to be in line with the beginnings of a more cosmopolitan, professionalized faculty. Of the thirty-six faculty members in 1881, seventeen were hired between 1875 and 1881 and twelve between 1868 and 1874.

The trustees' attempt to keep Charles A. Young, Appleton Professor of Natural Philosphy and professor of astronomy, from going to Princeton reflects their movement toward a more professionalized faculty[94] consistent with Quint's statements at the trial. Young was gaining an international reputation in his field. One of his most important achievements occurred in 1870 when he discovered the "reversing layer." He championed this discovery against the doubts of some scientists until it was confirmed in 1896. He visited numerous countries during this period to make scientific observations and made several important discoveries.[95] The board made appropriations for astronomical and physical apparatus, and the observatory was wholly renewed and enlarged.[96] Princeton offered Young the chair of astronomy. He indicated to the Dartmouth board that he might stay if he received $5,000 for more equipment, if his duties were confined to astronomy, and if his astronomical chair were endowed. They immediately granted his request regarding his duties and they absorbed the cost of the equipment. The trustees were not able to raise the endowment at once, but they told Young that they would do their best to secure it and in the interim his salary would not be reduced. Despite their efforts, they were not successful in keeping Young. He resigned in 1877.

The board's policies worked in conjunction with the faculty's changing interests, status groups, and aspirations. They, too, saw themselves as apart from the locale and region, with aspirations, audience, and success being defined exclusively in terms of their peers.[97] Probably unanticipated by the trustees were the assertions of the faculty of a sense of autonomy and their emergence as a collegiate faction seeking to gain power in the institution.

A shift in the pattern of financial support for the college accompanied these changes in the board's policies. During the Lord administration, the trustees appealed to the community of northern New England for funds and viewed the Congregational clergy as agents in this effort. During the Smith administration, funds began to come in from other sources. Although the community contributed funds, the trustees began to have trouble raising funds from this source. For example, in an attempt to raise $25,000 within the state for a chair called the New Hampshire Professorship, they were able to raise only $7,000.[98] In contrast to this, Smith secured $28,620 from his friends in New York for the endowment of the presidential chair within a short period of time.[99] He also was successful in securing some scholarship funds from this source. The college catalogue of the Academical Department in 1877 reveals that 32.7% of the individuals giving funds were from New York, 29.4% from New York City.[100] Smith had been minister of the Brainerd Presbyterian Church (Fourteenth Street Presbyterian Church) in New York City for twenty-nine years before accepting the presidency of Dartmouth. Historians of the college note that the trustees probably hoped his acquaintance with men of wealth in his congregation and in New York City would help the college financially.[101]

During the Smith administration the college received a number of individual gifts and bequests from individuals living in New York and Massachusetts. For example, George H. Bissell, class of 1845, a New York City lawyer, gave $23,850 for the construction of a gymnasium. John D. Willard, class of 1819, judge of the Court of Common Pleas of New York, left $10,000 for the establishment of a chair of rhetoric and oratory (the fund to accumulate until it reached $30,000). General Sylvanius Thayer, class of 1807, from Braintree, Massachusetts, left $70,000 for the establishment of the Thayer School of Civil Engineering; E. W. Stoughton, a New York City lawyer, left $12,000 for the Medical School; and Tappan Wentworth, a lawyer in Lowell, Massachusetts, left his entire estate estimated at $276,972.29.[102]

While financial aid from sources within the community did not disappear, the college began to get increasing support from individuals in other areas, especially those in New York and Massachusetts. And the alumni began to link their promises of funding to their demands for representation in the governance of the college. To this effect, in 1869 the alumni appointed a committee "to have in charge the whole matter of raising the fund and coming to a suitable understanding with the

Board."[103] When their demands were not met, the alumni abandoned the fundraising project.

Despite the gifts to the college and the increased assets, the college still faced financial problems. At the end of the Smith administration the total assets free from debts had risen to $475,973,[104] and President Smith issued a booklet indicating that the gifts to the college in the thirteen years of his administration totaled $960,590.[105] The college, however, ran at a deficit every year. Many of the funds were not available immediately; some were for restricted purposes; and expenses increased in certain areas,[106] such as faculty salaries. The college had no external debts, but the debts to itself rose to $122,125.[107] In addition, with the death of the treasurer in 1876, the trustees found a discrepancy of $47,840.73 in the accounts. This adverse balance was offset somewhat by the $20,000 of interest credited but not collected and with the $20,000 they received from his heirs.[108]

In fashioning this new college community, in addition to the appropriation of funds for an increase in faculty salaries and the allocation of funds for scientific equipment, especially for the department of Professor Young, the trustees allocated funds for the improvement of the appearance of the college. (This process was accelerated under Bartlett and Tucker.) Between 1862 and 1872 they repurchased land that had been granted to the settlers in the early days of the college. The trustees purchased property surrounding the college for $3,000, $3,300, and $6,849 (site for a library).[109] They built three new buildings—Bissell Hall,[110] Culver Hall,[111] and Conant Hall[112]—and remolded the Chandler and Medical buildings. The trustees introduced steam heating and gas lighting as well as repairing the buildings. They instituted some janitorial service and put Reed Hall (which housed the library and various equipment) under the charge of one individual. The trustees also planted seedling trees to improve the appearance of the grounds.[113] Dartmouth was not alone in this attempt to reconstruct the physical plant. At Yale, for instance, in the 1880s and 1890s the old Brick Row was largely replaced by handsome neo-Gothic structures.[114]

The trustees, then, as early as the period of the Smith administration, were beginning to introduce changes leading to the ultimate transformation of the character of the college. That the trustees were sensitive to pressure from the alumni, especially alumni in the leading metropolitan area, does not seem surprising in light of the potential resources they possessed. And as the trustees' reaction to the proposal from the New York alumni in 1876 regarding alumni representation illustrates, they were sensitive to alumni pressure even before the Bartlett controversy. By 1881 this general sensitivity to the alumni combined with what was a more youthful, cosmopolitan, and metropolitan-oriented board.[115]

Scene of Dartmouth College, 1881. Courtesy of Dartmouth College Library.

The problematic position of a majority of the board in not forcing Bartlett's resignation or dismissal seems to be due to the lingering of an older collegiate ideal and communal sense—the mutual concern, the sense of obligation, the affective ties, the peculiar nature of presidential authority in the nineteenth century—that retained a pressure of power during this period of changing values and relationships. The unexpected favorable financial position of the college at the time of the trial reinforced the power of this older ideal. This seems to have left just enough doubt in people's minds to enable Bartlett to stay on as president.

Within this context one should note that while the college was receiving new sources of support, the older sources did not dry up completely. Although more and more students were coming from outside northern New England, a majority still came from this area. And while the college received gifts from sources other than the community, the older sources of financial aid did not disappear. Bartlett, through his career and educational and religious activities, had connections with the Congregational clergy of New Hampshire and other areas and with people in the northern New England region and the Middle West (from which a number of Dartmouth students were coming).[116] In addition, $170,000 came into the college during the first four years of Bartlett's administration.[117] While it is true that at least $100,000 of these gifts was unsolicited and that the college was in a favorable financial position owing to the good fortune that most of the funds were for immediate use and in large part unrestricted, for the first time in many years the college was operating at a yearly surplus instead of a deficit. The college seemed to be moving toward a sound footing in a very short period of time and with little effort on their part. The trustees emphasized these points in their report following the trial: "The present financial condition of the college is the most satisfactory it has known for a long series of years. For the first time in a sadly protracted period, the annual revenue of the college has this past year met its annual expenses."[118]

The positions of Bartlett and the board and the public trial in the college community are indicative of a change in the organization of the college and the role of the president. While Bartlett in staying on was also acting within his conception of the president as a moral leader (choosing the role of savior as opposed to Lord's role of martyr), he was sufficiently able to separate the man from the office that he could participate in a public trial of the college community and stay on without the full confidence of the trustees. Although Bartlett's statements reveal a concern with what he perceived to be the questioning of his character,[119] he was living in a period different from that of Lord's with a transformation in American society of the notion of the organic community and its relationships.

The trustees began to emphasize important aspects of what would be the presidential role in modern guise within a more formal organization, differentiating personal and official roles and duties. They began to stress the president's ability to reconcile the various groups in the collegiate community and enhance the college's metropolitan reputation. In this context, the trustees noted with concern the inharmonious relations of the faculty with Bartlett, "in their official intercourse," despite the faculty's acknowledgement of the fine qualities of the man.[120] The emphasis in their report of placing the promising financial condition of the institution on the top of the list under the category, "Satisfactory Condition of the College," is indicative of an increasing emphasis on the president in his administrative capacity.[121] And the board's action in holding the trial on charges, not questioning "his high and long-established personal reputation, but his theories, methods, and the present conduct in the administration of the college," stresses the separation between personal and official roles and statuses.[122] The report, then, seems to emphasize a shift from a cohesive, closely knit communal order with expectations of a consenual orientation to one of collegiate factions that need to be reconciled and managed.

The Bartlett controversy received much press coverage,[123] especially from the metropolitan press of New York City and Boston. The newspapers not only chronicled the trial proceedings but presented arguments for and against Bartlett. These arguments and reports centered on the effect of the Bartlett presidency upon sources of support for the college, upon the college's growth and status, and upon conceptions of higher learning. They also reveal conceptions of culture in American society. In this process, the newspaper controversy sheds light on the pressures exerted upon the board and the interests involved.

The articles reveal the reach of the leading metropolitan areas into the college and the dominance of business values and growth in the late-nineteenth-century culture. The emphasis in many of the articles on the potential effect of the continuance of the Bartlett presidency upon alumni support in leading urban centers, especially New York City and Boston, highlights these developments. The *Boston Evening Transcript*, in an article critical of Bartlett, called attention to a resolution for Bartlett's resignation at a meeting of the New York association advanced by "a graduate of the college to whom its treasury is indebted for thousands of dollars."[124] Emphasizing the position of the alumni in Boston as well, the article noted: "If there is a single prominent graduate of the college in this vicinity who does not really believe that Dr. Bartlett would promote . . . [the] welfare, . . . of the college, by seeking another field of labor, we have not heard of him."[125] The *New York Tribune*, describing a meeting with the New York alumni, reported the following remark by an alumnus: "I know . . . of several men of millions who stand ready to give largely of their means to the support of the institution as soon as it shall secure a proper head."[126] The *Boston Post* warned that the college could not "afford to alienate any considerable body of her alumni and friends, from whom aid must come to replenish her treasury and keep up her numbers."[127] The *New York Times* emphasized the point that "the Alumni and wealthy friends of Dartmouth do not seem to be pressing eagerly forward with testamentary or other donations to complete the foundation for the Webster Professorship or swell the general fund."[128] And the *Springfield Republican* indicated that "with the advent of another president at Hanover, the alumni of New York would be under special obligations to rally to the support of their alma mater."[129]

On the other hand, a few of the publications representing the more rural areas noted the long history of the reciprocal relationship between the college and northern New England and their support of Bartlett.

The *Vermont Chronicle* commented:

> In Vermont and New Hampshire the influence upon the college of President Bartlett's scholarship and vigorous administration is recognized, and the Alumni and patrons generally support him. Upon these States the College must chiefly depend for the men who are more than money to build it up. Their support is more important, therefore, than that of New York, though the College needs all that all its friends everywhere can do to build it up.[130]

A Vermont newspaper, the *West Randolph Herald and News,* noted the importance of Dartmouth to Vermont. It praised Bartlett and stated: "Let Dartmouth keep the peace, do its best work, and it will receive most of the support and patronage we have to give to any college."[131] A report of the meeting of the General Association of the Congregational Churches (New Hampshire) noted the passage of a resolution regarding Bartlett and the college: "Resolved, That this Association has heard with great interest and pleasure the report of the President of Dartmouth College in respect to the moral and religious condition of its students."[132] And the *Congregationalist* cautioned:

> We venture to suggest as a lesson from this affair—and the remark is as true of Harvard, or Yale, as of Dartmouth—that while the cooperation of alumni is indispensable, the public interference of a body of alumni in some one city in the government of a college, while they are necessarily ignorant of the details of its affairs, may work an evil which it will take long and sad years to overcome.[133]

The articles emphasized the dominance of business values, of growth and numbers, for example, in the general culture and its application in judging the success of a college. Reflective of these points, a Boston paper commented:

> The size of the freshman class of any college is a fair gauge of the college's popularity at any time. The freshman classes at the different colleges the present year are 250 at Harvard (the largest class ever entered at this institution), ninety-seven at Amherst, eighty-five at Williams, 255 at Yale, seventy at Brown, thirty-three at Tufts, forty-five academics and eighteen scientifics at Dartmouth, and a first class of eighty-six at Smith's college. Seven of the forty-five academics are special course men, leaving but thirty-eight to pursue the regular and complete classical course. This is the smallest class

that has entered Dartmouth in twenty years with one exception, which exception was due to the demand of the war upon our young men. The number is but little if any more than half the average freshman classes four or five years ago. We notice President Bartlett is registered at Young's, and there are a number of Dartmouth men in Boston, who would be glad to have him appoint a time and place where they might assemble and hear his explanation of the reason why these things are so.[134]

The *New York Times* stated: "Instead of maintaining her place as third among New-England colleges, Dartmouth seems to be going down in the scale to the fifth or sixth in rank."[135] Another paper, noting some of the problems the college was having and revealing a metropolitan orientation, remarked that Bartlett seemed to be lacking in "that urbanity which is one of the chief requisites of a college president."[136]

Some articles, although much fewer in number, commented upon the course of study at Dartmouth. They expressed positions ranging from support for the traditional classical curriculum, praise for the newer courses, and support for the movement toward a more esoteric learning while upholding the importance of a broad general liberal arts education on the undergraduate level. In support of the classical education, the *West Randolph Herald and News* noted:

President Bartlett won distinction as a scholar, preacher and teacher before he came to Dartmouth, and if his views are out of tune with those of some modern agitators and would be reformers, we are inclined to think that he stands upon a sound basis and that time will prove this to be so. We have no sympathy with those who are making such vigorous assaults upon classical learning. . . . We believe that this modern science craze will have its day and pass by. . . . Dartmouth College proper is an institution that has given prominence to classical training. By means thereof it has fitted men for high and useful stations in life. We have no hesitation in saying that we believe that these men have been better fitted for their work than they would have been by sending them through the intricate and wild regions of modern scientific speculations. We hope that this college will preserve its character as a classical institution.[137]

In defense of the type of learning offered by the Chandler Scientific Department, a letter to the editor of the *Traveller* noted, "It sends out young men who take high positions in our own and foreign countries, who command high salaries from their marked ability."[138] Although the

Boston Transcript called Bartlett "a Conservative, a very Bourbon and Tory of college presidents,"[139] the paper seemed to support a more traditional liberal arts curriculum on the undergraduate level:

> There will be some who, while fully in sympathy with modern scientific thought and research, will hope to see an old-fashioned scholar here and there among the colleges holding stiffly out for the old-fashioned literary Latin-and-Greek college, conservator of the old-school lore, lumbering and impractical as it may seem to be, but the source of all the literary graces and honors of New England thus far.[140]

The articles illustrate, then, both some of the trustees' concerns that led to their sensitivity to alumni pressure and some of Bartlett's sources of strength. They also indicate the pervasiveness of late-nineteenth-century business standards in the general culture—numbers, growth, rank—as well as an emphasis on the power and influence of leading metropolitan areas and a reaction to this ascendancy.

Thus, the trustees were undergoing change, and they were turning Dartmouth into a college quite different from its 1851 counterpart. In general, the trustees were a younger and more cosmopolitan group with interests, aspirations, and status groups moving them away from the local community and linking them to peers in metropolitan areas. This movement was accentuated in Bartlett's opponents. The trustees' policies were transforming Dartmouth into an institution serving a different clientele—an upper-middle-class one. The college had a different relation to the community—a special place apart, and a different faculty, more cosmopolitan and professionalized. The trustees increasingly stressed the importance of the president in his executive capacity within a more formal organization separating personal and official roles and statuses.

While all the members of the 1881 board were sensitive to pressure from alumni because of their potential for sources of support, including students, jobs, and money, they did not want to completely reject the older values, so they left Bartlett in place.[141] But when it came to choosing Bartlett's successor, the board chose a minister who excelled in the mediator's role and who would attend to the wider world and the harsh realities of money.

CHAPTER VI

Conclusion

It is not too much to say that the necessity for the modernizing of the colleges virtually created the science of college administration, which in its inner working is the science of coordination and adjustment, and in its outer relations the scientific application of economic principles to the material necessities of the colleges.

—William Jewett Tucker (1919)

You are to be men in posit[i]on. You are to have the tremendous advantage of place as well as of personal training. You are to be lawyers, journalists, teachers, ministers, scientists, soldiers, men of affairs. You are to be, that is, recognized men. Make yourselves, I pray you, more and more worthy of your advantage by becoming more and more worthy of yourselves, true to the law of your being. Be right-minded men, true hearted men, men of determined faith.

—William Jewett Tucker (1898)

In 1893 at his inauguration, William Jewett Tucker told his audience, "Within the past year the phrase has become current amongst us,—the new Dartmouth. I interpret the phrase to express our decision and our enthusiasm in the work to which we are called in the readjustment and development of Dartmouth."[1] Tucker's administration has been portrayed as "a major turning point"[2] in the history of the college in which Dartmouth "broke loose from the restraining bonds of a nineteenth-century conservatism and took its place in the progressive world of the twentieth century."[3]

That the Dartmouth under Tucker in the late nineteenth and early twentieth centuries was quite different from the Dartmouth in the antebellum period under Lord, or even in degree, from that of Smith in the post–Civil War period, or Bartlett in the latter part of the century no one can deny. But that the nature of the change was one of conservatism versus liberalism, sectarianism versus secularism, or darkness versus light is not only a simplistic characterization from an ahistorical perspective but has the effect of masking the most important change, a historical change evolving before the advent of the Tucker administration. That change was rooted in the very conception of the college itself.[4] By 1881 Dartmouth had already evolved into an institution quite different from its 1851 counterpart. The Bartlett controversy highlighted all the significant aspects of that transformation. It dramatized the changing nature of the academic community and collegiate culture and forecast the shift in presidential power.

Within this context, the Bartlett trial itself seemed to be a forum for articulating and debating values. To this point, counsel for the prosecution remarked, "Every person connected with the investigation is on trial, on trial before the great public."[5] Although all sides disclaimed responsibility for making it a public trial, all parties were only too willing to participate in it. From the perspective of the alumni's actions, for example, their insistence on a direct, statutory voice in governance; their initiation of the investigation; their insistence on stenographic proceedings; and their display of legal talent[6] were all indicative of the use of legal forms for articulating values and for determining the direction of the college and their role in it. The use of the trial as such a forum was not unique to Dartmouth. The Bartlett trial was the first of several trials in educational institutions during the 1880s. Union and Hamilton College also experienced such trials,[7] as did Andover Theological Seminary, in which Tucker found himself a defendant in the trial.[8] These trials seemed to be particular manifestations of a general trend toward a "more self-conscious resort to law as the expression of values."[9]

Now that the role of each participant group in the Bartlett controversy has been traced, one must ask: Which collegiate faction ultimately won out? Or, which conception of community gained ascendancy and to whose advantage did it work? How did the new type of president now needed to administer the college, reflective of the altering notion of community, symbolize the changing character of the college and of the larger society as well? And with what conception of collegiate service did Dartmouth enter the twentieth century?

By 1881, as the preceding chapters reveal, the notion of community underwent marked change. The more centripetal notion of a closely knit communal order playing an integral role within the concentric ranges of the wider geographic and moral community began to erode. While the college did not completely abandon its services to the local community, the 1881 Dartmouth emerged as a special place apart with a more detached, introverted, impersonal collegiate sense. In contrast to the organic ideal of the 1851 period, the groups within the later college community evidenced a less affective, more fragmented, and more competitive vision of community, and a radical redefinition of the parameters of the larger community. For these various groups, community became, in essence, the separate select fellowship of associated peers, oriented to metropolitan systems of status, and associationally insulated from others not possessing the badge of common identity. This communal idea had significant centrifugal effects. The sense of group consciousness of these various groups, their metropolitan orientation, and open pursuit of interests were manifested in the Bartlett controversy with their emergence as collegiate factions. They sought to insure their interests (now extending beyond the college and locality) and influence the direction of the college by achieving power within the institution. And in contrast to a more personal, familial organization of 1851, with a unity of purpose and the accentuation of an underlying consensual orientation, the college community now provided for formal mechanisms for dealing with some intellectual diversity and professional competition.

This movement toward a more centrifugal notion of community, revealed in the Bartlett controversy, occurred in the larger society as well. Profound political, economic, and social changes were altering the very structure of American society and disrupting the older locality-based, organic communal patterns. Interest in, and concern for, questions of authority and patterns and styles of organization assumed great prominence. Late-nineteenth-century America emerged as a society that evidenced a great concentration of interest groups. These organizations ranged from the American Federation of Labor to the National Association of Manufacturers, from the Sons of the Revolution to the Scotch-Irish Society, from the American Philological Association and the American Association for the Advancement of Science, to the proliferation of metropolitan social clubs catering to an upper and middle class, to the publication of the *Social Register* in 1887. While the older communal ways did completely disappear, in important aspects of their lives people seemed to be identifying themselves on the basis of interests, skills, or class and looked for status and influence through these associations.[10]

Within the institutional setting of Dartmouth, the altered idea of community tended to favor these groups that could exert the most power and influence (real or potential) in determining the resources of the institution, financially or otherwise, and thus fulfill the "perceived" needs and interests of the institution. Beyond the conflict of the interest groups in the Bartlett controversy, the "new Dartmouth" was emerging, not as an institution that was an integral part of the organic community, but as a special place apart. While not offending democratic sensibilities, the institution was patterned after the ideals of its most significant constituency—a metropolitan-oriented, aspiring upper middle class. This constituency had a significant impact on the character of the college and its collegiate service. The direction of the college created its metropolitan reputation and its "place" as a leading Ivy League college and produced a sense of exclusiveness striking in contrast to the Dartmouth of 1851.

Within the context of the Bartlett controversy and its emergence into the "new Dartmouth," the faculty members were able to realize some of their demands and in the process demonstrate the power behind the movement toward their professionalization. In the report of the trustees regarding the charges in the memorial from the New York Association of Alumni, the trustees noted that they found "the most serious difficulty in the relations of the President and the Faculty,"[11] and they appointed a committee to go to Hanover to restore harmony. The sixteen members of the faculty who had signed the petition requesting Bartlett's resignation submitted their resignations to this committee. The trustees refused to accept their resignations, and when an article appeared in the Boston Advertiser indicating that the trustees were crushing the rebels in the faculty,[12] the trustees wrote a letter to the editor of the paper stating that, from their point of view, the faculty members concerned were not the rebels. Moreover, they stressed that they regarded "the professors of the college as gentlemen of the highest culture and character and unsurpassed as instructors."[13] While four out of ten members of the board officially registered no confidence in Bartlett, the board unanimously voted for a resolution expressing their confidence in the faculty.[14] In 1890, in response to petitions received from the faculty, the board raised their salaries to $2,200.[15] And in new appointments, especially during the Tucker administration, the faculty realized to a considerable extent their demands for a more professional faculty. While the emphasis on teaching and undergraduate education remained, many faculty members were hired with specialized training along disciplinary lines (some with reputations for original research). There was a more complete reorganization into departments, and the faculty were a more cosmopolitan group.[16]

Although the faculty did not realize all its demands for autonomy under Bartlett or Tucker, the faculty did gain some recognition with exposure of the issue. The trial testimony revealed the possible influence of the faculty's opinion on the board's decision regarding new appointments. The trustees evidently had asked Bartlett if the faculty approved of the Reverend Hewitt's appointment. When counsel for the prosecution asked one of the trustees what he would have done had he known that the faculty did not approve of Hewitt's appointment, although his answer was somewhat evasive, he indicated that it might have influenced his vote.[17] The trustee, Dr. Edward Spaulding, stated: "I cannot say what effect it might have had. I should have had a different feeling about it."[18] And the board's decision, in the only incident in which Tucker would be confronted with open faculty opposition, also evidences some recognition of peer evaluation. The trustees indicated that their general policy was not to consult with department heads in reference to promotions but that they would do so in reference to new appointments—and the recommendations would receive great weight (although they were not absolutely binding).[19]

The faculty members opposing Bartlett did not receive all they had desired, but that they were able to gain a limited measure of influence seems to be due to the coalescence of a number of factors. The concentrated group effort of sixteen out of twenty-three (treasurer included) permanent members of the faculty had a commanding effect in an institution of the size of Dartmouth, especially in light of the fact that the alumni, notably the New York group, and much of the press (probably through alumni influence) supported them. In addition, that such a faculty member as Arthur Sherburne Hardy would not be dismissed despite Bartlett's protests does not seem unusual, given Hardy's alliances with Hiram Hitchcock of the board, who had substantial connections in New York and alliances with the New York alumni. And Hardy himself, with his professional reputation and cosmopolitan background, was "likely," in the words of the metropolitan press, "to bring great distinction to the college."[20] This would be of special importance to a college trying to build up its metropolitan reputation.

The developments regarding the faculty at Dartmouth were not atypical, although there were important differences among institutions. As at Dartmouth, faculty members in many other colleges and universities identified with disciplinary peers in other institutions, viewed themselves as a distinct group within the college, and asserted claims for peer evaluation and some sense of faculty autonomy (with an increasing separation between themselves and the president).[21] During the late nineteenth and early twentieth centuries, at a number of other colleges adopting alternate collegiate routes (as well as at institutions such as Harvard), specialized graduate training along disciplinary lines became an important qualification for appointment to a position and for advancement.[22] At some colleges, at least, the movement to hire faculty with such training and in some cases with established academic reputations coincided with the institution's concern for growth and enhancing the college's metropolitan reputation.[23] During this period there also was a greater emphasis on departmental organization; and faculty at several other colleges and universities came into conflict with presidents over such issues as faculty autonomy. They met with varying degrees of success, and the type of influence faculty members received during this period usually related to their professional work (as opposed to overall policy) or to influence over appointments or course of study, for example. At Harvard, for instance, President Eliot retained a veto over appointments, but he increasingly depended upon the opinion of disciplinary specialists in the various departments.[24] At Amherst, when the president changed faculty assignments and placed a French professor in the history department without faculty consultation, the history professor resigned and the alumni flooded the board with petitions supporting the professor and attacking the president. Under this pressure, the board moved to guarantee to the head of the department (the professor in question) control over instruction in the history department. The trustees also guaranteed the other departments autonomy in course assignments and in teaching policies.[25] At Princeton faculty representatives seem to have met with the board on some regular basis.[26]

Highlighting the rise of alumni power, the alumni ultimately not only obtained the measure of influence in the governance of the institution that they had demanded but were brought into an even closer relationship to the college. Moving from the first step in 1876 to their assertions in the Bartlett controversy and the trustees' responsiveness to them, the alumni continued to press for their demands. Toward the end of the Bartlett administration, in 1891, the alumni obtained the recognition of their right to representation as alumni on the board of trustees. Excluding the president and the governor of New Hampshire, the alumni had gained one half of the seats on the board.[27] During the same period, at the suggestion of the Boston alumni, the executive committee of the Association of Alumni of Dartmouth College proposed to the board a plan whereby the alumni association would raise funds for the gymnasium and athletic apparatus, and also promote interest in athletics in the college, if they were given control of the management of athletics. In 1892 the board agreed to these demands, and the alumni partialy remodeled the gymnasium and built an Alumni Oval, with an athletic field, a track field, baseball and football fields, and a grandstand. Three alumni, three faculty members approved by the alumni, and three undergraduates (captains of the teams) formed the Athletic Council that managed athletics.[28] And Tucker, recognizing the importance of the alumni to the college, spent part of each year visiting the alumni associations; he visited the New York and Boston groups at least once each year.[29] From ten local alumni associations at his accession, eight more were added, and to the one Dartmouth Club, three more were added.[30] Tucker encouraged the formation of an association of class secretaries in 1905 and an alumni publication, the *Dartmouth Bi-Monthly* (called the *Dartmouth Alumni Magazine* since 1908).[31]

In the reconciliation of the increasingly powerful collegiate factions, the alumni's ultimate success does not seem surprising, given their potential power and influence over the resources of the institution. They could supply the students through recommendation, and screen students both in or out, thereby aiding in getting the type of student appropriate for Dartmouth.[32] They could help new graduates obtain jobs after college through recommendations and through access to social clubs and professional organizations. They could supply financial resources for the institution either directly through individual gifts or indirectly through their business and social contacts. To this point, Tucker remarked, "The financial asset of the historic college lies in the indebtedness of its alumni, greatly enhanced by the new sense of responsibility. Alumni government means alumni support. Representation calls for taxation as logically as taxation for representation."[33]

Financial support of Dartmouth by the alumni became especially evident after the turn of the century. When a fire destroyed Dartmouth Hall in 1904, the alumni contributed $250,000 for rebuilding it and erecting another hall. They also instituted a Tucker Alumni Scholarship and Instruction Fund,[34] and a number of alumni made individual donations to the college. Edward Tuck, class of 1862, of Paris, donated the largest gift the college ever received in the nineteenth century. He gave the college securities with a face value of $300,000 (actually valued at $500,000) for the establishment of new professorships in the college proper, or postgraduate, for the library, and for salaries for the president and faculty. Recognizing the importance of the field of business for graduates, Tucker approached Tuck regarding the use of part of the funds for the establishment of a school of business; Tuck agreed to this, and the Amos Tuck School of Administration and Finance was established. In 1901 Tuck gave $125,000 more for a building for the newly organized school.[35]

As chapter 4 revealed, Dartmouth was not alone in the demands of alumni for a voice in the governance of the institution. Several colleges and universities granted alumni representation on their governing boards during the last third of the nineteenth century and the early part of the twentieth century. While not all alumni groups were as successful as the Dartmouth group, trustees and college and university presidents recognized their potential for support of the institution.[36] At Princeton, for instance, after much struggle, in 1900 the trustees granted the alumni their seats on the board.[37] The language the Princeton alumni used in support of their case for alumni group representation—"taxation without representation"[38]—was the same sort of sentiment expressed by the Dartmouth alumni in their quest for a greater voice in the governance of the institution. And, as we saw, President Tucker turned the phrase around to encourage alumni support—"Representation calls for taxation as logically as taxation for representation"[39]—an idea several of his counterparts also advanced.

Presidents in numerous institutions courted the alumni, visited their associations (particularly in leading metropolitan areas), encouraged the further growth of associations and clubs, and in many cases supported alumni demands for representation. In the process of advancing a program for growth and developing the college's metropolitan reputation, President John Harris of Bucknell, for example, supported alumni demands for representation on the board and helped to turn the board into a group dominated by well-off alumni and outside businessmen.[40] In some cases, at least, where alumni were not given any voice in governance alumni associations tended to languish, and the institution sacrificed growth and expansion for older ties and aims.[41] At most institutions alumni also became intimately involved in the development, management, and support of athletics, and athletics frequently became a "rallying point" and recruitment tool.[42] Among women college graduates this period also saw the development of the American Association of Collegiate Alumnae (American Association of University Women).[43]

In keeping with the new role of the Dartmouth alumni, the changing character of the college, and the position of the college as a special place apart, the shift toward a more cosmopolitan, upper-middle-class student body continued to accelerate. A story related by a member of the class of 1893 points to this shift. The student reported that one of his classmates, who would become a football hero, was the son of a poor farmer; he waited on tables at the dining club to pay for his board, had a scholarship for tuition, and did odd jobs to earn extra money. "All this," said the student relating the story, "had no effect upon his relations with his classmates. Thank Heaven, there was never a bit of snobbery at Dartmouth."[44] The histories of the college also indicate an increase of students of wealth and a student body more widely distributed geographically.[45] Consistent with the developments evidenced in the Smith and Bartlett administrations, by the end of the Tucker administration (1908–9), students came from thirty-four different states, and only 27.1% of the students came from northern New England.[46] By 1900, indicative of the trend highlighted in the class of 1881, 39% of the students came from business backgrounds, and those from farming backgrounds declined to 13.5%.[47] The increase in expenses also evidences the changing nature of the student body. From the great rise in the mid-1870s, expenditures accelerated during the Tucker administration so that some students spent as much as $2,500 a year. According to one study, students spent an average of $700 a year as freshmen, $900 as sophomores, and $1,000 each as juniors and seniors.[48] The college fees rose to $125, and the college now linked scholarships to scholastic rank.[49]

In contrast to the students of 1851 and in keeping with the trend evidenced in the class of 1881, the closer the students approached the Dink Stover types, the more they were interested in "college life, not college work."[50] To these students, fraternities and athletics were important indicators of success. In addition to the fraternities and senior societies of the Bartlett period, the students instituted new fraternities, and all the fraternities began to acquire chapter houses.[51] Indicative of the sense of exclusiveness of the idea of community and a growing stratification among the students, an increasing number of students lacked fraternity affiliations,[52] and membership conferred status upon its members, providing a symbol of common identity and the kind of "crowd" one would "want to know all through life."[53] The divisions, however, did not appear to be as sharp as those at the more heterogeneous Harvard, or the competition quite as fierce as that evidenced in the Tap Day exercises at Yale.[54] Perhaps in an attempt to recapture at least some sense of community, the Dartmouth board passed a resolution prohibiting dining facilities in fraternity houses and limiting the number of students who could room together to fourteen.[55]

Organized athletics and intercollegiate competition increased, and leadership in athletics also influenced one's position in the campus status system. Athletics centered on football, baseball, and track; and in the view of one graduate, "The captain of the football team stood at the apex of the social system, and the less you resembled a football captain, the lower your social status was."[56] Another student noted in response to a game with Amherst, "Yell, Dartmouth, Yell! Be madmen if you will. Forget that you are young or old, rich, or poor, wise or foolish. Remember only that we have gloriously won a pennant."[57] They competed with Williams and Amherst and then with Brown, Harvard, and Princeton. The students also began to play basketball, hockey, and tennis on an intercollegiate basis. The Athletic Council hired a professional coach, a physical culture director, and a graduate manager.[58] And involvement in athletics gave the alumni an added opportunity to associate with the students and in this way to serve as surrogate parents and role models for them.

The pattern of the Dartmouth students is in keeping with developments in numerous other colleges and universities. Along this vein, Henry Seidel Canby, writing about his student days at Yale in the 1890s, noted, "College life was at least 90% of our felt experience, and therefore 90% of the college as we knew it."[59] And President Wilson of Princeton

remarked, "The side shows are so numerous, so diverting—so important if you will—that they have swallowed up the circus."[60] At some
of these institutions wealthy alumni helped to finance fraternity chapter
houses; alumni also helped to pay the bills of the exclusive eating clubs.[61]
At some of the eastern institutions such as Harvard, Yale, and Princeton,
the "caste system" reached back into the prep school, affecting students'
chances for admission to the right club, or fraternity.[62] At other institutions such as Amherst most of the students had fraternity affiliations,
and the distinctions were not as great.[63] At some of the western state
universities student life, judged by the standards of the exclusive eastern
institutions, developed at a somewhat slower pace.[64] By the 1880s, however, the University of Wisconsin had thirteen fraternities, and by 1894
ten of these fraternities had chapter houses.[65] Athletics, particularly
intercollegiate football, became a consuming interest at numerous colleges and universities. Expressive of this development, the students of
Yale shouted: "We toil not, neither do we agitate, but we play football."[66] And historians of the University of Wisconsin noted that the
development of intercollegiate athletics was the "most striking change"
in student life during the 1880s and 1890s.[67]

From the information available, out of college the class of 1881 replicated the pattern of collegiate associational involvements, and these
affiliations became important marks of success. Their club affiliations
ranged from elite clubs such as the University and Chevy Chase, to
professional and social organizations such as the American Bar Association and the Odd Fellows. More and more students came from business backgrounds and entered fields related to business and corporate
law. In the 1900–1905 period, for example, 52% of the Dartmouth graduates went into business and industrial pursuits.[68] They were attracted
to the metropolitan areas, especially New York and Boston;[69] in these
areas in order to get into the powerful firms and banks, the college one
attended and the fraternity and club to which one belonged could prove
a decisive factor in selection for a position.[70] The status referent here
is associational, this is one reason, no doubt, why the New York alumni
and similar alumni groups in leading urban centers were so concerned
with the status of the school. College graduates were competing with
one another in these metropolitan areas; and, with the altered communal
idea these associational involvements, rather than reputation in the local
community, began to confer status. In these metropolitan areas the
difference between the older communal ways and the newer pattern of
social relationships must have been the most severe. The "right" college,
fraternity, and club could provide the associations, subculture, values,
and skills needed for success.[71] With the growth of fraternities in all
types of institutions, this pattern of exclusiveness and stratification,

although on different levels, would seem to be replicated in other colleges and universities.

Thus, the emergence of the "new Dartmouth" evidenced in the Bartlett controversy continued in the aftermath of the trial and in the administration of Bartlett's successor; Tucker represented the new type of president now needed to administer and shape the college. In contrast to the Dartmouth of 1851, the college was now a special place apart, with a student body younger, more uniform in age, more cosmopolitan, from a higher socioeconomic background, and with a metropolitan orientation. The faculty was composed of a more professionalized and cosmopolitan group, within a formal organization more clearly defining its component roles. And the alumni were a metropolitan-oriented, aspiring, upper-middle-class group with a more intimate involvement in the direction of the institution. An assessment of Tucker's administration in relation to the conception of collegiate service, higher learning, and the administration of higher education illuminates not only the culmination of the historical shifts highlighted in the Bartlett controversy but also what the "new Dartmouth" represented and the changing nature of the larger society as well. It also illustrates how an institution choosing to remain a college—with its emphasis on undergraduate education, its homogeneous nature, the importance of teaching, and its religious character[72]—tried to maintain some sense of unity within an increasingly metropolitan-oriented college community divided into collegiate factions.

In Tucker's addresses to students, he emphasized their place in society as a privileged group that would provide leadership and fulfill a purposeful social service. Thus, he told the seniors in 1898:

You are to be men in posit[i]on. You are to have the tremendous advantage of place as well as of personal training. You are to be lawyers, journalists, teachers, ministers, scientists, soldiers, men of affairs. You are to be, that is, recognized men. Make yourselves, I pray you, more and more worthy of your advantage by becoming more and more worthy of yourselves, true to the law of your being. Be right-minded men, true hearted men, men of determined faith.[73]

In regard to this point, Tucker stressed the importance of Dartmouth as a college, not as a university. He noted that the professional schools that had been added to the college "are not in the direction of a University but to satisfy the College aim and method." "If our Colleges," he said, "are to remain as they have been in the past training schools for intellectual character and for effective public service, they must be allowed to carry their work to its natural conclusion."[74] Tucker emphasized the importance of undergraduate education, the broad liberal arts education, and the primacy of the teaching function in the process.[75]

But the type of collegiate service was quite different from its 1851 counterpart. In 1851, through uplifting the individual's character, a Christian kingdom would be achieved. In keeping with the notion of community, the college "served" the poor and lower-middle-class students from the rural towns of northern New England. The college provided access to middle-class status and to the professions, and in return it hoped that the students would live the life of the good Christian man in the organic community and thus help to fulfill the mission of creating a Zion. As with the idea of community and collegiate service, the individual was not set apart; he was an integral part of the organic community in which he lived.

In contrast to the emphasis on somehow uplifting the individual's character, character now became linked to demonstrable actions in insuring the quality of life through large-scale formal organizations. Evidencing this perspective and pointing toward his strategy of Christian reform through service, Tucker stated that men could not be defined apart from the institutions to which they belonged—the "corporations, . . . unions, . . . the complicated machinery, industrial, political and religious."[76] In many of his addresses and in his chapel talks to students, Tucker evidenced his emphasis on social causation, on the importance of what he called the "moral and spiritual outcome of the cities of Christendom,"[77] and on the linking of character to demonstrable actions in working in these institutions of society. In his address on the "Mind of the Wage Earner," for example, he noted that "a narrow and exclusive solidarity of wage earners" could be prevented by the acquisition of property and through access to higher education.[78]

With the emergence of the "new Dartmouth" as a special place apart, the stress centered on these students as a privileged group whose mission would be to guide society, conserve its values, and in this way provide meaningful social service. Similar to Tucker's comments to the seniors regarding their special place in society, Woodrow Wilson, in his inaugural address as president of Princeton, said that society would be directed by a special group of leaders who would "plan," "conceive," "superintend," and "mediate between group and group and . . . see the stage as a whole."[79] Students could provide a meaningful social service by conserving society's values and by introducing such changes for social improvement as, for example, Andover House, a social settlement house founded by Tucker. Thus, the college provided the students not only with the symbols of status to compete with others of similar backgrounds but with a purposeful social service as well.[80] After the turn of the century, perhaps in response to providing this collegiate service, two of the most prestigious universities—Princeton under Woodrow Wilson and Harvard under A. Lawrence Lowell—shifted their emphasis back to undergraduate education. And in this sense, Dartmouth seemed to serve as a model for these institutions.

Similar to the decline in the notion of the organic community and the emergence of the collegiate factions, the conception of higher learning evidenced a fragmentation of knowledge. In the words of Tucker, the older colleges were "organized around the idea of unity," while the colleges now were "organized around the idea of intensiveness."[81] And the faculty shifted from "a group of scholars of similar training, and pervaded by a common educational purpose," to "a body of specialists, or, . . . experts."[82] Thus, the basic unity of knowledge, the evangelical, the joining of faith and intellect, instructing the moral conscience, the uplifting of individual character gave way to a more rationalized and esoteric learning. Knowledge was divided into specific disciplines with particular methodologies and limited areas of study, and comparable to the stress in collegiate service, higher learning began to emphasize testable skills.[83] What had once flowed together in moral philosophy, for example, and had given the student an interpretation of life, now was divided into specific disciplines in the social sciences, such as economics and sociology.[84] Under Tucker one finds an increase in the number and types of courses[85] and a continuation and increase of faculty hired with advanced training along specific disciplinary lines. In an institution emphasizing undergraduate education and the primacy of teaching, faculty members also were able to pursue their interests, gain distinction in their particular areas of study, and thereby aid in the metropolitan reputation of the college. Thus, Tucker noted, "Contrary to the assertion of Cardinal Newman . . . that to discover and to teach are separate functions seldom united in the same person, I believe that discovery stimulates teaching, and that teaching necessitates discovery."[86] And Tucker, through his chapel talks, could concentrate further on the moral education of students, linking his talks to their social service mission.[87]

Reflective of the altered communal idea and symbolic of the changing character of the college and of the larger society, the notion of the president as pastoral head, interpreter of life, moral leader, and classroom teacher underwent marked change. While the conception of the president as a moral leader was not rejected at Dartmouth, it was altered and redefined. Added to this transformed notion was an increased stress on the president as an executive and administrative officer who could insure the college's metropolitan reputation and bring the college into the position of prominence in late-nineteenth-century America it had once held in the world of northern New England. In relation to the increased emphasis on his administrative role, Tucker observed:

> It is not too much to say that the necessity for the modernizing of the colleges virtually created the science of college administration, which in its inner working is the science of coordination and adjustment, and in its outer relations the scientific application of economic principles to the material necessities of the colleges.[88]

With the emphasis in the general culture on business standards, and with the metropolitan orientation of the college community concerned with rank (one element of which centered on growth and numbers), Tucker established a number of policies indicative of an application of "economic principles." Tucker stressed growth and expansion; he continued and accelerated the reconstruction of the physical plant and concentrated upon student enrollment. The number of the students in the college rose from 315 (academical and Chandler) in 1892–93 to 1,136 in 1908–9.[89] He continued the organization of the college on a more formal basis and instituted trustee and faculty standing committees for greater efficiency. He also courted the alumni who would be central to the college as the emphasis in college government shifted from administering funds to providing funds.[90]

In a related context, President Tucker's style and administrative policies bore similarities to methods used by some other college and university presidents during the late nineteenth and early twentieth centuries. For instance, in 1891 President Eliot of Harvard noted that he had tried to give "the institution the benefit of a business administration, attempting to extend business principles like a system of telegraph wires throughout the various departments," and that this had brought the institution "close to the hearts of our business men."[91] Although Eliot may have been overemphasizing the point in this newspaper interview, probably trying to consolidate financial support for Harvard and enhance his own reputation among businessmen, the trend evidenced in this statement does seem to be in keeping with developments in the later part of his administration.[92] In comparison with President Eliot, President Harris of Bucknell, "combined the modern entrepreneurial style of university presidents with a traditional concern for oversight and involvement in denominational affairs."[93] In the larger society, this period also saw a greater concentration on coordination and control and scientific management in the development of business corporations.[94]

Within Dartmouth's altered framework and reflective of the transformed role of the president as a moral leader, Tucker attempted to bring into harmony the factions in the college community by emphasizing a collegiate conception centering on their common identity as members of a select fellowship. This attempt to try to maintain a sense of community as an important value stood in contrast to the universities where interest groups were simply allowed to coexist as constituencies under a shared administration. Reflective of his own background and aspirations and of his conception of the college as an element of metropolitan culture, Tucker stressed the importance of the continuance of a nationalization of Dartmouth.[95] Building upon the notion of the college as a special place apart within that culture, he asserted the basic unity of the college community. To this point he said:

> The creation of a high college sentiment, not mere college spirit, was essential to the full institutional development of the College. . . . It is of special value in creating the institutional spirit in constructive periods. "The mind of the college" can be lifted at such times above the ordinary causes of enthusiasm and set upon the growths and advancements of the college itself. Such periods produce a fine community of feeling among members of the faculty, students, and alumni.[96]

To this effect, beginning in 1895, Tucker instituted "Dartmouth Night," encouraged the dormitory system, and emphasized the idyllic setting of Dartmouth. The purpose of "Dartmouth Night" centered on the perpetuation of the "Dartmouth Spirit" and the capitalization of the "history of the college."[97] The president, the faculty, and the alumni gathered together, and the undergraduate body was brought "into sympathetic and intelligent contact with the alumni, the living and the dead."[98] One historian of the college states that the freshman felt himself a "member, unworthy, perhaps, but still a member, of a great and growing whole. It did much to unify the college."[99] Tucker advanced the notion of the unity of this special group in an idyllic setting: "Probably there is no college where students are more closely related to one another or more personally related to the college. The Dartmouth democracy grows as a result of an accumulating inheritance and of a steadfast environment, especially of the latter."[100] He also encouraged an expansion of the dormitory system and the limitation upon the number of students who could room together in fraternities, not because he opposed what the fraternities symbolized, but because they could weaken the sense of community. Thus, in his convocation address in 1902 he declared:

> There should be abundant room for the free play of groups, for the coming together of men to their mutual tastes, but the condition should always exist for the spontaneous expression of a common

sentiment. The college spirit means more than an assumed loyalty; it means ready enthusiasm.[101]

Dartmouth, then, did not completely give up the ideal of a common ideology as a basis to insure cohesion, and outwardly the rhetoric of community and moral purpose continued under President Tucker and provided continuities of their own into the twentieth century.

Even under the rallying banner of unity, however, the sense of community of the Dartmouth of 1851 could not be recaptured. The college as a special place apart with metropolitan-oriented collegiate factions united under a rallying banner emphasizing the oneness of their position as a privileged group in an idyllic setting, with nevertheless a meaningful social purpose, was not the world of the Dartmouth of 1851. While such things as a more esoteric learning and a metropolitan reputation had been gained in the process of transformation, the world of the college as a closely knit community with policies expressive of its integral role in the wider community immediately outside the collegiate bounds had been lost. In the process of this shift in the notion of community, Dartmouth had been transformed dramatically in ways much more important than could be measured in terms of growth, numbers, an increase in the number of electives, or an expansion of the physical plant.

This study, then, has tried to demonstrate that more than the notion of community changed. The roles and identities of the various participant groups in the Bartlett controversy dramatized how changed was the character of the college, its relationship to the larger community, and the conception of higher learning. The shifts reconstituted the class of students the college served, the conception of collegiate service, the organization of the college, and the administration of higher education. The new type of president who would administer the college symbolized all these changes. The Bartlett controversy, underscoring the changing nature of the academic community and collegiate culture, highlighted the significant historical change of the "new Dartmouth." It illustrated the intrusion of the city and the metropolitan culture into the college. The controversy illuminated the contradictions promoted in a college with a president whose styles and policies were more in keeping with an older notion of community, college, and higher learning within a changing college community and society.

Within the context of the broader interpretation of the transformation of the academic community and collegiate culture, I have tried to use the Dartmouth experience and the comparative literature in the various chapters to illuminate the larger trends and dilemmas of nineteenth-century higher learning. While more detailed analyses of various institutions will be helpful in extending further our base of generalization, the pattern of institutional change revealed in this analysis seems representative of comparable institutions and provides important insights into the conflict and confusion over the various courses taken by colleges and universities in this period. The findings challenge the frequently simplistic characterization of change in nineteenth-century higher education as movement from darkness to light, from sectarianism to secularism, and from conservatism to liberalism. What happened at Dartmouth and the other institutions referred to in the text obviates the view that the transformation of higher learning was either isolated from changes in the rest of society or that the colleges slavishly responded to society's needs. Higher learning in American society was not operating in a vacuum, but was influenced by and in turn influencing the larger society. While there were similarities in the nature of change from the antebellum period to the alternate route colleges and universities followed in the late nineteenth century, not all institutions reacted exactly in the same way to the same set of forces. There were numerous competing conceptions of higher education, and the findings of this study challenge the view that the change was a one-way process—only universities influencing colleges "having" to adjust to the ascendancy of the university.

The findings of this study also underscore the needs for the type of model used in this analysis. The detailed study of the various groups in the college community challenges the view that change came about solely through the efforts of the academic "reformers." Studying such neglected elements of the college community as alumni and trustees, for example, helps to illuminate conceptions of culture, important sources of power, and the relationship between the college and the larger society. The use of historical sequences and the changing notion of community clarify the nature, process, and significance of change and the force of tradition on the nature of innovation in various institutions. It also telescopes significant changes in the larger society—social and organizational patterns, notions of culture, career patterns, the force of urbanization, for instance. This model for the analysis of institutional change also dramatizes the need for the study of shifts in power, the values underlying the changing structural arrangements, and the response of different institutions to conflict as a base upon which to build theories of institutionalization. And finally, the attempt by Dartmouth in the late nineteenth century to maintain some sense of community as a value itself within this altered framework, helps us to reexamine and ponder our nineteenth-century legacy and what was gained and lost in the process of transformation.

APPENDIX 1

Memorial of the New York Association of Alumni of Dartmouth College, 11 June 1881

The New York Association of Alumni of Dartmouth College, in support of the Memorial heretofore addressed to the Honorable Board of Trustees and by them referred to this Honorable Committee respectfully submit the following charges against the President, Samuel C. Bartlett:

First. That said Bartlett by his habitually insolent, discourteous and dictatorial manner in official intercourse with his associate members of the faculty has stifled all free and independent discussion of college matters and he has illegally, ignored and usurped the functions of the faculties of various departments of the College.

a. On the occasion of a vacancy in the Greek chair in the year 1881 upon request in a meeting of the faculty to disclose the name of the candidate he was to present to the Board of Trustees he declined so to do, and explicitly refused to discuss the matter, contrary to the best interests of the College and immemorial usage.

b. At a Meeting of the Board of Trustees held in the Spring of 1881 said Bartlett stated to the said Board that no member of the faculty objected to the Election of Professor Hewitt to fill the Greek Chair whereas he well knew that no opportunity had been given to object and that said Hewitt was not the choice of the faculty.

c. In the year 1878 said Bartlett requested Professor Worthen to accept a chair in the Chandler Scientific Department, and upon said Worthen stating that before deciding he would like to learn whether his acceptance would be agreeable to the faculty of that department said Bartlett replied "*No*, I want a friend in that Department and I have concluded that it is better not to mention the matter to any one, when you are once there you will have as much voice in the matter as any one."

d. In the year of 1879 upon the occasion of the case of Lewis' 79 coming up before the faculty of the Chandler Scientific Department for discipline, said Bartlett endeavored to get a vote but failed and the Meeting adjourned to a later date, but on the following morning and before final action had been taken by the faculty said Bartlett announced in chapel that the faculty had determined to suspend said Lewis.

e. In the Spring of 1880 on the date of a regular meeting of the faculty of the Chandler Scientific Department, said Bartlett, with the intent to affront said faculty and without excuse, not only was not present but locked the place of meeting and posted a notice on the door "At Prayer Meeting."

f. During the month of April 1880 at a Meeting of the faculty of the Chandler Scientific Department, he stated that he was surprised that Professor Jessup did not comprehend the matter under its discussion for he thought he had explained it two or three times so that a person of ordinary ability could understand.

g. In the month of May 1880 said Bartlett induced the faculty to reconsider a motion to have Wednesday Lectures from persons selected by a committee constituted for the purpose upon the express understanding that the whole subject should go over until the succeeding year and thus avoid offence to those whom he wished to exclude and then said Bartlett ignored said understanding and made his own selections and proceeded with the lectures.

h. In May 1879 said Bartlett stated to the Board of Overseers of the Thayer School of Engineering that there was no professor of Engineering in the Scientific Department then and would not be soon—giving them to understand that the Study would not thereafter be taught there which necessitated changes in the curriculum of said Thayer School and lowered the Standard of said School thus usurping the functions of the Board of Trustees.

i. That in June 1879 said Bartlett made a report to the Board of Trustees in explanation of his attitude toward the Chandler Scientific Department which Report was then and there referred to a committee of the said Board which Committee definitely overruled the views of said Bartlett, and thereafter on the 29th day of March 1880 read his own report so overruled to the faculty as the policy of the Board of Trustees, and suppressed the Report of the Committee of the Board above referred to and then refused to furnish his report to the faculty of the Chandler Scientific Department although so requested by them.

k. On April 19th 1881 said Bartlett stated to Professor Blanpied that he said Bartlett would favor a proposed change of name of the Degree to be conferred by the New Hampshire College of Agriculture and the Mechanic Arts in the Board of Trustees and Professor Blanpied and the faculty of said Department relying thereon made only a formal presentation of the matter to the Board; whereupon said Bartlett requested him to withdraw and then attacked the measure and by his vigorous opposition defeated it.

l. That in the Spring of 1880 said Bartlett assumed a right and authority to reprimand the Senior Professor of the faculty for writing a proper letter to a member of the Board of Trustees and did so in a most unjust and unwarrantable manner in an open faculty meeting.

Second. That said Bartlett has deliberately and intentionally imperiled the influence of the faculty with the Students and has improperly endeavored to bring certain members into disgrace in the eyes of the Students and the public.

a. At a faculty meeting held in March 1878 for the purpose of proving to the faculty the making of a certain Statement by one of the Professors said Bartlett called a student into the meeting and asked him to repeat there the statement made to him by the professor.

b. At a recitation of the Senior class of '80 he stated to them in effect that Professor Ruggles had interfered in the matter of prize speaking which did not concern him and at the same time impugned the veracity of Professor Ruggles and afterwards stated to different members of the faculty and others that the Board of Trustees had forbidden prize speaking in the College.

c. In the Spring of 1881 said Bartlett stated to the Editor of the Dartmouth that he must not publish anything from any member of the faculty in reference to the Election of Mr. Hewitt and threatened in case of non-compliance to suppress the magazine and call a meeting of the Board of Trustees to remove the writer of such article notwithstanding the fact that he himself had already furnished an article for publication by the same magazine upon the same subject.

d. In the Spring of 1880 said Bartlett stated to the correspondent of the

Associated prof. that there was a question of veracity between Professor Ruggles and Mullerse with the intent aforesaid.

Third. That said Bartlett has persistently and systematically exerted his official influence to impair and diminish the prosperity of different departments of the college.

a. On the 29th day of April 1879 at the annual commencement of the New Hampshire College of Agriculture and the Mechanic Arts, said Bartlett made a public address in which he stated that the education there obtained might fit a young man for Highway Surveyor, Selectman or perhaps the Legislature, but insinuated that only the classical education was worthy of ambition, thus ridiculing said Department and bringing it into disrepute.

b. Upon the graduation of Enright from the Chandler Scientific Department in 1879, said Bartlett stated to him in a conversation with him relative to the training in that Department "I am glad your father is going to give your *brother* an *education,*" meaning a classical course the result of which was that the brother referred to went to another college instead of Dartmouth.

c. In the Spring of 1879 said Bartlett wrote to an applicant for admission to the Chandler Scientific Department that he had better take the classical course and that if he could not do that he had better not go to Dartmouth.

d. In the year 1878 said Bartlett, with intent to discourage instructors in the classical department from furnishing instruction to the Chandler Scientific Department procured the passage of an illegal resolution of the Board of Trustees requiring one half of the money received for such instruction to be turned over to the College Treasury.

e. In July 1879 after consulting Professors Hardy and Pollens with reference to teaching in the Chandler Scientific Department, and learning from those Gentlemen that they were entirely willing to do so, said Bartlett stated to Professor Pollens that doing so would be construed by said Bartlett as a personal affront, and *then* said Bartlett informed the faculty of the Chandler Scientific Department that Professors Hardy and Pollens *declined* to teach there.

f. During the fall of 1880, said Bartlett stated to Dr. Chamberlin of New York in effect that these Departments referring to those other than the classical were Parasites eating away the life of the College and they should be swept away.

g. That said Bartlett has endeavored to rob the Chandler Scientific Department of whatever advantage might arise from its connection with the College by improper advertising and catalogue notices.

<u>Fourth</u>. That in his public official relations to the students said Bartlett has used such language as to necessarly [sic] humiliate and disgrace them and graduate them as enemies instead of friends of the college.

a. <u>Dur</u>ing the early part of the administration of said Bartlett he announced to the College in Chapel that he supposed he had been called to preside over a body of Gentlemen but if it proved to be a menagerie of babboons [sic] he thought he was equal to the occasion.

b. <u>In</u> criticising the habit of Students to place their feet upon the railing in front of them he stated that it showed the breeding of the families from which they had come.

c. <u>Upon</u> the occasion of finding an outhouse placed before the chapel door said Bartlett stated to the Students in chapel that it would remind them of their ancestral halls.

<u>Fifth</u>. That said Bartlett has so far lost the confidence of his associate members of the faculty that out of a total membership of twenty-three residents Sixteen openly express the belief that the best interests of the College require his resignation.

APPENDIX 2

Rank Structure of the 1851 and 1881 Dartmouth Faculty

Rank	1851 Faculty		1881 Faculty	
	N	%	N	%
Professor	13	92.9	22	61.0
Associate Professor	0	0	2	5.6
Instructor	0	0	4	11.1
Tutor	0	0	2	5.6
Assistant	0	0	1	2.8
Lecturer (Medical)	0	0	4	11.1
Demonstrator (Medical)	1	7.1	1	2.8
Total	14	100	36	100

Sources: Alumni files, Special Collections, Dartmouth College Library, Hanover, New Hampshire; Catalogue of the Officers and Students of Dartmouth College 1850-51 (Hanover, N.H., 1850); Catalogue of the Officers and Students of Dartmouth College and the Associated Institutions 1880-81 (Hanover, N.H., 1880); General Catalogue of Dartmouth College and the Associated Schools 1769-1910, 1769-1940 (Hanover, N.H., 1910, 1940).

Notes: The rank structure includes the faculty (resident and nonresident) of all the schools and departments. Where exact sum of percentages does not equal 100%, the numbers have been rounded off to equal 100%.

APPENDIX 3

Birthplace of the 1851 and 1881 Dartmouth Faculty

Birthplace	Academical Department 1851 N	1851 %	1881 N	1881 %	Medical College 1851 N	1851 %	1881 N	1881 %	Chandler Scientific Department 1881 N	1881 %	Thayer School 1881 N	1881 %	Agricultural College 1881 N	1881 %	Total All Departments 1851 N	1851 %	1881 N	1881 %
New Hampshire	5	62.5	3	23.1	5	83.3	1	8.3	1	20	0	0	1	25	10	71.4	6	16.7
Connecticut	1	12.5	0	0	0	0	1	8.3	1	20	0	0	0	0	1	7.1	2	5.6
Maine	1	12.5	1	7.7	0	0	1	8.4	1	20	0	0	0	0	1	7.1	3	8.3
Massachusetts	1	12.5	3	23.0	0	0	3	25.0	1	20	0	0	0	0	1	7.2	7	19.4
Rhode Island	0	0	1	7.7	0	0	0	0	0	0	0	0	0	0	0	0	1	2.8
Vermont	0	0	1	7.7	1	16.7	0	0	1	20	0	0	1	25	1	7.2	3	8.3
New England subtotal	8	100	9	69.2	6	100	6	50	5	100	0	0	2	50	14	100	22	61.1
New York	0	0	0	0	0	0	2	16.7	0	0	1	50	0	0	0	0	3	8.3
Ohio	0	0	2	15.4	0	0	1	8.3	0	0	0	0	1	25	0	0	4	11.1
Pennsylvania	0	0	0	0	0	0	1	8.3	0	0	0	0	0	0	0	0	1	2.8
Outside U.S.	0	0	2	15.4	0	0	2	16.7	0	0	0	0	1	25	0	0	4	11.1
Unknown	0	0	0	0	0	0	0	0	0	0	1	50	0	0	0	0	2	5.6
Non-New England subtotal	0	0	4	30.8	0	0	6	50	0	0	2	100	2	50	0	0	14	38.9
Total faculty	8	100	13	100	6	100	12	100	5	100	2	100	4	100	14	100	36	100

Sources: Alumni files, Special Collections, Dartmouth College Library; General Catalogue of Dartmouth College and the Associated Schools 1769-1910, 1769-1940 (Hanover, N.H., 1910, 1940).

Notes: This includes resident and nonresident faculty members, all ranks. Where exact sum of percentages does not equal 100%, the numbers have been rounded off to equal 100%.

APPENDIX 4

Undergraduate College of the 1851 and 1881 Dartmouth Faculty

Undergraduate College	Academical Department				Medical College				Chandler Scientific Department		Thayer School		Agricultural College		Total All Departments			
	1851		1881		1851		1881		1881		1881		1881		1851		1881	
	N	%	N	%	N	%	N	%	N	%	N	%	N	%	N	%	N	%
Dartmouth graduate	7	87.5	10	76.9	5[a]	83.3	5	41.7	4	80	1	50	2	50	12	85.7	22	61.1
Non-Dartmouth graduate	1	12.5	3	23.1	1	16.7	7	58.3	1	20	1	50	2[b]	50	2	14.3	14	38.9
Total Faculty	8	100	13	100	6	100	12	100	5	100	2	100	4	100	14	100	36	100

Sources: Alumni files, Special Collections, Dartmouth College Library, Hanover, New Hampshire; General Catalogue of Dartmouth College and the Associated Schools 1769-1910, 1769-1940 (Hanover, N.H., 1910, 1940).

Notes: This includes resident and nonresident faculty members, all ranks. Where exact sum of percentages does not equal 100%, the numbers have been rounded off to equal 100%.

[a]Those who hold no undergraduate degree, but hold a Dartmouth M.D., are also included in this category.

[b]The college of one faculty member was unknown, but he was not a Dartmouth graduate. Included in the total for non-Dartmouth graduates in 1881.

APPENDIX 5

Training Beyond Master's Degree of the 1851 and 1881 Dartmouth Faculty

Training Beyond Master's Degree[a]	Academical Department 1851 N	%	Academical Department 1881 N	%	Medical College 1851 N	%	Medical College 1881 N	%	Chandler Scientific Department 1881 N	%	Thayer School 1881 N	%	Agricultural College 1881 N	%	Total All Departments 1851 N	%	Total All Departments 1881 N	%
Ministerial training or graduate	6	75	4[b]	30.8	0	0	1	8.3	1	20	0	0	0	0	6	42.9	6	16.7
Legal training or graduate	1	12.5	0	0	1	16.7	1	8.3	0	0	0	0	0	0	2	14.3	1	2.8
Medical training or graduate	0	0	1	7.7	5	83.3	11	91.7	0	0	0	0	1	25	5	35.7	13	36.1
Post-professional medical training European	0	0	0	0	1	16.7	2	16.7	0	0	0	0	0	0	1	7.1	2	5.6
Engineering training or graduate	0	0	1	7.7	0	0	0	0	1	20	1	50	1	25	0	0	4	11.1
European specialized relating to discipline	0	0	3	23.1	0	0	0	0	1	20	0	0	0	0	0	0	4	11.1
European specialized during professorship (1883)	0	0	1	7.7	0	0	0	0	0	0	0	0	0	0	0	0	1	2.8
European Ph.D. or American Ph.D.	0	0	0	0	0	0	0	0	0	0	0	0	0	0	0	0	0[c]	0
None/unknown	2	25	5[d]	38.5	0	0	0	0	2	40	1	50	2	50	2	14.3	10[e]	27.8
Total faculty	8		13		6		12		5		2		4		14		36	

APPENDIX 5 (Continued)

Sources: Alumni files, Special Collections, Dartmouth College Library, Hanover, New Hampshire; Appleton's Cyclopedia of National Biography, rev. ed. (New York, 1898); The National Cyclopedia of American Biography (New York, 1907-44); Dictionary of American Biography (New York, 1929-64); Perry Baxter Smith, The History of Dartmouth College (Boston, 1878); Leon Burr Richardson, History of Dartmouth College, 2 vols. (Hanover, N.H., 1932); John King Lord, A History of Dartmouth College /Second Volume of History of Dartmouth College begun by Frederick Chase/ (Concord, N.H., 1913); Ralph Nading Hill, ed., The College on the Hill: A Dartmouth Chronicle (Hanover, N.H., 1964); General Catalogue of Dartmouth College and the Associated Schools 1769-1910, 1769-1940 (Hanover, N.H., 1910, 1940); Arthur Sherburne Hardy, Things Remembered (Boston, 1923); Faculty Manuscript Collections, Special Collections, Dartmouth College Library, Hanover, New Hampshire.

Notes: This includes resident and nonresident faculty members, all ranks. The percentages are based on percentage of total faculty with this training and therefore do not total to 100%, as some of the faculty have more than one type of training.

a During the 1851 and 1881 periods, a master's degree was awarded upon application and payment of a fee to all graduates of three years' standing.

b Two of these were professors in 1851.

c In the 1881 period some of the faculty held honorary Ph.D.s (American); they are not included in the figures for this table.

d Three of these were tutors, assistants, instructors.

e Five of these are in the category of tutors, assistants, and instructors.

APPENDIX 6

Age of Full Professors of the Dartmouth Faculty in 1851 and 1881

Age	Academical Department 1851		Academical Department 1881		Medical College 1851		Medical College 1881		Chandler Scientific Department 1881		Thayer School 1881		Agricultural College 1881		Total All Departments 1851		Total All Departments 1881	
	N	%	N	%	N	%	N	%	N	%	N	%	N	%	N	%	N	%
26-30	1	12.5	0	0	0	0	0	0	0	0	0	0	1	50	1	7.7	1	4.5
31-35	0	0	2	25	0	0	0	0	1	25	1	100	1	50	0	0	5	22.9
36-40	3	37.5	1	12.5	1	20	3	42.9	1	25	0	0	0	0	4	30.8	2	9.1
41-45	2	25	2	25	0	0	1	14.3	1	25	0	0	0	0	2	15.4	6	27.3
46-50	1	12.5	0	0	1	20	2	28.5	0	0	0	0	0	0	1	7.7	1	4.5
51-55	1	12.5	0	0	2	40	0	0	1	25	0	0	0	0	4	30.7	3	13.6
56-60	0	0	0	0	1	20	0	0	0	0	0	0	0	0	1	7.7	0	0
61-65	0	0	1	12.5	0	0	0	0	0	0	0	0	0	0	0	0	1	4.5
66-70	0	0	1	12.5	0	0	0	0	0	0	0	0	0	0	0	0	1	4.5
71-75	0	0	1	12.5	0	0	1	14.3	0	0	0	0	0	0	0	0	2	9.1
Total Faculty	8	100	8	100	5	100	7	100	4	100	1	100	2	100	13	100	22	100
Range	29-55		33-73		37-56		42-72		31-53		34		28-33					

Sources: Alumni files, Special Collections, Dartmouth College Library, Hanover, New Hampshire, General Catalogue of Dartmouth College and the Associated Schools 1769-1910, 1769-1940 (Hanover, N. H., 1910, 1940).

Note: Where exact sum of percentages does not equal 100%, the numbers have been rounded off to equal 100%.

APPENDIX 7

College Teaching Experience at Appointment as Full
Professor of the 1851 and 1881 Dartmouth Faculty

	Academical Department				Medical College				Chandler Scientific Department		Thayer School		Agricultural College		Total All Departments			
	1851		1881		1851		1881		1881		1881		1881		1851		1881	
	N	%	N	%	N	%	N	%	N	%	N	%	N	%	N	%	N	%
0-few months	5	62.5	0	0	2	40	0	0	1	25	0	0	0	0	7	53.8	1	4.5
1-3 years	3	37.5	4a	50	3	60	4b	57.1	2	50	1	100	1	50	6	46.2	12	54.5
4-6 years	0	0	0	0	0	0	1	14.3	1	25	0	0	0	0	0	0	2	9.1
7-10 years	0	0	2	25	0	0	1	14.3	0	0	0	0	1	50	0	0	4	18.2
Over 10 years	0	0	2	25	0	0	1	14.3	0	0	0	0	0	0	0	0	3	13.7
Total faculty	8	100	8	100	5	100	7	100	4	100	1	100	2	100	13	100	22	100

Sources: Alumni files, Special Collections, Dartmouth College Library, Hanover, New Hampshire; Faculty Manuscript Collections, Special Collections, Dartmouth College Library, Hanover, New Hampshire; General Catalogue of Dartmouth College and the Associated Schools 1769-1910, 1769-1940 (Hanover, N.H., 1910, 1940); Appleton's Cyclopedia of National Biography, rev. ed. (New York, 1898); The National Cyclopedia of American Biography (New York, 1907-44); Dictionary of American Biography (New York, 1929-64); Leon Burr Richardson, History of Dartmouth College, 2 vols. (Hanover, N.H., 1932); John King Lord, A History of Dartmouth College (Concord, N.H., 1913); Perry Baxter Smith, The History of Dartmouth College (Boston, 1878).

Notes: Experience may include teaching experience at other colleges prior to appointment as a full professor at Dartmouth as well as teaching experience at Dartmouth. Where exact sum of percentages does not equal 100%, the numbers have been rounded off to equal 100%.

aTwo of these were also faculty members in the 1851 period.
bOne of these was also a faculty member in the 1851 period.

APPENDIX 8

Age at Appointment to Full Professor of the 1851 and 1881 Dartmouth Faculty

Age	Academical Department 1851 N	%	1881 N	%	Medical College 1851 N	%	1881 N	%	Chandler Scientific Department 1881 N	%	Thayer School 1881 N	%	Agricultural College 1881 N	%	Total All Departments 1851 N	%	1881 N	%
23-26	2	25.0	0	0	0	0	0	0	0	0	1	100	1	50	2	15.4	2	9.1
27-30	4	50.0	1[a]	12.5	2	40	1	14.3	2	50	0	0	0	0	6	46.1	4	18.2
31-34	1	12.5	3	37.5	0	0	2	28.5	1	25	0	0	1	50	1	7.7	8	36.4
35-38	1	12.5	2	25.0	1	20	0	0	0	0	0	0	0	0	2	15.4	2	9.1
39-42	0	0	1	12.5	0	0	3	42.9	0	0	0	0	0	0	0	0	4	18.2
43-46	0	0	1	12.5	0	0	1	14.3	0	0	0	0	0	0	0	0	1	4.5
47-50	0	0	0	0	2	40	0	0	0	0	0	0	0	0	2	15.4	0	0
51-54	0	0	0	0	0	0	0	0	1	25	0	0	0	0	0	0	1	4.5
Total faculty	8	100	8	100	5	100	7	100	4	100	1	100	2	100	13	100	22	100

Sources: Alumni files, Special Collections, Dartmouth College Library, Hanover, New Hampshire; General Catalogue of Dartmouth College and the Associated Schools 1769-1910, 1769-1940 (Hanover, N.H., 1910, 1940).

Note: Where exact sum of percentages does not equal 100%, the numbers have been rounded off to equal 100%.

[a]The faculty member was a professor during the 1851 period.

APPENDIX 9

Associational Involvements of the 1851 and 1881 Dartmouth Faculty

Involvements	Academical Department 1851		Academical Department 1881		Medical College 1851		Medical College 1881		Chandler Scientific Department 1881	
	N	%	N	%	N	%	N	%	N	%
Clerical activities as preachers, licentiates, and ordained ministers	6	75	2	15.4	0	0	0	0	0	0
Local or regional civic and community associations	8	100	7	53.8	3	50	2	16.7	3	60
Association of peers related to particular discipline	1	12.5	7	53.8	1	16.7	7	58.3	5	100
State or county medical associations	0	0	0	0	4	66.7	5	41.7	0	0
Unknown[a]	0	0	3	23.1	1	16.7	5	41.7	0	0
Total faculty	8		13		6		12		5	

Sources: Alumni files, Special Collections, Dartmouth College Library, Hanover, New Hampshire; Appleton's Cyclopedia of National Biography, rev. ed. (New York, 1898); The National Cyclopedia of American Biography (New York, 1907-44); Dictionary of American Biography (New York, 1929-64); Perry Baxter Smith, The History of Dartmouth College (Boston, 1879); Leon Burr Richardson, History of Dartmouth College, 2 vols. (Hanover, N.H., 1932); John King Lord, A History of Dartmouth College (Concord, N.H., 1913); John King Lord, A History of the Town of Hanover, N.H., with an appendix on Hanover roads by Professor J. W. Goldthwait (Hanover, N.H., 1928); Francis Lane Childs, ed., Hanover, New Hampshire, a

APPENDIX 9 (continued)

Involvements	Thayer School 1881		Agricultural College 1881		Total All Departments 1851		Total All Departments 1881	
	N	%	N	%	N	%	N	%
Clerical activities as preachers, licentiates, and ordained ministers	0	0	0	0	6	42.9	2	5.6
Local or regional civic and community associations	1	50	2	50	11	78.6	15	41.7
Association of peers related to particular discipline	1	50	1	25	2	14.3	21	58.3
State or county medical associations	0	0	0	0	4	28.6	5	13.9
Unknown[a]	1	50	2	50	1	7.1	11	30.6
Total faculty	2		4		14		36	

Bicentennial Book: Essays in Celebration of the Town's 200th Anniversary (Hanover, N.H., 1961); Ralph Nading Hill, ed., The College on the Hill: A Dartmouth Chronicle (Hanover, N.H., 1964); Faculty Manuscript Collections, Dartmouth College Library, Hanover, New Hampshire.

Notes: This includes resident and nonresident faculty members, all ranks. The percentages are based on percentage of total faculty with this involvement and therefore do not total to 100%, as some of the faculty have more than one type of involvement.

[a]Primarily tutors, assistants, demonstrators, instructors.

APPENDIX 10

Birthplace of the Academical and Chandler Graduates of
Dartmouth College, Classes of 1851 and 1881

Birthplace	Academical Department				Chandler Scientific Department	
	1851		1881		1881	
	N	%	N	%	N	%
New Hampshire	24	52.2	23	45.1	3	25.0
Connecticut	0	0	0	0	0	0
Maine	4	8.7	3	5.9	0	0
Massachusetts	3	6.5	5	9.8	4	33.3
Rhode Island	1	2.2	0	0	0	0
Vermont	12	26.1	7	13.7	3	25.0
Subtotal northern New England (N.H., Vt.)	36	78.3	30	58.8	6	50.0
Subtotal New England	44	95.7	38	74.5	10	83.3
New York	2	4.3	4	7.8	0	0
New Jersey	0	0	0	0	0	0
Pennsylvania	0	0	0	0	0	0
Washington, D.C.	0	0	2	3.9	0	0
Subtotal Mid-Atlantic	2	4.3	6	11.7	0	0
Illinois	0	0	1	2	0	0
Michigan	0	0	0	0	0	0
Missouri	0	0	1	2	0	0
Ohio	0	0	3	5.8	1	8.3
Wisconsin	0	0	1	2	1	8.4
Subtotal West	0	0	6	11.8	2	16.7
Georgia	0	0	0	0	0	0
Outside U.S.	0	0	1	2	0	0
Unknown	0	0	0	0	0	0
Total	46	100	51	100	12	100

Sources: Alumni files, Special Collections, Dartmouth
College Library, Hanover, New Hampshire; General Catalogue
of Dartmouth College and the Associated Schools 1769-1940
(Hanover, N.H., 1940); George T. Chapman, Sketches of the
Alumni of Dartmouth College (Cambridge, Mass., 1867);
Myron W. Adams, The Class of 1881, Dartmouth College,
1881-1931 (Milford, N.H., 1931).

Note: Where exact sum of percentage does not equal 100%,
the numbers have been rounded off to equal 100%.

APPENDIX 11

Residence During College of the Academical and Chandler
Graduates of Dartmouth College, Classes of 1851 and 1881

Residence	Academical Department				Chandler Scientific Department	
	1851		1881		1881	
	N	%	N	%	N	%
New Hampshire	25	54.4	21	41.2	3	25.0
Connecticut	0	0	0	0	0	0
Maine	2	4.3	3	5.9	0	0
Massachusetts	2	4.3	8	15.6	3	25.0
Rhode Island	1	2.2	0	0	0	0
Vermont	14	30.5	6	11.8	4	33.3
Subtotal northern New England (N.H., Vt.)	39	84.9	27	53.0	7	58.3
Subtotal New England	44	95.7	38	74.5	10	83.3
New York	2	4.3	6	11.7	0	0
Washington, D.C.	0	0	1	2	0	0
Subtotal Mid-Atlantic	2	4.3	7	13.7	0	0
Illinois	0	0	1	2	0	0
Iowa	0	0	1	2	0	0
Kentucky	0	0	1	2	0	0
Montana	0	0	0	0	1	8.3
Ohio	0	0	3	5.8	1	8.4
Subtotal West	0	0	6	11.8	2	16.7
Total	46	100	51	100	12	100

Sources: Catalogue of the Officers and Students of Dartmouth
College 1850-51 (Hanover, N.H., 1850); Catalogue of the
Officers and Students of Dartmouth College and the Associated
Institutions 1880-81 (Hanover, N.H., 1880); Alumni files,
Special Collections, Dartmouth College Library, Hanover, New
Hampshire; Catalogue of the Officers and Students of Dartmouth
College 1847-1848, 1848-49, 1849-50 (Hanover, N.H., 1847, 1848,
1849); Catalogue of the Officers and Students of Dartmouth
College and the Associated Institutions 1879-80 (Hanover, N.H.,
1879); Catalogue of the Officers and Students of Dartmouth
College 1877-78, 1878-79 (Hanover, N.H., 1877, 1878).

Note: Where exact sum of percentages does not equal 100%, the
numbers have been rounded off to equal 100%.

APPENDIX 12

Fathers' Occupations, Academical and Chandler Graduates of
Dartmouth College, Classes of 1851 and 1881

Occupation	Academical Department				Chandler Scientific Department	
	1851		1881		1881	
	N	%	N	%	N	%
Farming	14	30.4	8	15.7	5	41.7
Law	3	6.5	2	3.9	0	0
Ministry	4	8.7	4	7.8	0	0
Medicine	2	4.3	0	0	0	0
Engineering	0	0	0	0	0	0
Education-teaching						
Below college level	0	0	0	0	0	0
College level	1	2.2	1	2	0	0
Business[a]						
Own or middle management of above	4	8.7	11	21.6	5	41.7
Office worker	0	0	2	3.9	0	0
Journalism	0	0	0	0	0	0
Skilled workers[b]	4	8.7	7	13.7	0	0
Other miscellaneous	1[c]	2.2	1[d]	2	0	0
Occupation not listed in census records	1	2.2	1	2	0	0
Unable to locate in census in location indicated as residence or birthplace	8	17.4	9	17.6	1	8.3
Father not listed in census; shows student living alone or with relatives, mother	4	8.7	5	9.8	1	8.3
Total	46	100	51	100	12	100

APPENDIX 12 (continued)

Sources: United States, National Archives, Seventh Census, 1850, and Tenth Census, 1880, Population Schedules, Manuscript Records of the Census; City Directories, Alumni files, Special Collections, Dartmouth College Library, Hanover, New Hampshire; George T. Chapman, Sketches of the Alumni of Dartmouth College (Cambridge, Mass., 1867); Myron W. Adams, The Class of 1881, Dartmouth College, 1881-1931 (Milford, N.H., 1931).

Note: Where exact sum does not equal 100%, the numbers have been rounded off to equal 100%.

[a]For exact breakdown of category for 1851 and 1881, see notes 30, 84, and 108, chapter 3.

[b]For exact breakdown of this category for 1851 and 1881, see notes 29 and 86, chapter 3.

[c]Captain.

[d]Artist.

APPENDIX 13

Age at Graduation of the Academical and Chandler
Graduates of Dartmouth College,
Classes of 1851 and 1881

Age at Graduation	Academical Department				Chandler Scientific Department	
	1851		1881		1881	
	N	%	N	%	N	%
20.0 - 20.11	5	10.9	5	9.8	2	16.7
21.0 - 21.11	7	15.2	11	21.6	2	16.7
22.0 - 22.11	4	8.7	14	27.5	3	25
23.0 - 23.11	3	6.5	6	11.8	1	8.3
24.0 - 24.11	12	26.1	8	15.6	0	0
25.0 - 25.11	4	8.7	2	3.9	1	8.3
26.0 - 26.11	4	8.7	5	9.8	3	25
27.0 - 27.11	4	8.7	0	0	0	0
28.0 - 28.11	0	0	0	0	0	0
29.0 - 29.11	0	0	0	0	0	0
30.0 - 30.11	2	4.3	0	0	0	0
31.0 - 31.11	1	2.2	0	0	0	0
Total	46	100	51	100	12	100
25 or over	15	32.6	7	13.7	4	33.3
Mean age[a]		24.3		22.10		23.1
Median age[b]		24.5		22 7		22.1

Sources: General Catalogue of Dartmouth College and the
Associated Schools 1769-1940 (Hanover, N.H., 1940); Alumni
files, Special Collections, Dartmouth College Library,
Hanover, New Hampshire; George T. Chapman, Sketches of the
Alumni of Dartmouth College (Cambridge, Mass., 1867); Myron
W. Adams, The Class of 1881, Dartmouth College, 1881-1931
(Milford, N.H., 1931).

Notes: Where exact sum of percentages does not equal 100%,
the numbers have been rounded off to equal 100%. Age at
graduation was as of commencement.

[a]Mean age was obtained from exact years and months at
graduation.

[b]Median age was obtained from exact years and months at
graduation.

APPENDIX 14

Occupation of Graduates of the Academical and Chandler
Scientific Departments of Dartmouth College,
Classes of 1851 and 1881

Occupation	Academical Department				Chandler Scientific Department	
	1851		1881		1881	
	N	%	N	%	N	%
Farming	0	0	0	0	0	0
Law	24	52.1	16	31.3	1	8.3
Ministry	4	8.7	2	3.9	0	0
Medicine	4	8.7	8	15.7	0	0
Engineering	0	0	0	0	6	50
Education-teaching						
Below college level	5	10.9	11	21.6	1	8.3
College level	3	6.5	2	3.9	0	0
Business						
Own or middle						
management of above	5	10.9	10	19.6	3	25
Journalism	1	2.2	1	2	0	0
Other miscellaneous	0	0	1[a]	2	1[b]	8.4
Occupation not listed on						
records	0	0	0	0	0	0
Total	46	100	51	100	12	100

Sources: General Catalogue of Dartmouth College 1880
(Hanover, N.H., 1880); Alumni files, Special Collections,
Dartmouth Library, Hanover, New Hampshire; George T. Chapman,
Sketches of the Alumni of Dartmouth College (Cambridge, Mass.,
1867); Myron W. Adams, The Class of 1881, Dartmouth College,
1881-1931 (Milford, N.H., 1931); General Catalogue of
Dartmouth College and the Associated Schools 1769-1910
(Hanover, N.H., 1910; General Catalogue of Dartmouth College
and the Associated Institutions (Hanover, N.H., 1880).

Notes: Where exact sum of percentages does not equal 100%,
the numbers have been rounded off to equal 100%. After an
examination of the above sources, the occupation chosen was
the one that seemed the most predominant.

[a]Died shortly after graduation.

[b]Inventor.

APPENDIX 15

Residence After College of the Academical and Chandler
Graduates of Dartmouth College,
Classes of 1851 and 1881

Residence	Academical Department				Chandler Scientific Department	
	1851		1881		1881	
	N	%	N	%	N	%
New Hampshire	6	13.0	2	3.9	0	0
Connecticut	2	4.3	0	0	0	0
Massachusetts	5	10.9	14	27.5	5	41.7
Rhode Island	1	2.2	0	0	0	0
Vermont	4	8.7	2	3.9	0	0
Subtotal northern New England (N.H., Vt.)	10	21.7	4	7.8	0	0
Subtotal New England	18	39.1	18	35.3	5	41.7
New York	3	6.5	10	19.6	1	8.3
New Jersey	0	0	1	2	0	0
Pennsylvania	2	4.3	2	3.9	0	0
Washington, D.C.	0	0	3	5.8	0	0
Subtotal Mid-Atlantic	5	10.8	16	31.3	1	8.3
Colorado	1	2.2	1	2.0	0	0
North Dakota	0	0	4	7.8	0	0
Illinois	6	13.1	2	3.9	0	0
Iowa	0	0	1	2	0	0
Kansas	3	6.5	2	3.9	0	0
Michigan	2	4.3	0	0	0	0
Minnesota	4	8.7	1	2.0	1	8.3
Montana	0	0	1	2.0	2	16.7
California	0	0	0	0	1	8.3
Ohio	3	6.5	3	5.8	1	8.4
Wisconsin	1	2.2	0	0	0	0
Indiana	1	2.2	0	0	0	0
Subtotal West	21	45.7	15	29.4	5	41.7
Georgia	1	2.2	1	2.0	0	0
Louisiana	1	2.2	0	0	0	0
Unknown	0	0	1[a]	2.0	1	8.3
Total	46	100	51	100	12	100

APPENDIX 15 (continued)

Sources: General Catalogue of Dartmouth College 1880 (Hanover, N.H., 1880); Alumni files, Special Collections, Dartmouth College Library, Hanover, New Hampshire; George T. Chapman, Sketches of the Alumni of Dartmouth College (Cambridge, Mass., 1867); Myron W. Adams, The Class of 1881, Dartmouth College, 1881-1931 (Milford, N.H., 1931); General Catalogue of Dartmouth College and the Associated Schools 1769-1910 (Hanover, N.H., 1910); General Catalogue of Dartmouth College and the Associated Institutions (Hanover, N.H., 1880).

Notes: Where exact sum of percentages does not equal 100%, the numbers have been rounded off to equal 100%. After an examination of the above sources, the residence chosen was the prime residence during the individual's active professional life.

[a]Died shortly after graduation.

APPENDIX 16

Birthplace of the Academical and Chandler Nongraduates of Dartmouth College and the Students of the Associated Schools, Classes of 1851 and 1881

Birthplace	Academical Nongraduates				Chandler Nongraduates		Medical College Graduates				Thayer School Graduates		Thayer School Non-graduates	
	1851		1881		1881		1851		1881		1881		1881	
	N	%	N	%	N	%	N	%	N	%	N	%	N	%
New Hampshire	8	50.0	4	18.2	1	33.3	6	37.5	11	37.9	0	0	0	0
Connecticut	0	0	2	9.1	0	0	0	0	1	3.4	0	0	0	0
Maine	0	0	3	13.6	0	0	0	0	6	20.7	0	0	0	0
Massachusetts	4	25.0	2	9.1	0	0	2	12.5	2	6.9	1	100	1	33.3
Rhode Island	1	6.3	0	0	0	0	0	0	0	0	0	0	0	0
Vermont	1	6.3	4	18.2	0	0	4	25.0	5	17.3	0	0	2	66.7
Subtotal northern New England (N.H., Vt.)	9	56.3	8	36.4	1	33.3	10	62.5	16	55.2	0	0	2	66.7
Subtotal New England	14	87.6	15	68.2	1	33.3	12	75	25	86.2	1	100	3	100
New York	0	0	2	9.1	1	33.3	1	6.3	1	3.4	0	0	0	0
New Jersey	0	0	1	4.5	0	0	0	0	0	0	0	0	0	0
Pennsylvania	0	0	0	0	0	0	0	0	1	3.5	0	0	0	0
Washington, D.C.	0	0	0	0	0	0	0	0	0	0	0	0	0	0
Subtotal Mid-Atlantic	0	0	3	13.6	1	33.3	1	6.3	2	6.9	0	0	0	0
Illinois	0	0	0	0	1	33.4	0	0	0	0	0	0	0	0
Michigan	0	0	1	4.5	0	0	0	0	0	0	0	0	0	0
Missouri	0	0	0	0	0	0	0	0	0	0	0	0	0	0
Ohio	0	0	2	9.1	0	0	0	0	0	0	0	0	0	0

Birthplace	Academical Nongraduates				Chandler Nongraduates		Medical College Graduates				Thayer School Graduates		Thayer School Nongraduates	
	1851		1881		1881		1851		1881		1881		1881	
	N	%	N	%	N	%	N	%	N	%	N	%	N	%
Wisconsin	0	0	0	0	0	0	0	0	0	0	0	0	0	0
Subtotal West	0	0	3	13.6	1	33.4	0	0	0	0	0	0	0	0
Georgia	1	6.2	0	0	0	0	0	0	1	3.4	0	0	0	0
Outside U.S.	1	6.2	1	4.6	0	0	0	0	0	0	0	0	0	0
Unknown	0	0	0	0	0	0	3	18.7	1	3.5	0	0	0	0
Total	16	100	22	100	3	100	16	100	29	100	1	100	3	100

Sources: Alumni files, Special Collections, Dartmouth College Library, Hanover, New Hampshire; General Catalogue of Dartmouth College and the Associated Schools 1769-1940 (Hanover, N.H., 1940); Myron W. Adams, The Class of 1881, Dartmouth College, 1881-1931 (Milford, N.H., 1931).

Note: Where exact sum of percentages does not equal 100%, the numbers have been rounded off to equal 100%.

APPENDIX 17

Residence During College of the Academical and Chandler Nongraduates and the Students of the Associated Schools, Dartmouth College, Classes of 1851 and 1881

Residence	Academical Nongraduates				Chandler Nongraduates		Medical College Graduates				Thayer School Graduates		Thayer School Nongraduates		Agricultural College Graduates	
	1851		1881		1881		1851		1881		1881		1881		1881	
	N	%	N	%	N	%	N	%	N	%	N	%	N	%	N	%
New Hampshire	7	43.8	5	22.7	1	33.3	7	43.7	11	37.9	0	0	2	66.7	4	28.5
Connecticut	0	0	1	4.5	0	0	0	0	0	0	0	0	0	0	1	7.2
Maine	0	0	3	13.6	0	0	0	0	5	17.2	0	0	0	0	0	0
Massachusetts	4	25.0	4	18.2	0	0	3	18.7	6	20.7	1	100	1	33.3	1	7.2
Rhode Island	1	6.3	0	0	0	0	0	0	1	3.5	0	0	0	0	0	0
Vermont	2	12.5	4	18.2	0	0	4	25.0	4	13.5	0	0	0	0	8	57.1
Subtotal northern New England (N.H., Vt.)	9	56.3	9	40.9	1	33.3	11	68.7	15	51.7	0	0	2	66.7	12	85.6
Subtotal New England	14	87.6	17	77.2	1	33.3	14	87.4	27	93.1	1	100	3	100	14	100
New York	0	0	2	9.1	0	0	1	6.3	1	3.5	0	0	0	0	0	0
New Jersey	0	0	1	4.5	0	0	0	0	0	0	0	0	0	0	0	0
Pennsylvania	0	0	0	0	0	0	0	0	1	3.4	0	0	0	0	0	0
Subtotal Mid-Atlantic	0	0	3	13.6	0	0	1	6.3	2	6.9	0	0	0	0	0	0
Illinois	0	0	0	0	1	33.3	0	0	0	0	0	0	0	0	0	0
Minnesota	0	0	0	0	1	33.4	0	0	0	0	0	0	0	0	0	0
Ohio	0	0	2	9.2	0	0	0	0	0	0	0	0	0	0	0	0
Subtotal West	0	0	2	9.2	2	66.7	0	0	0	0	0	0	0	0	0	0

Residence	Academical Nongraduates				Chandler Nongraduates		Medical College Graduates				Thayer School Graduates		Thayer School Non-graduates		Agricultural College Graduates	
	1851		1881		1881		1851		1881		1881		1881		1881	
	N	%	N	%	N	%	N	%	N	%	N	%	N	%	N	%
Georgia	1	6.2	0	0	0	0	0	0	0	0	0	0	0	0	0	0
Unknown	1	6.2	0	0	0	0	1	6.3	0	0	0	0	0	0	0	0
Total	16	100	22	100	3	100	16	100	29	100	1	100	3	100	14	100

Sources: Catalogue of the Officers and Students of Dartmouth College, 1847-48, 1848-49, 1849-50, 1850-51 (Hanover, N.H., 1847, 1848, 1849, 1850); Alumni files, Special Collections, Dartmouth College Library, Hanover, New Hampshire; Catalogue of the Officers and Students of Dartmouth College 1877-78, 1878-79 (Hanover, N.H., 1878, 1879); Catalogue of the Officers and Students of Dartmouth College and the Associated Institutions 1879-80, 1880-81 (Hanover, N.H., 1879, 1880).

Note: Where exact sum of percentages does not equal 100%, the numbers have been rounded off to equal 100%.

APPENDIX 18

Fathers' Occupations, Academical and Chandler Nongraduates of Dartmouth College, and Students of the Associated Schools, Classes of 1851 and 1881

Occupation	Academical Nongraduates				Chandler Nongraduates		Medical College Graduates				Thayer School Graduates		Thayer School Non-graduates		Agricultural College Graduates	
	1851		1881		1881		1851		1881		1881		1881		1881	
	N	%	N	%	N	%	N	%	N	%	N	%	N	%	N	%
Farming	5	31.2	4	18.2	0	0	2	12.5	6	20.7	0	0	0	0	6	42.9
Law	0	0	2	9.1	0	0	0	0	0	0	0	0	0	0	0	0
Ministry	1	6.2	1	4.5	0	0	0	0	0	0	0	0	0	0	0	0
Medicine	0	0	1	4.5	0	0	1	6.2	3	10.3	0	0	0	0	0	0
Engineering	0	0	0	0	0	0	0	0	0	0	0	0	0	0	0	0
Education-teaching																
Below college level	0	0	0	0	0	0	0	0	0	0	0	0	0	0	0	0
College level	0	0	0	0	0	0	0	0	1	3.5	0	0	0	0	0	0
Business																
Own or middle management of above	0	0	5	22.8	3	100	0	0	1	3.5	0	0	0	0	0	0
Office workers	1	6.3	0	0	0	0	0	0	0	0	0	0	0	0	0	0
Journalism	0	0	0	0	0	0	0	0	0	0	0	0	0	0	0	0
Skilled workers	1[a]	6.3	2[b]	9.1	0	0	0	0	1	3.5	0	0	0	0	2	14.3
Other miscellaneous	1[a]	6.3	2[b]	9.1	0	0	2[c]	12.5	5[d]	17.2	1[e]	100	0	0	0	0
Occupation not listed in census records	0	0	1	4.5	0	0	0	0	2	6.9	0	0	0	0	0	0
Unable to locate in census in location indicated as residence or birthplace	4	25.0	1	4.5	0	0	9	56.3	7	24.1	0	0	1	33.3	3	21.4

Occupation	Academical Nongraduates 1851 N %	Academical Nongraduates 1881 N %	Chandler Nongraduates 1881 N %	Medical College Graduates 1851 N %	Medical College Graduates 1881 N %	Thayer School Graduates 1881 N %	Thayer School Nongraduates 1881 N %	Agricultural College Graduates 1881 N %
Father not listed in census; shows student living alone or with relatives, mother	3 18.7	3 13.7	0 0	2 12.5	3 10.3	0 0	2 66.7	3 21.4
Total	16 100	22 100	3 100	16 100	29 100	1 100	3 100	14 100

Sources: United States, National Archives, Seventh Census, 1850, Tenth Census, 1880, Population Schedules, Manuscript Records of the Census; City Directories; Alumni files, Special Collections, Dartmouth College Library, Hanover, New Hampshire; Myron W. Adams, The Class of 1881, Dartmouth College, 1881–1931 (Milford, N.H., 1931).

Note: Where exact sum does not equal 100%, the numbers have been rounded off to equal 100%.

[a]Residence not indicated in any of the sources consulted, and birthplace was out of the United States.

[b]Sea captain, colonel.

[c]Unable to verify first name.

[d]Same as note c, above.

[e]Same as note c, above.

APPENDIX 19

Age at Graduation of the Academical and Chandler Nongraduates and the Students of the Associated Schools of Dartmouth College, Classes of 1851 and 1881

Age at Graduation	Academical Nongraduates				Chandler Nongraduates		Medical College Graduates				Thayer School Graduates		Thayer School Nongraduates	
	1851		1881		1881		1851		1881		1881		1881	
	N	%	N	%	N	%	N	%	N	%	N	%	N	%
19.0 - 19.11	0	0	1	4.5	0	0	0	0	0	0	0	0	0	0
20.0 - 20.11	0	0	1	4.5	0	0	0	0	0	0	0	0	0	0
21.0 - 21.11	0	0	4	18.2	0	0	1	6.3	1	3.5	0	0	0	0
22.0 - 22.11	2	12.5	4	18.2	0	0	2	12.5	3	10.3	0	0	0	0
23.0 - 23.11	1	6.2	2	9	2	66.7	0	0	5	17.2	1	100	2	66.7
24.0 - 24.11	1	6.2	6	27.3	1	33.3	1	6.3	4	13.8	0	0	0	0
25.0 - 25.11	1	6.2	1	4.6	0	0	1	6.3	3	10.3	0	0	0	0
26.0 - 26.11	0	0	1	4.6	0	0	2	12.5	2	6.9	0	0	1	33.3
27.0 - 27.11	3	18.8	1	4.6	0	0	1	6.2	0	0	0	0	0	0
28.0 - 28.11	0	0	0	0	0	0	1	6.2	1	3.5	0	0	0	0
29.0 - 29.11	0	0	0	0	0	0	0	0	1	3.5	0	0	0	0
30.0 - 30.11	0	0	0	0	0	0	1	6.2	2	6.9	0	0	0	0
31.0 - 31.11	1	6.3	1	4.5	0	0	0	0	1	3.5	0	0	0	0
32.0 - 32.11	0	0	0	0	0	0	1	6.3	1	3.4	0	0	0	0
33.0 and over	0	0	0	0	0	0	3	18.7	3	10.3	0	0	0	0
Unknown	7	43.8	0	0	0	0	2	12.5	2	6.9	0	0	0	0
Total	16	100	22	100	3	100	16	100	29	100	1	100	3	100
25 or over	5	31.3	4	18.2	0	0	10	62.5	14	48.3	0	0	1	33.3
Mean age[a]	25.6		23.6		24.1		29.3		27.4		24.1		24.4	
Median age[b]	25.4		23.7		23.6		27.1		25.6		24.1		23.4	

Sources: General Catalogue of Dartmouth College and the Associated Schools 1769-1940 (Hanover, N.H., 1940); Alumni files, Special Collections, Dartmouth College Library, Hanover, New Hampshire; Myron W. Adams, The Class of 1881, Dartmouth College, 1881-1931 (Milford, N.H., 1931).

Notes: Where exact sum of percentages does not equal 100%, the numbers have been rounded off to equal 100%. Age at graduation was as of commencement. In the case of the nongraduates, it was as of commencement had they graduated with their class.

[a]Mean age was obtained from exact years and months at graduation and, in the case of the nongraduates, if they had graduated with their class.

[b]Median age was obtained from exact years and months at graduation and, in the case of the nongraduates, if they had graduated with their class.

APPENDIX 20

Occupation of the Academical and Chandler Nongraduates and Students of
the Associated Schools, Dartmouth College, Classes of 1851 and 1881

Occupation	Academical Nongraduates 1851		Academical Nongraduates 1881		Chandler Nongraduates 1881		Medical College Graduates 1851		Medical College Graduates 1881		Thayer School Graduates 1881		Thayer School Nongraduates 1881		Agricultural College Graduates 1881	
	N	%	N	%	N	%	N	%	N	%	N	%	N	%	N	%
Farming	0	0	1	4.5	0	0	0	0	0	0	0	0	0	0	2	14.3
Law	2	12.5	6	27.3	0	0	0	0	0	0	0	0	0	0	2	14.3
Ministry	2	12.5	1	4.5	0	0	0	0	0	0	0	0	0	0	0	0
Medicine	3	18.7	2	9.1	2	66.7	16	100	29	100	0	0	0	0	1	7.1
Engineering	0	0	1	4.5	0	0	0	0	0	0	0	0	2	66.7	0	0
Education-teaching Below college level	1	6.3	1	4.5	0	0	0	0	0	0	0	0	0	0	0	0
College level	0	0	1	4.6	0	0	0	0	0	0	1	100	0	0	1	7.1
Business Own or middle management of above	0	0	6	27.3	1	33.3	0	0	0	0	0	0	0	0	3	21.5
Office worker	0	0	1	4.6	0	0	0	0	0	0	0	0	0	0	3	21.5
Journalism	0	0	0	0	0	0	0	0	0	0	0	0	0	0	0	0
Workers, mechanics, blacksmiths, etc.	0	0	0	0	0	0	0	0	0	0	0	0	0	0	1b	7.1
Other miscellaneous	0	0	2a	9.1	0	0	0	0	0	0	0	0	0	0	1b	7.1
Occupation not listed on records	8	50	0	0	0	0	0	0	0	0	0	0	1	33.3	0	0
Total	16	100	22	100	3	100	16	100	29	100	1	100	3	100	14	100

Sources: Alumni files, Special Collections, Dartmouth College Library, Hanover, New Hampshire; General Catalogue of Dartmouth College 1769-1910, 1769-1925, 1769-1940 (Hanover, N.H., 1910, 1925, 1940); Myron W. Adams, The Class of 1881, Dartmouth College, 1881-1931 (Milford, N.H., 1931).

Notes: Where exact sum of percentages does not equal 100%, the numbers have been rounded off to equal 100%. After an examination of the above sources, the occupation chosen was the one that seemed the most predominant.

[a] Horse breeder.

[b] Pharmacist.

APPENDIX 21

Residence After College of the Academical and Chandler Nongraduates and the Students of the Associated Schools, Dartmouth College, Classes of 1851 and 1881

Residence	Academical Nongraduates 1851		Academical Nongraduates 1881		Chandler Nongraduates 1881		Medical College Graduates 1851		Medical College Graduates 1881		Thayer School Graduates 1881		Thayer School Nongraduates 1881		Agricultural College Graduates 1881	
	N	%	N	%	N	%	N	%	N	%	N	%	N	%	N	%
New Hampshire	1	6.3	0	0	1	33.3	2	12.5	6	20.7	1	100	0	0	4	28.6
Connecticut	0	0	0	0	0	0	0	0	1	3.4	0	0	0	0	0	0
Maine	0	0	2	9.1	0	0	0	0	3	10.4	0	0	0	0	0	0
Massachusetts	1	6.3	3	13.6	0	0	5	31.3	12	41.4	0	0	0	0	1	7.1
Vermont	1	6.2	2	9.1	0	0	0	0	0	0	0	0	0	0	7	50
Subtotal northern New England (N.H., Vt.)	2	12.5	2	9.1	1	33.3	2	12.5	6	20.7	0	0	0	0	11	78.6
Subtotal New England	3	18.8	7	31.8	1	33.3	7	43.8	22	75.9	1	100	0	0	12	85.7
New York	1	6.3	4	18.2	0	0	1	6.3	1	3.4	0	0	0	0	0	0
New Jersey	0	0	1	4.5	0	0	0	0	0	0	0	0	0	0	0	0
North Carolina	1	6.2	0	0	0	0	0	0	0	0	0	0	0	0	0	0
South Carolina	0	0	1	4.5	0	0	0	0	0	0	0	0	0	0	0	0
Pennsylvania	0	0	1	4.6	0	0	0	0	1	3.5	0	0	0	0	0	0
Maryland	0	0	1	4.6	0	0	0	0	0	0	0	0	0	0	0	0
Subtotal Mid-Atlantic	2	12.5	8	36.4	0	0	1	6.3	2	6.9	0	0	0	0	0	0
Colorado	0	0	0	0	0	0	0	0	1	3.4	0	0	0	0	0	0
North Dakota	0	0	1	4.5	0	0	0	0	0	0	0	0	0	0	1	7.1
Illinois	1	6.3	0	0	1	33.3	2	12.5	0	0	0	0	0	0	0	0

Residence	Academical Nongraduates 1851		Academical Nongraduates 1881		Chandler Nongraduates 1881		Medical College Graduates 1851		Medical College Graduates 1881		Thayer School Graduates 1881		Thayer School Nongraduates 1881		Agricultural College Graduates 1881	
	N	%	N	%	N	%	N	%	N	%	N	%	N	%	N	%
Iowa	0	0	1	4.5	0	0	1	6.2	0	0	0	0	0	0	0	0
Kansas	0	0	0	0	0	0	1	6.2	0	0	0	0	0	0	0	0
Missouri	0	0	0	0	0	0	0	0	0	0	0	0	1	33.4	0	0
Minnesota	0	0	1	4.6	1	33.4	0	0	0	0	0	0	0	0	1	7.2
Montana	0	0	0	0	0	0	0	0	0	0	0	0	0	0	0	0
California	0	0	1	4.6	0	0	0	0	2	6.9	0	0	0	0	0	0
Ohio	0	0	1	4.6	0	0	2	12.5	0	0	0	0	0	0	0	0
Wisconsin	1	6.2	0	0	0	0	0	0	0	0	0	0	0	0	0	0
Nebraska	0	0	0	0	0	0	0	0	0	0	0	0	1	33.3	0	0
Nevada	0	0	0	0	0	0	0	0	0	0	0	0	1	33.3	0	0
Subtotal West	2	12.5	5	22.8	2	66.7	6	37.4	3	10.3	0	0	3	100	2	14.3
Florida	1	6.2	1	4.5	0	0	0	0	0	0	0	0	0	0	0	0
Unknown	8	50	1	4.5	0	0	2	12.5	2	6.9	0	0	0	0	0	0
Total	16	100	22	100	3	100	16	100	29	100	1	100	3	100	14	100

Sources: Alumni files, Special Collections, Dartmouth College Library, Hanover, New Hampshire; General Catalogue of Dartmouth College and the Associated Schools 1769-1910, 1769-1925, 1769-1940 (Hanover, N.H., 1910, 1925, 1940); Myron W. Adams, The Class of 1881, Dartmouth College, 1881-1931 (Milford, N.H., 1931).

Notes: Where exact sum of percentages does not equal 100%, the numbers have been rounded off to equal 100%. After an examination of the above sources, the residence chosen was the prime residence during the individual's active professional life.

APPENDIX 22

Percentage of Graduates by Occupation, Academical and Chandler
Graduates of Dartmouth College, 1771 - 1910
(by 40- and 50-Year Periods)

Occupation	1771-1820	1821-1870	1861-1910	1871-1910
Law	36	32	18	17
Ministry	30	21	6	5
Teaching	14	21	17	18
Medicine	10	12	9	9
Subtotal learned professions	90	86	50	49
Business	..	..	29	31
Engineering	..	..	8	..
Other fields	10	14	13	20
Subtotal nontraditional fields	10	14	50	51
Total	100	100	100	100

Source: Adapted from General Catalogue of Dartmouth College and the
Associated Schools 1769-1910 (Hanover, N.H., 1910), p. 839.

APPENDIX 23

Percentage of Graduates by Occupation, Academical and Chandler Graduates of Dartmouth College, 1801-1890 (by Classes)

Classes	Law	Ministry	Medicine	Teaching	Learned Professions	Business	Engineering	Journalism	Farming	Government Service	Misc. and Unknown
1801-10	48.0	20.5	11.0	9.8	89.3	3.0	0	.6	1.2	1.2	4.7
1811-20	39.6	30.1	10.4	10.7	90.8	4.8	.3	.6	.6	0	2.9
1821-30	33.8	34.7	9.4	14.9	92.8	2.0	0	.3	.6	.3	4.0
1831-40	31.6	31.4	9.5	17.3	89.8	4.1	.3	.7	2.9	0	2.2
1841-50	33.3	18.9	16.7	15.4	84.3	6.7	1.5	.7	2.4	.3	4.1
1851-60	35.6	15.4	9.3	15.8	76.1	13.0	2.0	1.0	3.5	.6	3.8
1861-70	27.8	12.6	11.0	15.8	67.2	17.7	4.9	2.3	1.9	.7	5.3
1871-80	29.3	10.6	11.0	16.1	67.0	17.6	4.6	2.1	3.6	0	5.1
1881-90	21.6	9.0	10.4	21.7	62.7	20.4	8.4	4.0	1.0	0	3.5
Average %											
1821-50	32.9	28.3	11.9	15.9	89.0	4.3	.6	.6	2.0	.2	3.4
1851-80	30.9	12.9	10.4	15.9	70.1	16.1	3.8	1.8	3.0	.4	4.7

Source: Adapted from Frank H. Dixon, "Statistics of Vocations of Dartmouth College Graduates," Yale Review (May 1901), p. 84.

APPENDIX 24

Occupation of the Members of the New York Association
of Alumni, Academical and Chandler Departments of
Dartmouth College, 1809-1880

Occupation	Academical and Chandler Graduates				Chandler Scientific Dept. Only	
	1809-1880		1851-1880		1855-1880	
	N	%	N	%	N	%
Law	84	27.2	70	31.1	2	5.4
Medicine	40	12.9	28	12.4	0	0
Ministry	49	15.9	25	11.1	1	2.7
Education	57	18.4	36	16.0	7	18.9
Business[a]	56	18.1	47	20.9	15	40.6
Journalism	4	1.3	4	1.8	0	0
Engineering	7	2.3	7	3.1	7	18.9
Other[b]	12	3.9	8	3.6	5	13.5
Total	309[c]	100	225	100	37[d]	100

Sources: Nineteenth Annual Dinner, Dartmouth College Association
of New York, 1883. The printed announcement contains a list of
graduates in the New York metropolitan area with their year of
graduation and occupation. The General Catalogue of Dartmouth
College and the Associated Schools 1769-1910 (Hanover, N.H., 1910)
was also consulted in the few cases where the occupation was not
listed.

Note: Where exact sum of percentages does not equal 100%, the
numbers have been rounded off to equal 100%.

[a]Business includes categories such as: insurance business,
president, mining company; financial broker; bank president,
treasurer; real estate; general business; publishing; flour
business; merchant; vice-president, New Haven Railroad; paper
business; military goods business; secretary, I.B.& W. Railroad;
iron business; lumber business; president, 23rd St. Railway.

[b]Other includes such categories as artist, dentist, architect,
farmer, postmaster, druggist, mechanic, stenographer, architect,
librarian.

[c]The 1883 list also includes 12 members of the class of 1881 and
9 members of the class of 1882; 2 members of this group were
Chandler graduates, the rest were academical graduates. The
announcement also lists the graduates of the medical college (55)
and those in the area holding honorary degrees from Dartmouth (21),
in addition to the graduates listed in this table.

[d]The 37 members from 1855 to 1880 can be subtracted from the 225
total to get the total of academic graduates alone from 1851 to
1880.

APPENDIX 25

Members of the New York Association of Alumni of the
Academical and Chandler Departments of Dartmouth
College by Year of Graduation, 1809-1880

Year of Graduation	N	%
1809-50		
Subtotal	84	27.2
1851-59	62	20.0
1860-69	46	14.9
1870-80	117	37.9
Subtotal (1851-80)	225	72.8
Total	309[a]	100

Source: Nineteenth Annual Dinner, Dartmouth College
Association of New York, 1883. The printed announcement
contains a list of graduates in the New York metropolitan
area with their year of graduation and occupation.

Note: Where exact sum of percentages does not equal 100%,
the numbers have been rounded off to equal 100%.

[a]See note c, appendix 24.

APPENDIX 26

Occupation of Graduates of New Hampshire College of
Agriculture and the Mechanic Arts,
Dartmouth College, 1871-1892

Occupation	N	%
Clergymen	2	1.5
Lawyers	5	3.6
Physicians	13	9.6
Professors of agriculture	2	1.5
Others connected with agriculture	28	20.6
Other teachers	8	5.9
Civil and mechanical engineers	12	8.8
Architects	2	1.5
Chemists	3	2.2
Electricians	1	.7
Journalists	1	.7
Manufacturers and mechanics	8	5.9
Weather bureau	9	6.6
Business pursuits	38	27.9
Unclassified	2	1.5
Unknown	2	1.5
Total	136	100.0

Source: Adapted from the Catalogue of the New
Hampshire College of Agriculture and the Mechanic
Arts 1890-92 (Concord, N.H., 1892), p.66.

Notes: Where exact sum of percentages does not equal
100%, the numbers have been rounded off to equal 100%.
The school was separated from Dartmouth College and
moved to Durham in 1893.

APPENDIX 27

Age of the Members of the Board of Trustees of Dartmouth College (1851, 1863, 1877, and 1881 Boards)

Age	1851 Board[a]		1863 Board[b]		1877 Board[c]		1881 Board[d]	
	N	%	N	%	N	%	N	%
40-44	0	0	0	0	0	0	1	10
45-49	0	0	0	0	3	30	3	30
50-54	2	20	2	28.6	1	10	3	30
55-59	3	30	0	0	0	0	0	0
60-64	2	20	3	42.8	3	30	0	0
65-69	3	30	1	14.3	1	10	2	20
70-74	0	0	1	14.3	0	0	0	0
75-79	0	0	0	0	2	20	0	0
80-84	0	0	0	0	0	0	1	10
Total	10	100	7	100	10	100	10	100

Sources: General Catalogue of Dartmouth College and the Associated Schools 1769-1910, 1769-1940 (Hanover, N.H., 1910, 1940).

Notes: Where exact sum of percentages does not equal 100%, the numbers have been rounded off to equal 100%. The president of the college and the governor of the state of New Hampshire are not included in this table; they held their seats on the board by virtue of their position.

[a] As of 31 July 1851.

[b] As of 24 July 1863—includes those present and voting regarding the resolutions from the Merrimack County Association of Congregational Churches.

[c] As of 30 January 1877—the date the board chose Bartlett.

[d] As of 28 July 1881—-the date of the report by the board regarding the Bartlett trial.

APPENDIX 28

Occupation of the Members of the Board of Trustees of Dartmouth
College (1851, 1863, 1877, and 1881 Boards)[a]

Occupation	1851 Board		1863 Board		1877 Board		1881 Board	
	N	%	N	%	N	%	N	%
Ministry	4	40	3	42.9	3	30	3	30
Law	5	50	4	57.1	4	40	4	40
Business	1	10	0	0	0	0	1	10
Education	0	0	0	0	1	10	1	10
Medicine	0	0	0	0	2	20	1	10
Total	10	100	7	100	10	100	10	100

Sources: General Catalogue of Dartmouth College and the
Associated Schools 1769-1910, 1769-1940 (Hanover, N. H.,
1910, 1940).

Notes: Where exact sum of percentages does not equal 100%, the
numbers have been rounded off to equal 100%. The president of the
college and the governor of the state of New Hampshire are not
included in this table; they held their seats on the board by
virtue of their position.

[a]See notes a - d, appendix 27.

APPENDIX 29

Occupation of Members of Boards of Trustees of
Fifteen Comparable Institutions, 1860-1890

Occupation	1860-61 %	1870-71 %	1880-81 %	1890-91 %
Clergymen	39.1	34.4	33.3	28.5
Businessmen	22.8	25.4	25.4	24.8
Bankers	4.6	8.4	8.8	11.5
Lawyers	20.6	19.8	21.8	23.7
Educators	5.0	6.8	6.2	7.6
Physicians	4.6	3.1	2.3	3.1
Engineers	.7	.6	.6	0
Farmers	2.1	1.2	.8	.6
Housewives	0	0	.8	.3
Unknown	.4	.3	0	0

Source: Adapted from Earl J. McGrath, "The Control of
Higher Education." Reprinted from Educational Record,
Vol. 18, No. 2 ©️ 1936 by American Council on Education,
Washington, D.C. Used by permission.

Note: The fifteen institutions are Williams, Lafayette,
Amherst, Wesleyan, Lawrence, Hamilton, Wabash, Knox, Yale,
Pennsylvania, Cornell (founded in 1868), Princeton, Beloit,
Carleton (founded in 1866), and Dartmouth.

APPENDIX 30

Occupation of Members of Boards of Trustees of
Five State Universities, 1860-1890

Occupation	1860-61 %	1870-71 %	1880-81 %	1890-91 %
Businessmen	23.9	22.6	28.3	20.8
Lawyers	39.1	33.9	28.3	39.6
Bankers	4.4	3.2	13.0	12.5
Farmers	15.2	6.5	4.3	6.3
Educators	8.7	16.1	13.0	14.6
Physicians	2.1	6.5	8.7	6.3
Clergymen	4.4	11.3	4.3	0
Housewives	0	0	0	0
Engineers	2.2	0	0	0

Source: Adapted from Earl J. McGrath, "The Control of
Higher Education." Reprinted from Educational Record,
Vol. 18, No. 2 ⓒ 1936 by American Council on Education,
Washington, D.C. Used by permission.

Note: The five institutions are Nebraska (founded in 1871),
Missouri, Minnesota, Iowa, and Michigan.

NOTES

Chapter I
Introduction

1. Memorial of the New York Association of Alumni of Dartmouth College, 7 April 1881, in "In the Matter of a Memorial of the New York Association of Alumni Vs. President Bartlett." 10 vols. [17 June 1881–13 July 1881], 10:472 Special Collections, Dartmouth College Library. Hereafter cited as "N.Y. Alumni Assoc. v. Pres. Bartlett."

2. After the trustees invited the faculty and alumni to present their charges in a final hearing, Bartlett demanded that the charges be specific and not just generalizations about tendencies and policies. The New York alumni submitted 5 general charges and 25 specifications against Bartlett. For a list of the specific charges, see appendix 1.

3. "The Trial at Hanover," *New York Times*, 19 June 1881, p. 1.

4. A number of major works in the humanities and social sciences utilize this type of approach. The authors draw broad conclusions from small or specific concrete events, situations, or cases that are representative of larger changes in society. See, for example, Clifford Geertz, *The Interpretation of Cultures: Selected Essays* (New York, 1973); Michael B. Katz, *The Irony of Early School Reform: Educational Innovation in Mid-Nineteenth-Century Massachusetts* (Boston, 1968); Thomas Bender, *Toward an Urban Vision: Ideas and Institutions in Nineteenth-Century America* (Lexington, Ky., 1975); Paul H. Mattingly, *The Classless Profession: American Schoolmen in the Nineteenth Century* (New York, 1975); Samuel P. Hays, "A Systematic Social History," in *American History: Retrospect and Prospect*, ed. George A. Billias and Gerald Grob (New York, 1971), pp. 315–366; Peter L. Berger and Thomas Luckmann, *The Social Construction of Reality: A Treatise in the Sociology of Knowledge* (New York, 1966).

5. There are a number of new historical studies challenging this approach to the study of nineteenth-century higher education. See, for example, James Axtell, "The Death of the Liberal Arts College," *History of Education Quarterly* 11 (1971): 339–352; Hugh Hawkins, "The University-Builders Observe the Colleges," ibid.: 353–362; David B. Potts, "American Colleges in the Nineteenth Century: From Localism to Denominationalism," ibid.: 363–380; Jurgen Herbst, "American College History: Reexamination Underway," ibid. 14 (1974): 259–266; Natalie A. Naylor, "The Ante-Bellum College Movement: A Reappraisal of Tewksberry's Founding of American Colleges and Universities," ibid. 13 (1973): 261–274; David F. Allmendinger, Jr., *Paupers and Scholars: The Transformation of Student Life in Nineteenth-Century New England* (New York, 1975); Wilson Smith, "Apologia pro Alma Matre: The College as Community in Ante-Bellum America," in *The Hofstadter Aegis*, ed. Stanley Elkins

and Eric McKitrick (New York, 1974), pp. 125–153; Lawrence Stone, ed., *The University in Society*, 2 vols. (Princeton, N.J., 1974); Paul H. Mattingly, "The Meaning of Professional Culture," *The Review of Education* 3 (1977): 435–445, and the same author's study, *Classless Profession*. The concepts and methodology developed in this book are important for an assessment of changes in the college faculty as well. See also Douglas Sloan, "Harmony, Chaos, and Consensus: The American College Curriculum," *Teacher's College Record* 73 (1971): 221–251; Thomas Bender, "Science and the Culture of American Communities: The Nineteenth Century," *History of Education Quarterly* 16 (1976): 63–77, and in relation to foundations of intellectual community see his essay, "The Cultures of Intellectual Life: The City and the Professions," in *New Directions in American Intellectual History*, ed. Paul K. Conkin and John Higham (Baltimore, 1979), pp. 181–195; Daniel J. Boorstin, "Universities in the Republic of Letters," *Perspectives in American History* 1 (1967): 369–379; David B. Potts, "'College Enthusiasm!' As Public Response, 1800–1860," *Harvard Educational Review* 47 (1979): 28–42.

6. For a perceptive critique of the problems of a purely functionalist approach, see Floyd Morgan Hammack, "Rethinking Revisionism," *History of Education Quarterly* 16 (1976): 53–66.

For an excellent inquiry into institutionalization and education and the problems of structural functionalism, see Thomas Bender, Peter H. Hall, Thomas Haskell, and Paul H. Mattingly, "Institutionalization and Education in the Nineteenth and Twentieth Centuries," *History of Education Quarterly* 20 (1980): 449–472.

7. See, for example, Richard Hofstadter, "The Revolution in Higher Education," in *Paths of American Thought*, ed. Arthur M. Schlesinger and Morton White (Boston, 1963), pp. 269–290, and Richard Hofstadter and C. DeWitt Hardy, *The Development and Scope of Higher Education in the United States* (New York, 1952).

In histories of this type the main focus is on the curriculum. The curriculum is treated as a "barometer" of educational progress (Hofstadter and Hardy, p. 11). For insights into the limits of this approach for gauging the changing nature of higher education, see authors cited in note 5. Axtell provides a good summary in "Death of the Liberal Arts College." See also the comments of Thomas Le Duc in an older work, *Piety and Intellect at Amherst College 1865–1912* (New York, 1946), especially pp. vii–viii. For a successful attempt to analyze the antebellum curriculum in a broader context, see Sloan, "Harmony, Chaos, and Consensus," For a recent historical survey of the curriculum since 1626, see Frederick Rudolph, *Curriculum: A History of the American Undergraduate Course of Study Since 1626* (San Francisco, 1977). See reviews of Rudolph's book by Wilson Smith, *Academe* 65 (1979): 62–64, and Jurgen Herbst, *History of Education Quarterly* 18 (1978): 481–483.

8. Bernard Bailyn, *Education in the Forming of American Society: Needs and Opportunities for Study* (Chapel Hill, N.C., 1960), p. 9. See also Wilson Smith's critique of the study of the history of education and his suggestions for "the new historian of education," in "Some Notes for a Portrait," *Harvard Educational Review* 31 (1961): 136–143.

9. A number of diverse studies provide critiques of this schema and alternative frameworks. See, for example, Thomas S. Kuhn, *The Structure of Scientific Revolutions*, 2d ed. enl. (Chicago, 1970); Thomas Bender, *Community and Social Change in America* (New Brunswick, N.J., 1978); Anthony F. C. Wallace, *Rockdale: The Growth of an American Village in the Early Industrial Revolution* (New York, 1978); Michael Foucault, *Discipline and Punish: The Birth of the Prison*, trans. Alan Sheridan (New York, 1978).

10. For theoretical frameworks of generation, see Julian Marias, *Generations: A Historical Method*, trans. Harold C. Raley (University, Ala., 1967); Karl Mannheim, "The Problem of Generations," in *Essays on the Sociology of Knowledge*, ed. Paul Kecskemeti (London, 1952), pp. 276–320; Alan B. Spitzer, "The Historical Problem of Generations," *American Historical Review* 78 (1972): 1353–1385.

For an excellent example of the generational approach in relation to the changing nature of professional culture, see Mattingly, *Classless Profession*.

11. In a broader context, changes in the nature of social relations resulting from the growth of a market economy are discussed in Karl Polanyi, *The Great Transformation: The Political and Economic Origins of Our Time* (Boston, 1944). In relation to the altering structure and experience of community in America, Thomas Bender's excellent book, *Community and Social Change in America*, provides the most incisive, probing analysis. For a thoughtful inquiry into changes in human relationships and intellectual changes, see R. Jackson Wilson, *In Quest of Community: Social Philosophy in the United States, 1860–1920* (New York, 1968).

12. For a critique of grand strategic theory as regards educational development, see Stone, *University in Society*, 2:vi.

13. Smith, "Apologia pro Alma Matre," p. 128. I am grateful to Professor Smith for the questions he poses in his essay in relation to the concept of community.

14. C[harles] B. Haddock (professor at Dartmouth), *Collegiate Education: An address on Behalf of the Society for the Promotion of Collegiate and Theological Education at the West, delivered in Tremont Temple, Boston, May 31, 1848* (Boston, 1848), p. 15.

15. *Cincinnati Commercial*, 23 December 1881, n.t., correspondence from Henry C. Lord, an alumnus ["Scrapbook of Newspaper Clippings Relating to the Charges Brought Against President Bartlett by the Dartmouth Alumni Association of New York 1880–1882"], compiled by Henry Griswold Jesup (Dartmouth professor in the 1881 period). Hereafter cited as "Scrapbook." Special Collections, Dartmouth College Library. The "Scrapbook" contains newspaper clippings and handwritten notes regarding the controversy.

16. Nathaniel Hawthorne described students such as these at the commencement of 1838 at Williams College. See *Passages from the American Note-book of Nathaniel Hawthorne* (Boston, 1833), pp. 162, 164.

17. Dink Stover represented the students of the boarding schools and elite clubs who came to college for the pleasant associations. See Owen Johnson, *Stover at Yale*, with an introduction by Kingman Brewster, Jr. (New York, 1968). Johnson was a graduate of Lawrenceville and Yale (1900).

18. Phrase used by Tucker in his description of many of the students of the period, "The Part Which Our Colleges Must Henceforth be Expected To Take in the Training of the Gentleman" [Convocation Address of 1905], *Dartmouth Bi-Monthly* 1 (October 1905): 14.

19. The problem of the generation of institutional theory is discussed by Peter Hall in "Veritas and Pecunias: The Historical Economy of Education," *History of Education Quarterly* 14 (1974): 501; The publication of Thomas Bender's seminal work, *Community and Social Change in America*, has brought us a long way in this process in dealing with changes in community.

The discussion of institutionalization and education by Professors Bender, Hall, Haskell, and Mattingly, in "Institutionalization and Education in the Nineteenth and Twentieth Centuries," provides important insights into problems and opportunities for the generation of theory.

Chapter II
The Faculty

1. C[harles] B. Haddock, *Collegiate Education: An Address on Behalf of the Society for the Promotion of Collegiate and Theological Education at the West, delivered in Tremont Temple, Boston, May 31, 1848* (Boston, 1848), p. 15.

2. Memorial of the Faculty to the Board of Trustees of Dartmouth College, 29 April 1881, cited by Leon Burr Richardson, *History of Dartmouth College*, 2 vols. (Hanover, N.H., 1932), 2:600–601. The document has not survived, but its oral history is noted by Richardson, letters from the period, and the second memorial.

3. Second Memorial of the Faculty to the Board of Trustees of Dartmouth College, 12 July 1881, introduced as evidence (marked Exh. E) in "N.Y. Alumni Assoc. v. Pres. Bartlett," 6:265.

4. Hovey was referring to Eleazar Wheelock, the first president of Dartmouth. "Eleazar Wheelock," in Richard Hovey, *Dartmouth Lyrics*, ed. Francis Lane Childs (Hanover, N.H., 1938), p. 28.

5. John Ordronaux, *Dartmouth College Class of 1850: Report of its golden anniversary meeting, June 26, 1900* (n.p., n.d.), p. 10.

6. Haddock, *Collegiate Education*, p. 11.

7. For varying approaches to the question of professionalism and professional culture, see Burton J. Bledstein, *The Culture of Professionalism: The Middle Class and the Development of Higher Education in America* (New York, 1976); Paul H. Mattingly, "The Meaning of Professional Culture," *The Review of Education* 3 (1977): 435–445; Charles D. Biebel, "Higher Education and Old Professionalism," *History of Education Quarterly* 17 (1977): 319–325 (both authors provide perceptive critiques of Bledstein's work); Thomas Bender, "The Cultures of Intellectual Life: The City and the Professions," in *New Directions in American Intellectual History*, ed. Paul K. Conkin and John Higham (Baltimore, 1979), pp. 181–195; Bender, "Science and the Culture of American Communities: The Nineteenth Century," *History of Education Quarterly* 16 (1976): 63–77; Paul H. Mattingly, *The Classless Profession: American Schoolmen in the Nineteenth Century* (New York, 1975); Magali Sarfatti Larson, *The Rise of Professionalism: A Sociological Analysis* (Berkeley, 1977); Samuel Haber, "The Professions and Higher Education in America: A Historical View," in Margaret Gordon, ed., *Higher Education and the Labor Market* (New York, 1974), pp. 237–280; Thomas L. Haskell, *The Emergence of Professional Social Science: The American Social Science Association and the Nineteenth Century Crisis of Authority* (Urbana, Ill., 1977); Mary O. Furner, *Advocacy and Objectivity: A Crisis in the Professionalization of American Social Science, 1865–1905* (Lexington, Ky., 1975); R. Jackson Wilson, *In Quest of Community: Social Philosophy in the United States, 1860–1920* (New York, 1968); Daniel H. Calhoun, *Professional Lives in America: Structure and Aspiration 1750–1850* (Cambridge, Mass., 1965).

8. Robert A. McCaughey, "The Transformation of American Academic Life: Harvard University, 1821–1892," *Perspectives in American History* 8 (1974): 246.

9. William R. Johnson, "Education and Professional Life Styles: Law and Medicine in the Nineteenth Century," *History of Education Quarterly* 14 (1974): 203. See also William R. Johnson, "Professions in Process: Doctors and Teachers in American Culture," ibid. 15 (1975): 185–199.

10. Biographical information relating to the faculty (both for 1851 and a generation later in 1881) was obtained from the following sources: Alumni Files, Special Collections, Dartmouth College Library, Hanover, N.H.; *Appleton's Cyclopedia of National Biography*, rev. ed. (New York, 1898); *National Cyclopedia of American Biography* (New York, 1907–44); *Dictionary of American Biography* (New York, 1929–44); Richardson, *History of Dartmouth College*, 2 vols.; John King Lord, *A History of Dartmouth College* (Concord, N.H., 1913); Perry Baxter Smith, *The History of Dartmouth College* (Boston, 1878); John King Lord, *A History of the Town of Hanover, N.H.*, with an appendix on Hanover roads by Professor J. W. Goldthwait (Hanover, N.H., 1928); Faculty Manuscript Files, Special Collections, Dartmouth College Library, Hanover, N.H.; Ralph Nading Hill, ed., *The College on the Hill: A Dartmouth Chronicle* (Hanover, N.H., 1964); *General Catalogue of Dartmouth College and the Associated*

Schools 1769–1910, 1769–1940 (Hanover, N.H., 1910, 1940); Arthur Sherburne Hardy, *Things Remembered* (Boston, 1923).

11. With the exception of the professor of medical jurisprudence, the members of the medical faculty were all practicing physicians.

12. Pastoral as used here is not meant to imply proselytizing in the narrow sectarian sense, but as relating to the care and guidance of one's "flock" in building a Christian nation.

13. The faculty member is included in the academical faculty because until 1866 his major duties were in the Academical Department.

14. The literature indicates that Edwin David Sanborn was one of the best examples of college teachers during this period. He has been called "an example of the college teacher at his best in the days before productive scholarship, in the technical sense, became a requirement of the professor." *Dictionary of American Biography*, under Sanborn, Edwin David. The age range of the academical faculty in 1851 reveals a clustering around Sanborn's age of forty-three. All but two of the faculty were forty-three, plus or minus seven years. The clustering around Sanborn's age seems to indicate a commonality in terms of *vigencia*—customs, usages, beliefs, traditions, "that currently prevail in a given society or collectivity." Julian Marias, *Generations: A Historical Method*, trans. Harold C. Raley (University, Ala., 1967), p. 81.

15. Some of the faculty also served in the position of professor emeritus and thus had an affiliation with Dartmouth beyond that listed here as their active status.

16. David B. Potts, "American Colleges in the Nineteenth Century: From Localism to Denominationalism," *History of Education Quarterly* 11 (1971): 367; see also for community-college orientation, Potts, " 'College Enthusiasm!' As Public Response, 1800–1860," *Harvard Educational Review* 47 (1979): 28–42; Wilson Smith, "Apologia pro Alma Matre: The College as Community in Ante-Bellum America," in *The Hofstadter Aegis*, ed. Stanley Elkins and Eric McKitrick (New York, 1974), pp. 125–153.

17. In reference to the idea and significance of the concepts of audience and status and changes during the nineteenth century, see Bender, "Science and the Culture of Communities," and by the same author, "The Cultures of Intellectual Life."

18. *Dictionary of American Biography*, under Brown, Samuel Gilman.

19. For an analysis of the cultural significance of the rural cemetery movement in mid-nineteenth-century America, see Thomas Bender, *Toward an Urban Vision: Ideas and Institutions in Nineteenth-Century America* (Lexington, Ky., 1975), pp. 80–87.

20. For a description of Haddock's activities as a moral philosopher, see Wilson Smith, *Professors & Public Ethics: Studies of Northern Moral Philosophers before the Civil War* (Ithaca, N.Y., 1958), pp. 111–127. Smith characterizes Haddock as "the best Yankee example of a moral philosopher-political economist translating his classroom dictum into legislative action and corporate enterprise." *Professors & Public Ethics*, p. 112.

21. George Adams Boyd, *Three Stimsons and a Bartlett*, with family data compiled by Dorothy Stimson (Stonington, Conn., 1967), p. 80.

22. Henry A. Hazen, *Congregational and Presbyterian Ministry and Churches in New Hampshire* (Boston, 1875), cited by Calhoun, *Professional Lives in America* p. 122.

23. Haddock, as quoted in Richardson, *History of Dartmouth College*, 2:457.

24. Within this context, it should also be noted that the former occupations of the faculty consisted of a teaching or ministry background. Seven of the faculty members had some experience as schoolmen.

For an excellent study of schoolmen during the nineteenth century, see Mattingly, *Classless Profession*. The concepts and methodology utilized in this study are important for an assessment of the changing nature of nineteenth-century college faculty as well.

25. Mattingly, *Classless Profession*, p. 22.

26. See, for example, Natalie A. Naylor, "The Theological Seminary in the Configuration of American Higher Education," *History of Education Quarterly* 17 (1977): 23–26; James Findlay, "The SPECTEW and Western Colleges: Religion and Higher Education in Mid-Nineteenth-Century America," *History of Education Quarterly* 17 (1977): 47; Thomas Le Duc, *Piety and Intellect at Amherst College 1865–1912* (New York, 1946); Frederick Rudolph, *Mark Hopkins and the Log: Williams College, 1836–1872* (New Haven, 1956).

27. Calhoun, *Professional Lives in America*, pp. 166, 161.

28. Ibid., p. 168.

29. Hopkinton Association Records, 1804–40, New Hampshire Historical Society, cited by Calhoun, *Professional Lives in America*, p. 168.

30. Sidney E. Mead, "The Rise of the Evangelical Conception of the Ministry in America, 1607–1850," in *The Ministry in Historical Perspective*, ed. H. Richard Niebuhr and Daniel D. Williams (New York, 1956), p. 228.

31. Ibid.

32. Ibid., p. 229.

33. Ordronaux, *Class of 1850*, p. 10.

34. Amos N. Currier, "Dartmouth College Fifty Years Ago," *Dartmouth Bi-Monthly* 1 (1906): 245.

35. Albea Godbold, *Church Colleges of the Old South* (Durham, N.C., 1944), pp. 96–100.

36. Haddock, *Collegiate Education*, p. 7.

37. Students were sent to a minister or some responsible person for special care for a period of time.

38. Records of the Faculty, 30 April 1851, Special Collections, Dartmouth College Library, Hanover, N.H. Although these were the usual punishments, in extreme cases students might be separated permanently from the college.

39. Currier, "Dartmouth College Fifty Years Ago," p. 253.

40. For explanations of the influence and significance of moral philosophy and the instructed conscience, see Smith, *Professors & Public Ethics*, and D. H. Meyer, *The Instructed Conscience* (Philadelphia, 1972).

41. Samuel Gilman Brown, "The Spirit of a Scholar," *Bibliotheca Sacra and Theological Review* 6 (1849): 127. David Potts, in an article on Baptist colleges in nineteenth-century America ("American Colleges"), notes that the colleges in the antebellum period were not the narrow sectarian institutions usually described in traditional histories but local enterprises very much a part of the community. This study of Dartmouth would seem to indicate that his view is correct, but his underestimation of the religious element in terms of the guidance and care of one's "flock" for the social and moral progress of a Christian nation gives us only a partial picture of the college during this period.

42. Brown, "Spirit of a Scholar," p. 129.

43. Ibid., p. 133.

44. Quoted in ibid., p. 134. The quotation is set in capitals in the article.

45. Haddock, *Collegiate Education*, p. 7. Although this was probably written in the vein of a promotional effort, the collected data seem to indicate that he held these views.

46. *Remarks of E[dwin] D. Sanborn, in the State Constitutional Convention on the Resolution to Create a Superintendent of Public Instruction, December 21, 1850* (Concord, N.H., 1850), p. 3.

47. Ibid., p. 9.

48. "Speech of Professor Sanborn," *Boston Daily Journal*, 3 November 1853, Alumni Files, under "Sanborn."

49. Haddock, *Collegiate Education*, p. 11.

50. Sanborn to Fairbanks, 9 July 1851, Sanborn Manuscript File. The students went to St. Johnsbury to participate in a public celebration.

51. Ibid.

52. Ibid.

53. This is consistent with a more general pattern suggested by Smith that antebellum colleges were "meant to 'serve' the outside community by codifying and inculcating the community's own best principles, and thus to function as an integral part of civic life." "Apologia pro Alma Matre," p. 132.

54. *Hanover Gazette*, n.d., Alumni Files, under "Sanborn."

55. Smith, *Professors & Public Ethics*, p. 111.

56. For changes in intellectual style as well as in the concepts of audience and status, see Bender, "Cultures of Intellectual Life" and "Science and the Culture of American Communities."

57. For illuminating developments of this point, see Bender, *Toward an Urban Vision*, and Michael H. Frisch, *Town into City: Springfield, Massachusetts, and the Meaning of Community 1840–1880* (Cambridge, Mass., 1972), and especially Thomas Bender, *Community and Social Change in America*, (Rutgers, N.J., 1978).

58. Along with their lack of teaching experience, they became professors at a young age. This seems to parallel developments in the ministry during this period. A study of New Hampshire Congregational and Presbyterian clergy confirms complaints of ministers that churches were looking for young men—"not the man of maturity and profundity, but . . . the fresh personality." Calhoun, *Professional Lives in America*, p. 152.

59. William S. Tyler, *Prayer for Colleges*, new ed. (Boston, 1877), p. 164, quoted in Thomas Le Duc, *Piety and Intellect at Amherst College 1865–1912* (New York, 1946), p. 9.

60. President William A. Stearns to Samuel Williston, 30 January 1856, quoted in Le Duc, *Piety and Intellect*, p. 11. For an interesting discussion of the pastoral ideal and the development of good citizens, see Leo Marx, *The Machine in the Garden* (New York, 1964).

61. Haddock, *Collegiate Education*, p. 15.

62. See, for example, Le Duc, *Piety and Intellect*, p. 6.

63. See, for example, Anne Firor Scott, "The Ever Widening Circle: The Diffusion of Feminist Values from the Troy Female Seminary 1822–1872," *History of Education Quarterly* 19 (1979): 7, and Phillida Bunkle, "Sentimental Womanhood and Domestic Education 1830–1870," *History of Education Quarterly* 14 (1974): 21.

64. The data regarding the Harvard faculty are derived from McCaughey's study of the Harvard faculty in 1845, "Transformation of American Academic Life."

65. While McCaughey notes that the faculty were locally rooted, he provides little information regarding their associational involvements in the community, so one cannot begin to assess the extent of their community involvement.

66. McCaughey, "Transformation of American Academic Life," pp. 327, 332, 256, 258, 331.

67. See, for example, Edward Everett [President of Harvard], *Orations and Speeches on Various Occasions*, 2 vols. (Boston, 1850), 2:493–518.

68. For an excellent portrayal of the medical profession in nineteenth-century America, see Johnson, "Education and Professional Life Styles." For an example of competition among physicians in New York, see Calhoun, *Professional Lives in America*, pp. 20–58. For a treatment of the medical profession in Stuart England and the relationship between education and status, see James Axtell, "Education and Status in Stuart England: The London Physicians," *History of Education Quarterly* 10 (1970): 141–159. One might compare the pattern of the London physicians and the apothecaries and the "regular" and "irregular" physicians in early-nineteenth-century America; cf. Johnson, "Education and Professional Life Styles," and Johnson, "Professions in Process."

69. No information was available regarding the age of the demonstrator; he did not remain on the faculty.

70. For a description of their contributions to the literature of the period, see *Dictionary of American Biography*, under Peaslee, Edmund Randolph; *National Cyclopedia of American Biography*, under Peaslee, Edmund Randolph; *Dictionary of American Biography*, under Parker, Joel.

71. Phineas Sanborn Conner, "Historical Address," in *Centennial Exercises, Dartmouth College Medical School, June 29, 1897* (Hanover, N.H., 1897), pp. 17–18.

72. From J. W. Barstow's obituary notice in the *New York Medical Journal* (November 1873), quoted in Smith,*History of Dartmouth College*, p. 356.

73. Ibid., pp. 356–357; Conner, "Historical Address," pp. 22–23; for a description of the outstanding accomplishments of Peaslee, however, for his era, see Dr. T. A. Emmet of New York regarding Peaslee, quoted in Smith, *History of Dartmouth College*, pp. 358–360.

74. Conner, "Historical Address," p. 18.

75. See Lord, *History of Dartmouth College*, p. 662.

76. Hill, *College on the Hill*, p. 105.

77. Conner, "Historical Address," p. 17.

78. Peaslee moved to New York and held numerous positions in other medical institutions.

79. Quoted in Conner, "Historical Address," p. 11.

80. Ibid.

81. A committee made an examination of the school on a yearly basis and reported to the board. See Lord, *History of Dartmouth College*, p. 262.

82. "Officers of the Faculty," in *Centennial Exercises*, p. 75.

83. Conner, "Historical Address," p. 7, and Richardson, *History of Dartmouth College*, 1:421.

84. Established in 1852 through a bequest.

85. Established in 1871 through a bequest.

86. Established in 1866 through the will of David Culver for the establishment of an agricultural school at Dartmouth College and through the Morrill Act. Through an act passed in 1891, the school was separated from Dartmouth College, and in 1893 the school opened at its new site in Durham.

87. The original document has not survived, and the two historians of the college differ as to the exact number. One says seven out of twelve; the other says six out of eleven. See Lord, *History of Dartmouth College*, p. 432, and Richardson, *History of Dartmouth College*, 2:601. The difference seems to relate to including or not including the tutor.

88. One of Bartlett's supporters was his son, Edwin J. Bartlett. One of those who did not sign the documents was neutral throughout the controversy. Another one, according to Bartlett's biographer, was not really in sympathy with Bartlett either. See Boyd, *Three Stimsons and a Bartlett*, p. 108.

89. Hardy regarding Bartlett, "N.Y. Alumni Assoc. v. Pres. Bartlett," 2:37; see also Bartlett, 8:360–361.

90. Hardy, "N.Y. Alumni Assoc. v. Pres. Bartlett," 2:28. Professors John K. Lord and Daniel Noyes followed Hardy on this point. But Bartlett replied that it was "unwise to discuss the matter there; it would complicate matters." Hardy regarding Bartlett, "N.Y. Alumni Assoc. v. Pres. Bartlett," 2:28. Bartlett made the remarks regarding their reputation and their lack of influence at the second faculty meeting, after the faculty forced the issue.

91. Bartlett, "N.Y. Alumni Assoc. v. Pres. Bartlett," 8:364, 366–67.

92. Hardy, "N.Y. Alumni Assoc. v. Pres. Bartlett," 2:29–30.

93. Louis Pollens [professor of French], "N.Y. Alumni Assoc. v. Pres. Bartlett," 2:86.

94. Lord, "N.Y. Alumni Assoc. v. Pres. Bartlett," 2:55,49.

95. McCaughey, "Transformation of American Academic Life," p. 298, n. 8.

96. Hardy, "N.Y. Alumni Assoc. v. Pres. Bartlett," 2:37. See also Bartlett, 8:360–361.

97. Bartlett, "N.Y. Alumni Assoc. v. Pres. Bartlett," 9:420.

98. Ibid., 8:361, 362, 370.

99. Cosmopolitan as used here refers to faculty members whose backgrounds, associations, identities, aspirations, and experiences are not connected just to the local area or institution.

100. Professionalized characterizes a new professorial style emphasizing the values of specialization in a discipline, advanced training in that discipline, apprenticeship in the form of college teaching, identification with one's peers in that discipline in other colleges and universities, reputation based on publication in the form of original research for the consumption of other scholars, and peer evaluation for appointment.

101. For Princeton see Patricia Albjerg Graham, *Community & Class in American Education 1865–1918* (New York, 1974), p. 188. For Harvard see McCaughey, "Transformation of American Academic Life."
For analyses of those who studied at the German universities and their influence on American higher education, see Carl Diehl, "Innocents Abroad: American Students in German Universities, 1810–1870," *History of Education Quarterly* 16 (1976): 321–339, and Jurgen Herbst, *The German Historical School in American Scholarship* (Ithaca, N.Y., 1969).

102. McCaughey, "Transformation of American Academic Life," p. 331.

103. See Le Duc, *Piety and Intellect*, p. 50, and Rudolph, *Mark Hopkins and the Log*, p. 131.

104. For Franklin and Marshall College, see W. Bruce Leslie, "A Comparative Study of Four Middle Atlantic Colleges, 1870–1915: Bucknell University, Franklin and Marshall College, Princeton University, and Swarthmore College" (Ph.D. diss., Johns Hopkins University, 1971), pp. 64, 163.

105. The age range of the full professors in 1881 was between thirty-three and seventy-three. Nearly two thirds, however, were between thirty-three and forty-five, seeming to form a younger cohort group (see appendix 6). If one includes the lower ranks such as associate professors, the younger cohort group becomes even more accentuated.

106. McCaughey, "Transformation of American Academic Life," p. 332.

107. Ibid., p. 327.

108. Ibid., p. 329.

109. Ibid., pp. 330, 329.

110. Some of the faculty served in the position of professor emeritus beyond their active service noted here.

111. Probably in an attempt to attract and keep a more cosmopolitan, professionalized faculty, in 1869 the trustees raised the faculty salaries considerably. While their salaries were lower than those in upper-middle-class positions, the salary scale did not compare unfavorably with that of other colleges, and the cost of living in a rural area such as Hanover probably was lower than in some other areas. For a discussion of this point see p. 118 of this study.

112. See, for example, McCaughey, "Transformation of American Academic Life," p. 244, and Alvin W. Gouldner, "Cosmopolitans and Locals: Toward an Analysis of Latent Social Roles," *Administrative Science Quarterly* 2 (1957–58): 281–306.

113. See Bender, *Community and Social Change in America*, p. 93; see also comments of Mattingly regarding "vertical vision" in reference to careers, "Meaning of Professional Culture."

114. Within the context of the shift in audience and status, see Bender, "Science and the Culture of Communities" and "Cultures of Intellectual Life."

115. For a discussion of why the local involvement remained despite the growing metropolitan orientation, see pp. 51–52 of this study.

116. For changes in intellectual styles as well as the changing institutional context, see Bender, "Science and the Culture of Communities" and "Cultures of Intellectual Life." See also Wilson, *In Quest of Community.*

117. William Jewett Tucker, Bartlett's successor, describes the changed societal environment from his perspective in *My Generation: An Autobiographical Interpretation* (Boston, 1919), pp. 1–18.

118. To this point, R. Jackson Wilson notes, for example, "The emphasis shifted (to oversimplify the matter considerably) from moral insight to matter-of-fact knowledge, from Emerson's poet at the one extreme, to Thorstein Veblen's 'engineer' at the other." *In Quest of Community*, p. 40.

119. This is not meant to imply that the emphasis on character and the evangelical was abandoned completely; see p. 138 of this study.

120. For an analysis of this point in relation to a shift in the qualities of intelligence that were developed and valued, see Daniel Calhoun, *The Intelligence of a People* (Princeton, N.J., 1973).

121. For the development of this point as it applied to the undergraduate curriculum and from the perspective of a Dartmouth professor from this period, see John Henry Wright, "The Place of Original Research in College Education," *Journal of Addresses and Proceedings of the National Educational Association* (1882); 91–117. Wright hints at the concentration of majors in the junior and senior years eventually adopted by Dartmouth and other colleges.

122. Hill, *College on the Hill*, p. 139.

123. For a portrayal of students who studied in Germany before 1870 and their influence upon American higher education, see Diehl, "Innocents Abroad." For students in the later period, see Herbst, *German Historical School.*

124. Edwin B. Frost, *An Astronomer's Life* (Boston, 1933), p. 22.

125. "The Church and the Men of the Seventies," *Hanover Gazette*, 1 December 1921.

126. Richardson, *History of Dartmouth College*, 2:612.

127. Robert H. Wiebe, *The Search for Order 1877–1920*, with an introduction by David Donald (New York, 1967), p. 112.

128. Testimony of Professor Pollens, "N.Y. Alumni Assoc. v. Pres. Bartlett," 2:86.

129. While one does not find the complete segmentation into departments that would emerge later in the century, another faculty member's testimony illustrates the beginnings of such assertions. Bartlett indicated to instructor Thomas W. D. Worthen that a place might be available for him in the Chandler school, probably in theoretical and applied mechanics. Worthen replied, "My first impulse is to consult the faculty of that department, to ascertain their wishes with reference to this matter." "N.Y. Alumni Assoc. v. Pres. Bartlett," 2:100.

130. George E. Peterson, *The New England College in the Age of the University* (Amherst, 1964), p. 102.

131. Ibid., p. 116.

132. Pollens, "N.Y. Alumni Assoc. v. Pres. Bartlett," 2:82.

133. Hardy, "N.Y. Alumni Assoc. v. Pres. Bartlett," 7:312. Hardy seems to be referring to James Joseph Sylvester and Benjamin Peirce, two of the greatest mathematicians of the period. *See Dictionary of American Biography*, under Sylvester, James Joseph, and Peirce, Benjamin.

134. Parker, "N.Y. Alumni Assoc. v. Pres. Bartlett," 10:452.

135. Worthen, regarding Bartlett, "N.Y. Alumni Assoc. v. Pres. Bartlett," 2:100.

136. Hardy, "N.Y. Alumni Assoc. v. Pres. Bartlett," 2:28.

137. Pollens, "N.Y. Alumni Assoc. v. Pres. Bartlett," 2:86–87.

138. Hardy, "N.Y. Alumni Assoc. v. Pres. Bartlett," 2:41.

139. "General Answer," inserted in a volume of testimony. It has no signature, but it has a watermark. This probably was a document, not only of the academical faculty, but of the sixteen members who signed the memorials.

140. Records of the Faculty, 31 August 1881. See also Peterson, *New England College*, p. 227, n. 4, regarding formal designation of faculty meetings at Union College (rather than by presidential decision) after complaints by the faculty.

141. By age in 1881, they also seemed to form a younger cohort group. The age range of the full professors was between thirty-one and fifty-three; three of these were between thirty-one and forty-five (see appendix 6).

Their stay at Dartmouth ranged from twenty-two years to forty-one years. The tutor stayed at Dartmouth eight years. He was promoted to the position of instructor and then left to accept a position as a professor at Northwestern.

142. Edward R. Ruggles, "N.Y. Alumni Assoc. v. Pres. Bartlett," 7:254.

The department was established as a result of a $50,000 bequest by Abiel Chandler. Instruction was to be "in the practical and useful arts of life, comprised chiefly in the branches of mechanics and civil engineering, the invention and manufacture of machinery, carpentry, masonry, architecture, and drawing, the investigation of the properties and uses of the materials employed in the arts, the modern languages, and English literature, together with book-keeping and such other branches of knowledge as may best qualify young persons for the duties and employments of active life." Will of Abiel Chandler, quoted in Lord, *History of Dartmouth College*, p. 294.

143. In 1857 John Woodman became director of the school and professor of civil engineering. Under Woodman the course was increased to four years, the curriculum was expanded, and the admissions standard raised. The board went along with this and seemed to have permitted the Chandler faculty to determine policy, including a further increase in admission requirements, until a permanent policy could be decided upon by the board (see statement of Wheelock G. Veazey, board member, "N.Y. Alumni Assoc. v. Pres. Bartlett," 6:211). This was the policy when Bartlett became president. The Chandler Department had a separate faculty, but many of the members of the academical faculty taught in the Chandler school. (Name changed to "Department" in 1865, by vote of the board.)

Some of the measures passed by the board were the following: (a) No notice or advertisement should be issued by any department in the college without the approval of the president. (b) A larger share of the general college expenses were assigned to the Chandler school. (c) Members of the academical faculty who taught in the Chandler school had to turn over one half of their compensation to the college treasury. (d) The entrance requirements were revised so that most of the algebra requirements and all of the plane geometry requirements were eliminated. (e) The bachelor of letters degree was established in the Academical Department. It eliminated Greek from the course of study and added some courses in modern languages, science, and mathematics. At the same time, the board voted that it was opposed to any changes that would debase or degrade the Chandler Scientific Department. They left the course of study essentially the same. At the time of the trial, with the added insistence of the alumni, they restored the entrance requirements, one of the most hotly debated points.

144. Bartlett to the Secretary of the Boston Correspondents, quoted in Richardson, *History of Dartmouth College*, 2:625.

145. Ruggles, regarding Bartlett, "N.Y. Alumni Assoc. v. Pres. Bartlett," 6:234.

In reference to Bartlett's concern that the scientific section was attracting students away from the "pure" liberal arts, one should note that around 1880 some educators began to believe whether correctly or not that a majority of the "bright young men" were entering scientific fields. "Pres. Report," College of New Jersey, 10 November 1881, quoted in Laurence R. Veysey, *The Emergence of the American University* (Chicago, 1965), p. 175.

146. Samuel C. Bartlett, "Inaugural Address," June 1877, quoted in Smith, *History of Dartmouth College*, p. 206.

147. Ibid., p. 200.

148. Ruggles, "N.Y. Alumni Assoc. v. Pres. Bartlett," 6:261.

149. Ruggles, regarding Bartlett, "N.Y. Alumni Assoc. v. Pres. Bartlett," 6:227.

150. Ibid.

151. Bartlett, "N.Y. Alumni Assoc. v. Pres. Bartlett," 8:391.

152. Ruggles, regarding Bartlett, "N.Y. Alumni Assoc. v. Pres. Bartlett," 2:110.

153. The school was established through a gift of $40,000 for this purpose from Gen. Sylvanus Thayer of Braintree, Massachusetts, a graduate of Dartmouth and of West Point. Thayer increased his donation so that it equalled $70,000.

154. Bartlett, regarding Fletcher, "N.Y. Alumni Assoc. v. Pres. Bartlett," 9:405.

155. Diary of Robert Fletcher, 1877 (no page number is indicated, but the notation is on a page with the date 8 March 1877 crossed out). Special Collections, Dartmouth College Library, Hanover, N.H.

156. Hazen to Carr, 2 March 1881, Hazen Manuscript File.

157. See Daniel H. Calhoun, *The American Civil Engineer: Origin and Conflict* (Cambridge, Mass., 1960).

For an interpretation of the professionalization of engineers after 1880 and their role in shaping modern industrial society, see David F. Noble, *America by Design: Science, Technology, and the Rise of Corporate Capitalism* (New York, 1977).

158. See Monte A. Calvert, "The Search for Engineering Unity: The Professionalization of Special Interest," in *Building the Organizational Society*, ed. Jerry Israel, with an introduction by Samuel P. Hayes (New York, 1972), pp. 44, 46.

159. There were occasional lecturers in agriculture as well.

160. Blanpied regarding Bartlett, "N.Y. Alumni Assoc. v. Pres. Bartlett," 5:174.

161. Blanpied quoting Bartlett, "N.Y. Alumni Assoc. v. Pres. Bartlett," 5:174.

162. Bartlett, "N.Y. Alumni Assoc. v. Pres. Bartlett," 9:411.

163. Blanpied, "N.Y. Alumni Assoc. v. Pres. Bartlett," 5:175.

164. Pettee, "N.Y. Alumni Assoc. v. Pres. Bartlett," 5:191.

165. The professor of chemistry in the Academical Department and the assistant in that department also lectured as instructors in the Medical College.

166. Johnson discusses these points in "Professions in Process."

167. Conner to Veazey, 6 March 1881, Conner Manuscript File.

168. U.S. Department of the Interior, Census Office, *Statistics of the Population of the United States at the Tenth Census, June 1, 1880* (Washington, D.C., 1883).

169. In line with this point, see Ronald C. Tobey, "How Urbane Is the Urbanite? An Historical Model of the Urban Hierarchy and the Social Motivation of Service Classes," *Historical Methods Newsletter* 7 (1974): 259–275. Tobey notes that during this period, places having populations between 1,501 and 7,201 are not cities and do not have "urbane social structures." "Urban Hierarchy," p. 271.

170. See, for example, L. A. Wait, "Advanced Instruction in American Colleges," *Harvard Register* 3 (1881): 129–130; F. W. Clarke, "The Appointment of College Officers," *Popular Science Monthly* 21 (1882): 171–178; W. T. Hewett, "University Administration," *Atlantic Monthly* 50 (1882): 512–513, cited by Veysey, *American University*, p. 175.

171. For a Dartmouth faculty member's discussion of the new ideas and standards of higher learning and the problematic question of how to keep some framework of unity in undergraduate liberal arts education, see Arthur Sherburne Hardy, "The New Departure

in Education," *Lectures, Discussions, and Proceedings of the American Institute of Instruction* 57 (1887): 55–75.

For an analysis of the debates among faculty and presidents over the goals and aims of the university, see Veysey, *The Emergence of the American University.*

Chapter III
The Students

1. Frederick Rudolph, "Neglect of Students as a Historical Tradition," in *The College and the Student,* ed. Lawrence E. Dennis and Joseph F. Kaufman (Washington, D.C., 1966), p. 47.

2. For an analysis of the recent literature on college students, see David B. Potts, "Students and the Social History of American Higher Education," *History of Education Quarterly* 15 (1975): 317–327.

For overall changes in youth in American society, see Joseph F. Kett, *Rites of Passage: Adolescence in America, 1790 to the Present* (New York, 1977).

3. Rudolph, "Neglect of Students as a Historical Tradition," p. 53, and Frederick Rudolph, *The American College and University* (New York, 1962), chaps. 7, 18.

4. David F. Allmendinger, Jr., *Paupers and Scholars: The Transformation of Student Life in Nineteenth-Century New England* (New York, 1975), p. 129.

5. Lawrence Stone provides an excellent discussion of the significance of this type of approach. See Introduction to *The University in Society* (Princeton, N.J., 1974), 2:v–vi.

6. While Allmendinger describes how poor students brought changes to antebellum college life, it has also been suggested that wealthy students in antebellum colleges were the prime agents of student disturbances and that these disturbances were found primarily in colleges with a predominance of such students. See Wilson Smith, "Apologia pro Alma Matre: The College as Community in Ante-Bellum America," in *The Hofstadter Aegis,* ed. Stanley Elkins and Eric McKitrick (New York, 1974), pp. 125–153. Kathryn Moore has found a similar relationship in eighteenth-century Harvard; see "The War with the Tutors: Student-Faculty Conflict at Harvard and Yale, 1745–1771," *History of Education Quarterly* 18 (1978): 115–127.

For another interpretation of student protests in the very early part of the nineteenth century, see Steven J. Novak, *The Rights of Youth: American Colleges and Student Revolt, 1798–1815* (Cambridge, Mass., 1977). David Allmendinger provides a perceptive critique of this study; see *American Historical Review* 83 (1978): 272.

7. Dr. J. W. Barstow, class of 1846, quoted in John King Lord, *A History of Dartmouth College: 1815–1909* (Concord, N.H., 1913), p. 330.

8. Quoted in Leon Burr Richardson, *History of Dartmouth College* (Hanover, N.H., 1932) 2:472.

9. Richardson, *History of Dartmouth College,* 2:472.

10. Hon. J. W. Patterson, class of 1848, quoted in Lord, *History of Dartmouth College,* p. 330.

11. The document is cited in the histories of the college and articles from the period. See Richardson, *History of Dartmouth College,* 2:602, and "Dr. Bartlett on Trial," *New York Times,* 18 July 1881, p. 5. This article notes that only six students declined to sign it and that the others were not consulted for lack of time.

There also seems to have been other petitions circulated against Bartlett—one shortly after he assumed the presidency, and one in 1879 that was presented to Governor Prescott (member of the board of trustees). See "N.Y. Alumni Assoc. v. Pres. Bartlett," 9:433–434, and "Dartmouth College: How the Seniors Look at It," *Boston Journal*, 11 May 1881, "Scrapbook."

12. Memorial of the New York Association of Alumni of Dartmouth College, 11 June 1881, Special Collections, Dartmouth College Library, Hanover, N.H. See appendix 1, pp. 145–149 of this study.

13. Junior, "Some Students' Views of Dartmouth's Crisis," *Boston Journal*, 7 May 1881, "Scrapbook." President Bartlett's son was a member of the class of 1882, and some members of that class wrote a letter signed Junior to which the seniors responded accusing the writer of being a friend of Bartlett or his son. See "Dartmouth College: How the Seniors Look at It."

The only other general comment favorable to the president seems to be one in the *Dartmouth* (student publication) in 1883 in which the author of the article expresses the support of the students for Bartlett and the faculty. The article is quoted in Richardson, *History of Dartmouth College*, 2:612.

14. "How the Seniors Look at It."

15. "Pocket Elucidator," *Aegis*, class of 1883, p. 94.

16. The reference here seems to be to the story of a Christian who was struck dead after lying about his church donation. It seems to be used here in reference to Bartlett's lying about the 1881 charges.

17. *New York World* quoted in *Wesleyan Argus* 20 (8 March 1887): 116–117, cited in George E. Peterson, *The New England College in the Age of the University* (Amherst, 1964), p. 97.

18. Amos N. Currier, "Dartmouth College Fifty Years Ago," *Dartmouth Bi-Monthly* 1 (1906): 249.

19. Mellen Chamberlain, *Address at the Dedication of Wilson Hall, Dartmouth College Library, June 22, 1885* (n.p., n.d.), p. 2.

20. Clarence B. Little, *History of the Class of Eighty-One: Freshman History '81* (n.p., 1881), p. 6.

21. The General Catalogue lists only the graduates of the Medical College. Although one can find lists of when students spent some time at the medical school without graduating, it is difficult to assign a particular class to them as to the year when they might have graduated. Tables relating to the medical graduates, the other students of the associated schools, and the academical and Chandler nongraduates appear in appendixes 16–21.

22. Northern New England as defined here includes New Hampshire and Vermont. These areas remained largely agricultural as opposed to southern New England, which turned to manufacturing. See Harold Fisher Wilson, *The Hill Country of Northern New England: Its Social and Economic History 1790–1930* (New York, 1936), pp. 4–5. Although Maine to a lesser degree is included in the division of northern New England, it is not included in this category because New Hampshire and Vermont were the major recruiting areas for Dartmouth students during this period.

During the early part of the Lord administration, 84.3% of the students came from New Hampshire and Vermont (74.6% of these were from New Hampshire). See Ralph Nading Hill, ed., *The College on the Hill: A Dartmouth Chronicle* (Hanover, N.H., 1964), p. 74.

23. Wilson, *The Hill Country of Northern New England*, pp. 48–50.

24. Such students included George Bell, the son of Governor Bell; Redfield Proctor, the son of a manufacturer who held numerous state offices and who would himself become governor of Vermont; and Nathan Lord, the son of the president of Dartmouth.

25. See Allmendinger's *Paupers and Scholars* for the general patterns in New England colleges.

26. That they were the sons of farmers does not necessarily imply that they were of limited financial circumstances. One would need to know the wealth of the students to support definitely this conclusion. But, in the case of Dartmouth students during this

period, the writings from the period and the other collected data indicate that they were of limited financial circumstances.

27. For a description of such students at the commencement of 1838 at Williams College, see Nathaniel Hawthorne, *Passages from the American Note-books of Nathaniel Hawthorne* (Boston, 1883), pp. 162, 164.

28. John Ordronaux, *Dartmouth College, Class of 1850: Report of its golden anniversary meeting at commencement, June 26, 1900* (n.d., n.p.), p. 11.

29. This category includes carpenter, blacksmith, shoe cutter, printer. For occupational divisions in the nineteenth century see Michael B. Katz, "Occupational Classification in History," *Journal of Interdisciplinary History* 3 (1972): 63–68. See also Paul H. Mattingly, *The Classless Profession: American Schoolmen in the Nineteenth Century* (New York, 1975), p. 217.

30. Business includes manufacturer, merchant, agent, treasurer, railroad company.

31. Alumni Files under "Shepard," Special Collections, Dartmouth College Library, Hanover, N.H.

32. The Catalogue for 1850–51 states: "Students whose circumstances render it necessary for them to take schools in the winter, are permitted to be absent fourteen weeks from the close of the Fall Terms." *Catalogue of the Officers and Students of Dartmouth College 1850–51* (Hanover, N.H., 1850), p. 22.

33. See Allmendinger, *Paupers and Scholars*.

34. Samuel E. Herrick, class of 1859, *An Address in Memory of William Seymour Tyler* (n.p., n.d.), p. 10, quoted in Thomas Le Duc, *Piety and Intellect at Amherst College 1865–1912* (New York, 1946), p. 7, n. 12.

35. Le Duc, *Piety and Intellect*, p. 6.

36. From the enrollment lists in the annual catalogues of the college, cited by Le Duc, *Piety and Intellect*, p. 7, n. 13.

Harvard seems to have been unusual among the New England colleges in the composition of students from large towns and cities. Many students from such areas came from Boston. See Allmendinger, *Paupers and Scholars*, p. 25, n. 18.

37. See David F. Allmendinger, Jr., "Mt. Holyoke Students Encounter the Need for Life Planning, 1837–1850," *History of Education Quarterly* 19 (1975): 27–46.

38. Ibid.: 29–33, 37–38.

39. See, for example, Albea Godbold, *Church Colleges of the Old South* (Durham, N.C., 1944), pp. 54, 56, 47, and David B. Potts, "'College Enthusiasm!' As Public Response, 1800–1860," *Harvard Educational Review* 47 (1977): 37–38.

40. See Potts, "'College Enthusiasm,'" pp. 33, 38; Potts, "American Colleges in the Nineteenth Century: From Localism to Denominationalism," *History of Education Quarterly* 11 (1971): 367–368; Potts, "Baptist Colleges in the Development of American Society, 1812–1860" (Ph.D. diss., Harvard University, 1967), chap. 3, for instance.

41. "The Columbian College, D.C.," *Christian Index*, 16 January 1846, as cited in Potts, "'College Enthusiasm,'" p. 38.

42. C[harles] B. Haddock, *Collegiate Education*: An Address on Behalf of the Society for the Promotion of Collegiate and Theological Education at the West, delivered in Tremont Temple, Boston, May 31, 1848 (Boston, 1848), pp. 7–8; John Todd, *Plain Letters Addressed to a Parishioner in Behalf of Collegiate and Theological Education at the West* (New York, 1847), p. 22.

43. For the occupational trends of Dartmouth students in this period and for general trends for college graduates and the general population, see chapter 4 of this study.

44. Percy Wells Bidwell, *Rural Economy in New England at the Beginning of the Nineteenth Century* (New Haven, 1916), p. 390, quoted in Wilson, *Hill Country of Northern New England*, p. 57.

45. Although the economic motive may have been dominant for many, others went west to "help save the West for God." Wilson, *Hill Country of Northern New England*, p.

62. References to the *Vermont Chronicle*, 13 December 1853, 5 December 1854, 11 September 1855, 12 January 1858.

For a discussion of this point in this chapter, see p. 64 of this study.

For an analysis of the migration of students to and from colleges, see Colin B. Burke, "The Quiet Influence: The American Colleges and Their Students, 1800–1860" (Ph.D. diss., Washington University, 1973), pp. 206–224. Burke notes that his sample is loaded toward the smaller non–New England institutions. Contrary to the analysis of students in this study, he calculates the migration from the place they were educated rather than from the residence or birthplace. While his findings regarding the out-migration (over 50%) for students at New England institutions seems in keeping with the information we have about the Dartmouth students, his statements regarding the in-migration to ante-bellum colleges seems to differ from the Dartmouth case and from other studies that reveal the local character of many antebellum colleges.

46. Lord, *History of Dartmouth College*, p. 559. For information about the Handel Society and students singing at concerts for the people of the community, see Samuel Willey, *Dartmouth Reminiscence, 1840–1845* (Hanover, N.H., 1955), pp. 10–11.

47. Jocabed Skivers (pseud.), "Pedagography," *Dartmouth*, June 1840, p. 236.

Students boarding with local townspeople as an extension of the school-community relationship is also noted by James McLachlan in his study of boarding schools. See *American Boarding Schools: A Historical Study* (New York, 1970), p. 47.

48. We (pseud.), "Talk by the Way," *Dartmouth*, June 1840, p. 243.

49. *Catalogue of Dartmouth College 1850–51*, p. 25.

50. Lord, *History of Dartmouth College*, p. 527.

51. *True Democrat*, 30 July 1847, cited by Lord, *History of Dartmouth College*, p. 273.

52. Lord, *History of Dartmouth College*, p. 307.

53. Ibid., pp. 566–569.

54. Ibid., p. 274.

55. Details of the students' actions were reported in the *True Democrat*, 18 April 1845, and statements of Dr. J. W. Barstow, class of 1846. The five students who were present at the dancing were dismissed. Records of the Faculty, cited in Lord, *History of Dartmouth College*, pp. 577–578.

56. Quoted in Lord, *History of Dartmouth College*, pp. 577–578.

57. See, for example, Potts, "American Colleges," pp. 367–368.

58. *Dartmouth Advertiser*, September 1853, quoted in Lord, *History of Dartmouth College*, p. 305.

59. "Republican Institutions," *Dartmouth*, May 1842, p. 226. To this point, Richard Powers notes that many of the New England colleges such as Amherst, Bowdoin, Dartmouth, Yale, and Williams carried on a crusade to extend Yankee culture. See Richard Lyle Powers, "A Crusade to Extend Yankee Culture, 1820–1865," *New England Quarterly* 13 (December 1940): 638–658.

60. C. (pseud.), "The Moral Hero," *Dartmouth*, March 1844, p. 157.

61. William Badger to his brother (1845), quoted in Richardson, *History of Dartmouth College*, 2:482.

62. Ordronaux, *Class of 1850*, p. 11.

63. Currier, "Dartmouth Fifty Years Ago," p. 245.

64. The organized athletic events centered on activities such as freshman and sophomore contests involving kicking the ball (football).

65. The Library of the Social Friends contained 6,773 books in 1850–51. The United Fraternity had 6,602 books, and the College Library had 6,600 books. *Catalogue of Dartmouth College, 1850–51*, p. 26. For the range of books at Dartmouth and at other libraries of the northern literary societies, see Thomas S. Harding, *College Literary Societies: Their Contri-*

bution to Higher Education in the United States 1815–76 (New York, 1971). See chaps. 3 and 8 for the 1815–65 period.

66. Chamberlain, *Address at the Dedication of Wilson Hall*, p. 3.

67. An illuminating inquiry into the nature of student literary societies at Princeton and the broader significance of these societies in the history of American higher education is provided by James McLachlan in "The *Choice of Hercules*: American Student Societies in the Early 19th Century," in Stone, ed., *University in Society*, 2:449–494. For a survey of the literary societies in nineteenth-century colleges, see Harding, *College Literary Societies*. For an interpretation of the literary societies as an integral part of collegiate life, see Rita S. Saslaw, "Student Societies: Nineteenth Century Establishment" (unpublished paper presented at the annual meeting of the American Educational Research Association, San Francisco, April 9, 1979).

68. The literary societies had been in existence since the mid-1780s. During the 1850s they were in a period of decline, and by 1860 they died out. Beginning with 1825, students were assigned to the literary societies by lot.

69. Currier, "Dartmouth College Fifty Years Ago," p. 251.

70. Most of the work in rhetoric was not included in the recitations. Assignments included compositions and then declamations before the college. See Richardson, *History of Dartmouth College*, 2:431.

For a perceptive analysis of the antebellum curriculum, see Douglas Sloan, "Harmony, Chaos, and Consensus: The American College Curriculum," *Teacher's College Record* 73 (1971): 221–256.

71. For an excellent treatment of the relationship between moral philosophy and the social sciences that emerged in the late nineteenth century, see Gladys Bryson, "The Comparable Interests of the Old Moral Philosophy and the Modern Social Sciences," *Social Forces* 11 (October 1932): 19–27.

For moral philosophy in the women's colleges, see Anne Firor Scott, "The Ever Widening Circle: The Diffusion of Feminist Values from the Troy Female Seminary 1822–1872," *History of Education Quarterly* 19 (1979): 7.

72. Unidentified source from obituary of Samuel Gilman Brown in *Utica Morning Herald*, 1885, in Alumni Files under "Brown."

73. William R. Johnson, "Education and Professional Life Styles: Law and Medicine in the Nineteenth Century," *History of Education Quarterly* 14 (1974): 188, 190.

74. Bartlett, "N.Y. Alumni Assoc. v. Pres. Bartlett," 8:357.

75. Two of those listed as academical graduates left before 1881 but were awarded degrees from Dartmouth later. The Catalogue includes them as graduates of the class of 1881, and they are so included in this chapter.

76. As in 1851, it is difficult to assign the nongraduates in the medical school to a specific class, as they are listed just by the year they entered.

77. Only the agricultural graduates seem to be included in the catalogue of the agricultural school. See *Catalogue of the New Hampshire College of Agriculture and the Mechanic Arts 1890–92* (Concord, N.H., 1892).

78. Tables for the academical and Chandler nongraduates and for students in the associated schools appear in appendixes 16–21.

79. Wilson, *Hill Country of Northern New England*, p. 151.

80. Frederick Rudolph, *Mark Hopkins and the Log: Williams College, 1836–1872* (New Haven, 1956), pp. 71–72.

81. Potts, "American Colleges," p. 369.

82. Without an index of wealth, one cannot definitely conclude that this was the trend (higher socioeconomic status than their 1851 counterparts). Farmers, for example, can be rich or poor. But from the other collected data and writings, it seems that this was the case at Dartmouth. For classifications, see Katz, "Occupational Classification in History."

83. See, for example, Rudolph, *Mark Hopkins and the Log*, pp. 70–72. Movement toward students of a higher socioeconomic status seems to have begun somewhat earlier at Williams.

An analysis of the first class of Smith College (1879) indicates that while the women were not wealthy, over half of them came from "well-off, middle class families" in which the father was engaged in business or professional employment. See Sarah H. Gordon, "Smith College Students: The First Ten Classes, 1879–1888," *History of Education Quarterly* 15 (1975): 150.

84. Within this category, 21.5% were merchants, bank president, owner furniture business, insurance agents, owner building and carpentry company, owner warp and woof business, advertising agent, wool manufacturer. Another 3.9% were in the category of bookkeeper and clerk.

85. The figures for the 1882–96 period seem to suggest this. In addition, 17.6% of the fathers could not be found in the area indicated as student's residence and birthplace, 9.8% of the students were not living with the father, and in 2% of the cases no occupation was listed. Thus, some of those not identified may have been farmers.

86. This category includes machinist, tanner, saddler, cabinetmaker, harnessmaker, papermaker.

87. Frank H. Dixon, "Statistics of Vocations of Dartmouth College Graduates," *Yale Review*, May 1901, p. 87. No breakdown is given as to exactly who is included in each of these general categories. Other categories include engineering, 0.1%; journalism, 0.5%; government service, 1.3%; miscellaneous/unknown, 7.4%.

88. Samuel C. Bartlett, *Dartmouth College, As It Has Been, Is, Should Be, and Can Be: A statement to its graduates and friends, and to all intelligent New Hampshire men, at home or abroad, Jan. 1, 1881* (n.d., n.p.), pp. 1, 4. Bartlett also noted that because of the unattractive appearance of some of the buildings and because of the contrast of the more comfortable circumstances from which some of these students came, they were in danger of losing the wealthier students as well. This address, of course, was a plea for money, but the general trend as to types of students at the college seems accurate.

89. See p. 117 of this study.

90. See p. 116 of this study.

91. "Editorial Department," *Dartmouth*, September 1973, p. 295.

92. Ibid. The editorial also advised against this practice and noted that the alumni counseled against it.

93. "Editorial Department," *Dartmouth*, June 1873, p. 254.

94. J. M. Hulbert (class historian), *Recollections of a Freshman Year, Read before the Class of '85, Sept. 25, 1882*, (Hanover, N.H., 1882), pp. 35–36.

95. Most of the statistics involving those engaged in the traditional learned professions include individuals in that category even if they are engaged in other pursuits at the same time (unless the profession is abandoned and the individual's time is spent overwhelmingly in the other pursuit). In order to ascertain clearly the extent of the fields in which the individual was involved, it is necessary to consult individual biographies as well as general catalogues and reports. This was done in this chapter primarily through the report of the class secretary tracing each individual in the class of 1881. See Myron W. Adams, *The Class of 1881, Dartmouth College, 1881–1931* (Milford, N.H., 1931).

96. Johnson, "Education and Professional Life Styles," pp. 202–203. For changes in the legal profession, see also Johnson, *Schooled Lawyers: A Study in the Clash of Professional Cultures* (New York, 1978).

97. Adams, *Class of 1881*, p. 35.

98. As of the writing of the class report in 1931, the corporation was the largest in the world as regards the number of its shareholders.

99. Adams, *Class of 1881*, pp. 54–55.

100. Ibid., p. 90.

101. For an analysis of the significance of the rise of the superintendency, see Mattingly, *Classless Profession*, chap. 8.

102. Bailey B. Burritt, *Professional Distribution of College and University Graduates*, U.S. Office of Education Bulletin No. 19 (Washington, D.C., 1912), pp. 46, 62–73, 76–78. For a discussion of the general trends among Dartmouth graduates, other college graduates, and the general population, see chapter 4 of this study.

103. Clinton Johnson, "The Deserted Homes of New England," *Cosmopolitan* 15 (May–October 1893): 218, quoted in Wilson, *Hill Country of Northern New England*, p. 140.

104. Correspondence from Clarence Belden Little, in Myron W. Adams and Edward L. Kimball, *First Class Report of the Secretaries of the Class of 1881, Dartmouth College* (Hartford, 1883), p. 9.

105. The ages had leveled out so that Dartmouth students and Harvard students would be about the same. The average age at entrance at Harvard was nineteen in 1882 and 1883. President's Report for 1884–85 (President Eliot) in Samuel Eliot Morison, ed., *The Development of Harvard University Since the Inauguration of President Eliot 1869–1929* (Cambridge, Mass., 1930), p. xliv.

106. Dink Stover symbolized the students of the boarding schools and elite clubs who attended college for the pleasant associations. See Owen Johnson, *Stover at Yale*, with an introduction by Kingman Brewster, Jr. (New York, 1968). Johnson was a graduate of Lawrenceville and Yale (1900).

107. One third of the students showed a different residence from birthplace. In addition, 8.3% could not be found in the area indicated as birthplace or residence, and 8.3% were not living with the father (as of the census of 1880 from reported residence and birthplace). In some cases the student may have been living with relatives, and in other cases the father may have been deceased.

108. This category includes bobbin spool and shuttle manufacturer; axle grease manufacturer; owner, lumber business; ranchman; president, cemetery association (also mayor of town).

109. Johnson, *Stover at Yale*, p. 79.

110. George Hunt Hutchinson to William B. Greeley, Class Secretary of '81, 21 August 1941, Alumni Files, under "Hutchinson."

111. "A Week at Hogglestock," *Dartmouth*, November 1867, p. 365.

112. Diary of Cuthbert Payson (pseud.), probably belonged to Professor Edwin J. Bartlett, class of 1872, quoted in Hill, *College on the Hill*, p. 227.

113. "Dartmouth Items," *Dartmouth*, November 1874, p. 347.

114. "Editorial Notes," *Dartmouth*, January 1871, p. 33.

115. Little, *Freshman History '81* (n.p., 1881), p. 6.

116. Richard Hovey to his mother, 23 April 1882, Special Collections, Dartmouth College Library, Hanover, N.H. Hovey noted he loafed that day.

117. Announcement from E. W. Woodman & Sons, Tailors and Importers, Concord, N.H., in the *Dartmouth*, 27 June 1883.

118. George Walker, "The Usefulness of a College Education to Business Men," *Dartmouth*, February 1873, pp. 62–63.

119. Ibid., p. 64.

120. "Dartmouth College and Its Alumni," *Dartmouth*, January 1872, pp. 1, 2.

121. For specifications, see pp. 147–149 of this study.

122. "N.Y. Alumni Assoc. v. Pres. Bartlett," 2:72–74.

123. Ibid., p. 74.

124. Ibid.

125. See, for example, W. Bruce Leslie, "A Comparative Study of Four Middle Atlantic Colleges, 1870–1915: Bucknell University, Franklin and Marshall College, Princeton University, and Swarthmore College" (Ph.D. diss., Johns Hopkins University, 1971), p. 102; for summary regarding newspaper coverage and students, see also George E. Peterson, *The New England College in the Age of the University* (Amherst, 1964), pp. 83–84, and suggestions by Le Duc, *Piety and Intellect*, pp. 125–126.

126. Quoted in Richardson, *History of Dartmouth College*, 2:566.

127. Myron W. Adams, "The Fifty Year Class: Class of 1881," *Dartmouth Alumni Magazine* (July 1931): 611. In 1886 Dartmouth, Amherst, and Williams formed a new league.

128. See, for example, Le Duc, *Piety and Intellect*, pp. 124–126; Rudolph, *American College and University*. For development of fraternities and athletics and student life in the latter part of the century, see chapter 6 of this study.

129. This probably was due in part to the smallness of the institution, the required prayer meetings, and the limited electives and optionals.

130. Quoted in Allan Houston Macdonald, *Richard Hovey: Man & Craftsman* (New York, 1968), p. 7.

131. "Pocket Elucidator," *Aegis*, class of 1883, p. 94.
For a description of cribbing at institutions in the 1880s, see C. H. Patton and Walter T. Field, *Eight O'Clock Chapel: A Study of New England College Life in the Eighties* (Boston, 1927), pp. 329–331.

132. Little, *Freshman History '81*, pp. 13–14.

133. Ibid., p. 15.

134. Quoted in Macdonald, *Richard Hovey*, p. 25.

135. Ibid.

136. Rudolph, *American College and University*, pp. 148–149.

137. Ibid., p. 148.

138. In 1880–81, with the support of the trustees, the faculty began a revision of the curriculum. They introduced electives in the sophomore year; these were increased in the junior and senior years. This system was limited as compared with Harvard, but it marked the beginning of the elective system of the late nineteenth century.
Dartmouth was not the only college to introduce electives. See Leslie, "Comparative Study of Four Mid-Atlantic Colleges," for Swarthmore and Bucknell, pp. 79, 84, and James Axtell, "The Death of the Liberal Arts College," *History of Education Quarterly* 11 (1971): 347–348.

139. William Jewett Tucker, *My Generation: An Autobiographical Interpretation* (Boston, 1919), p. 333.

140. Little, *Freshman History '81*, p. 20.

141. "N.Y. Alumni Assoc. v. Pres. Bartlett," 8:356–357. The reference to treating some indecorums by ridicule refers to the specifications listed on p. 149 of this study.
The disciplinary case in 1878 was a case of aggravated assault. Two students were expelled, seven finally separated, and two suspended until the end of the term. There seems to have been some division within the faculty over this, but the majority voted with the president for these penalties.

142. Little, *Freshman History '81*, p. 18.

143. Ibid., p. 20.

144. Ibid.

145. Ibid. Students at Williams also circulated a similar handbill calling for the delivery of Saul A. Shadbourne, an escapee from "Williamstown Philanthropical Lunatic Asylum." Handbill, Chadbourne Manuscripts, Williams College, cited in George E. Peterson, *New England College in the Age of the University*, p. 123.

146. *Journal of Education*, 2 May 1881, "Scrapbook."

147. Ibid.

148. For conflicts and disturbances at other New England colleges see, for example, Peterson, *New England College in the Age of the University*, chap. 5.

149. Chadbourne to Bartlett, March 22, 1878, Dartmouth College Library, cited in Peterson, *New England College in the Age of the University*, p. 137.

150. *Dartmouth*, 1892, quoted in Hill, *College on the Hill*, pp. 39–40. See also "Biographical Notes of Prof. A. S. Hardy," *Aegis*, class of 1889.

151. "Pocket Elucidator," *Aegis*, class of 1883, p. 94.

152. Ordronaux, *Class of 1850*, p. 11.

153. Memorial of the New York Association of Alumni of Dartmouth College, 11 June 1881. See also "N.Y. Alumni Assoc. v. Pres. Bartlett," 6:281.

154. "N.Y. Alumni Assoc. v. Pres. Bartlett," 6:282.

Chapter IV
The Alumni

1. Webster Schultz Stover, *Alumni Stimulation by the American College President* (New York, 1930). Alumni associations were not new in themselves, but the nature of these associations began to change in the late nineteenth century and to incorporate demands for a voice in governance. Stover notes that some presidents encouraged the development of alumni associations in the last third of the century, and the number of associations increased greatly. But there was little thought that the alumni would demand a voice in governance. The presidents hoped that the associations would stimulate alumni spirit and raise money.

2. Merle Curti and Roderick Nash, *Philanthropy in the Shaping of American Higher Education* (New Brunswick, N.J., 1965).

3. Now part of the Council for Advancement and Support of Education.

4. Daniel J. Boorstin, "Universities in the Republic of Letters," *Perspectives in American History* 1 (1967), p. 376.

5. "N.Y. Alumni Assoc. v. Pres. Bartlett," 10:472.

6. For example, two of the resolutions passed by the New York Alumni were:

"Resolved. That in the opinion of the New York Alumni Dr. Bartlett does not possess the qualities essential to a successful administration of the affairs of the college."

"Resolved. That in view of the action of the Faculty and the state of feeling it reveals, reconciliation or other happy issue being hopeless. It is our conviction that Dr. Bartlett should immediately retire from the Presidency."

See "The Strife at Dartmouth," *New York Times*, 8 June 1881, "Scrapbook."

7. See "Dartmouth Alumni at Dinner," *New York Tribune*, 9 February 1882, and *Boston Transcript*, 9 February 1882 (n.t.), "Scrapbook."

8. In reference to the policy that Bartlett urged and that the board adopted in modified form, Chandler alumni stated that its effect was to degrade the school and alienate the alumni. See, for example, Memorial of the Chandler Alumni, 5 May 1881, Special Collections, Dartmouth College Library, Hanover, N.H.

Bartlett also incurred the disfavor of graduates of the agricultural school by his attitude toward agricultural education. See, for example, "N.Y. Alumni Assoc. v. Pres. Bartlett," 2:174–77.

9. "Old Dartmouth Crisis," *New York Times*, 3 May 1881, "Scrapbook." A handwritten notation indicates that Charles R. Miller, secretary of the N.Y. alumni and an editor of the *New York Times*, wrote the article.

For example, while the Boston Alumni Association passed a resolution for a fair and impartial investigation, they talked about replacing Bartlett, and the name of Dr. Tucker was received with much favor. See proceedings reported in "The Boston Alumni on the Troubles at Dartmouth," *Boston Transcript*, 17 May 1881, and "Dartmouth College Troubles," *Boston Journal*, 18 May 1881, "Scrapbook."

10. Richardson, *History of Dartmouth College*, 2:613. This situation was not reversed until the Tucker administration. Just before Bartlett resigned, the board of trustees granted alumni what was in effect the right to elect five members of the board. When Tucker became president, he worked very closely with the alumni and was very popular with them.

11. Remarks of Joel Parker, President of the Alumni Association, in *An Address, Delivered before the Society of the Alumni of Dartmouth College at Their First Triennial Meeting July 25, 1855 by Samuel Gilman Brown, with an Account of the Proceedings of the Society* (Concord, N.H., 1856).

12. As in the chapter on the students, the academical and Chandler graduates are covered in this chapter. The Thayer graduates ordinarily entered the field of engineering, and the medical graduates were almost always physicians. For information relating to individual graduates, see *General Catalogue of Dartmouth College and the Associated Schools 1769–1940* (Hanover, N.H., 1940). For information regarding the agricultural graduates, see appendix 26.

13. Bailey B. Burritt, *Professional Distribution of College and University Graduates*, U.S. Office of Education Bulletin No. 19 (Washington, D.C., 1912).

14. Ibid., p. 77.

15. James McLachlan, *American Boarding Schools: A Historical Study* (New York, 1970), p. 183.

16. Using a factor analysis of student occupations, Colin Burke (in an important study of students in the nineteenth century) states that there was much more continuity in the choice of occupations than the figures presented in Burritt's study seem to reveal. Burke states that most college alumni chose the traditional learned professions throughout the nineteenth century, that there was not a sharp break in the post–Civil War period as some historians have indicated, and that it was not until the 1890s that there was a significant break with the past. While Burke makes an important point in reminding us to look for patterns of continuity as well as change, he does not indicate that the traditional learned professions were themselves undergoing change. Law, for example, a very popular field for college graduates, was more and more related to the field of business, with many of those in this field having business interests or representing corporations. And while there were important differences among institutions, contemporary writings and other data do point to aspirations of students and alumni toward positions in leading business concerns in metropolitan areas. Similar to the findings of Buritt's study, for example, a study of Yale graduates (through 1893) notes that the "most striking fact" revealed in the study is the "great increase" of those going into business careers. While the conclusion that "the industrial leaders are . . . largely recruited from among college graduates" may be an overstatement, it does highlight the popularity of the field for a significant segment of the population and the general interest among college alumni in opportunities in such fields. See "Statistics of the Vocations of College Graduates," *Yale Review* (November 1898), pp. 344, 345 and Colin B. Burke, "The Quiet Influence: The American Colleges and Their Students, 1800–1860" (Ph.D. diss., Washington University, 1973), pp. 267–273.

For the popularity of the fields of business and engineering among nongraduates as well as graduates of the Academical Department and the Chandler Scientific Department, class of 1881, Dartmouth College, see appendix 20.

17. *Vidette* 2 (4 July 1868), cited in Frederick Rudolph, *Mark Hopkins and the Log: Williams College, 1836–1872* (New Haven, 1956), p. 127.

18. In 1850, 44.1% of the working population were engaged in agricultural pursuits, 3.1% in professional service, 18.8% in domestic and personal service, 9.3% in trade and transportation, and 24.8% in manufacturing and mechanical pursuits. By 1900, 36% were engaged in agricultural pursuits, 4% in professional service, 13.4% in domestic and personal service, 19.8% in trade and transportation, and 26.8% in manufacturing and mechanical pursuits. U.S. Department of Commerce and Labor, Bureau of the Census, *A Century of Population Growth from the First Census of the United States to the Tenth* (Washington, D.C., 1909), p. 143.

19. For occupations for the individual ten-year periods (1821–30 through 1880–90), see appendix 23.

20. For the statistics at five-year intervals, see Burritt, *College and University Graduates*, p. 95 (academical and Chandler graduates). In some cases there are variations in individual percentages between Burritt's statistics and those in appendix 23, but the general trends are the same.

21. Many of the agricultural graduates also engaged in business pursuits; see appendix 26.

22. Business included such categories as president of railroad, lumber business, publishing, and insurance.

23. For example, out of a class of sixty-three in 1881, twelve were Chandler graduates. On the national level in 1895–96, 20% of degree candidates were candidates for a B.S. degree. See W. T. Harris, "Higher Education in the United States," in *Universities and Their Sons*, ed. Joshua L. Chamberlain (Boston, 1901), p. 3.

24. Burritt gives figures for five-year intervals. The average percentages are derived from these figures. See Burritt, *College and University Graduates*, p. 144.

For insights into the careers and occupational distribution of women college graduates, particularly from different women's colleges, see Roberta Frankfort, *Collegiate Women: Domesticity and Career in Turn-of-the-Century America* (New York, 1977); David F. Allmendinger, Jr., "Mount Holyoke Students Encounter the Need for Life Planning, 1837–1850," *History of Education Quarterly* 19 (1979): 27–46; Allmendinger, "History and the Usefulness of Women's Education," ibid.: 117–124; Anne Firor Scott, "The Ever Widening Circle: The Diffusion of Feminist Values from the Troy Female Seminary, 1822–72," ibid.: 3–25.

25. As with the students of the class of 1881, if one includes lawyers who were also engaged in business pursuits, the figures would be even higher; see p. 9 of this study.

26. The average percentages were derived from the statistics provided in "Statistics of the Vocations of College Graduates," *Yale Review*, November 1898, p. 342.

27. The average percentages were derived from the statistics provided by Burritt, *College and University Graduates*, pp. 79–80.

28. The percentages include academical and Chandler alumni. See appendix 24, note c.

The membership list seems to include some graduates who were deceased in 1883, so that one cannot conclude that the predominance of the later classes was due simply to the death of members from earlier classes.

29. "Statistics of College Graduates," *Yale Review*, May 1899, p. 93.

30. Remarks of Joel Parker in *First Triennial Meeting July 25, 1855*, p. 36. Parker tried to form an association earlier in the century. He stated that one of the reasons for its lack of success was the dispersion of the graduates and the poor transportation facilities. President Lord encouraged the formation of the association founded in 1854.

31. Remarks of Nathan Lord in *First Triennial Meeting July 25, 1855*, p. 40.

Along this vein, Wilson Smith has suggested that the expectation of fashioning a Zion may have been what antebellum colleges in general asked of their graduates. See "Apologia pro Alma Matre: The College as Community in Ante-Bellum America," in *The Hofstadter Aegis*, ed. Stanley Elkins and Eric McKitrick (New York, 1974), p. 135.

32. John Ordronaux, *Dartmouth College Class of 1850: Report of its golden anniversary meeting, June 26, 1900* (n.p., n.d.), pp. 10, 12.

33. This stands in marked contrast to the observations of some historians that a college education was of little value in the antebellum period. See, for example, Richard Hofstadter and C. DeWitt Hardy, *The Development and Scope of Higher Education in the United States* (New York, 1952).

For the growth of colleges between 1800 and 1860, see David F. Allmendinger, Jr., *Paupers and Scholars: The Transformation of Student Life in Nineteenth-Century New England* (New York, 1975), Table 1, p. 10. Allmendinger notes that "the number of students graduating in the New England region tripled." *Paupers and Scholars*, p. 3. See also Burke, "Quiet Influence," pp. 16–18.

34. Nathan Lord, *Letter to the Alumni of Dartmouth College, On Its Hundredth Anniversary* (New York, 1869), p. 40.

35. Richard B. Kimball, *The True Life of the Scholar, An Address Delivered before the Literary Societies of Dartmouth College, July 24, 1844* (New York, 1844).

36. Ordronaux, *Class of 1850*, pp. 11–12.

37. In a similar context, see remarks of Mark Hopkins before the Williams alumni. *An Address, Delivered before the Society of Alumni of Williams College, at the Celebration of the Semi-centennial Anniversary*, p. 31, as cited in Rudolph, *Mark Hopkins and the Log*, p. 47.

38. For an interpretation of this sense of commonwealth and how it was transformed from the 1820s through mid-century, see Oscar Handlin and Mary Flug Handlin, *Commonwealth. A Study of the Role of Government in the American Economy: Massachusetts 1774–1861* (New York, 1947), pp. 219–246.

39. For perceptive treatments of the transformation of community, see Thomas Bender, *Community and Social Change in America* (New Brunswick, N.J., 1978), Bender, *Toward an Urban Vision: Ideas and Institutions in Nineteenth-Century America* (Lexington, Ky., 1975); and Michael H. Frisch, *Town into City: Springfield, Massachusetts, and the Meaning of Community 1840–1880* (Cambridge, Mass., 1972).

40. For a thoughtful treatment of this point in relation to the field of law, see James Willard Hurst, *Law and the Conditions of Freedom in the Nineteenth-Century United States* (Madison, Wis., 1956).

41. "Dr. Bartlett at Dartmouth," *New York Times*, 4 May 1881, "Scrapbook." Handwritten insertion indicates that it was written by Charles R. Miller.

42. Ibid.

43. "N.Y. Alumni Assoc. v. Pres. Bartlett," 10:472.

44. Samuel Colcord Bartlett, *Christianity in the College: A Baccalaureate Sermon Preached at Dartmouth College, June 20, 1886* (Hanover, N.H., 1886), pp. 7, 17.

45. Samuel Colcord Bartlett, *Dartmouth, As It Has Been, Is, Should Be: A statement to its graduates and friends and to all intelligent New Hampshire men, at home or abroad, Jan. 1, 1881* (n.d., n.p.), pp. 11, 10.

46. In the 1881–90 decade, those going into business increased to an even greater percentage at Harvard, Yale, and Dartmouth. But the percentage was higher at Harvard and Yale during this period. A comparison of the three schools indicates the following: Yale (1851–80), 20.8% and (1881–90), 28.5%; Harvard (1851–80), 24.1% and (1881–90), 31.4%; Dartmouth—New York Alumni (1851–80), 20.9%. See "Statistics of the Vocations of College Graduates," p. 342; Burritt, *College and University Graduates*, p. 80; appendix 24

of this study provides statistics for Dartmouth graduates in general entering the fields of business from 1881 to 1890; see appendix 23.

47. George Walker [alumnus from New York], from remarks before the New York Alumni Dinner, "The Usefulness of a College Education to Business Men," *Dartmouth,* February 1873, pp. 62, 63, 65.

48. Arthur M. Comey, "The Growth of New England Colleges," *Educational Review* 1 (March 1891): 214–215.

49. See Daniel H. Calhoun, *The American Civil Engineer: Origin and Conflict* (Cambridge, Mass., 1960).

For an interpretation of the development of engineers since 1880 and the role of engineers in the growth of corporate capitalism, see David F. Noble, *America by Design: Science, Technology, and the Rise of Corporate Capitalism* (New York, 1977).

50. See Comey, "Growth of New England Colleges," pp. 214–215. M.I.T. grew from 224 in 1870 to 233 in 1880 to 914 in 1890. The Sheffield School grew from 21 in 1850 to 38 in 1860 to 125 in 1870 to 190 in 1880 to 350 in 1890. Comey, "Growth of New England Colleges," p. 215.

51. See also p. 70 of this study.

52. See also p. 69 of this study.

53. Thomas Le Duc, *Piety and Intellect at Amherst College* (New York, 1946), p. 135.

54. Frederick Law Olmstead, "Autobiographical Passages," in *Frederick Law Olmstead: Landscape Architect, 1822–1903,* ed. Frederick Law Olmstead, Jr., and Theodora Kimball, 2 vols. in one (New York: Benjamin Blom, 1970; orig. ed. 1922–28), 1:43, quoted in Bender, *Toward an Urban Vision,* p. 159.

The 1910 catalogue indicates that more graduates (all classes included) lived in New York City and Boston than in any other area. See *General Catalogue of Dartmouth College and the Associated Schools* (Hanover, N.H., 1910), pp. 836–837.

55. Rudolph, *Mark Hopkins and the Log,* pp. 71–72.

56. For a discussion of these points in relation to the aftermath of the trial and through the Tucker administration, see chap. 6 of this study.

57. See p. 96 of this study.

58. "Old Dartmouth Crisis," "Scrapbook."

59. "Dr. Bartlett at Dartmouth," *New York Times,* 4 May 1881, "Scrapbook."

60. "Dartmouth's Decline," *New York Times,* 12 September 1881, "Scrapbook"; handwritten insertion indicates C. R. Miller (class of 1872) wrote the article; "Dr. Bartlett at Dartmouth"; Report of the meeting of New York Alumni in *Boston Evening Transcript* and statement by an alumnus introducing a resolution for Bartlett's resignation, "Dartmouth's Embarrassments," *Boston Evening Transcript,* 24 February 1882.

61. *Springfield Republican,* 11 October 1881 (n.t.); handwritten insertion indicates it was written by C. B. Evans, class of 1870; "Scrapbook."

62. *Cincinnati Commercial,* 23 December 1881 (n.t.); correspondence from Henry C. Lord, "Scrapbook." Handwritten insertion indicates paper and date.

63. "Dartmouth's Decline," "Scrapbook".

64. Ibid.

65. Bartlett to the Secretary of the Boston Correspondents, quoted in Richardson, *History of Dartmouth College,* 2:625. He expresses a similar opinion in his inaugural address.

66. One of the members of the board noted that the trustees had received a series of memorials from over 100 alumni of the Chandler Department. See George W. Nesmith to Wheelock G. Veazey, 18 July 1881, Nesmith Manuscript File, Special Collections, Dartmouth College Library, Hanover, N.H. A committee of graduates also presented a petition to the trustees at the annual meeting of the trustees. See Annual Meeting, 1881, Records of the Trustees, Special Collections, Dartmouth College Library, Hanover, N.H.

67. Ernest Martin Hopkins, "The Beginnings of Dartmouth's Alumni Organization," *Dartmouth Alumni Magazine* 47 (March 1955): 17.

68. *Boston Post*, 29 June 1881 (n.t.), "Scrapbook." Handwritten insertion indicates the paper and the date.

69. Samuel H. Ranck, "Alumni Representation in College Government," *Education* 22 (October 1901): 107.

70. Stover, *Alumni Stimulation*, p. 14. For example, associations were formed at Princeton in 1826, Oberlin in 1839, Harvard in 1840, and Brown and Amherst in 1842.

71. In the last decade of the century, due to increasing financial needs, many college presidents began to join alumni in these demands. See Stover, *Alumni Stimulation*, pp. 16, 17, 19, 42; and Ranck "Alumni Representation in College Government," p. 109.

72. Stover, *Alumni Stimulation*, p. 18. In 1865 the Massachusetts state legislature passed an act transferring the power to elect the overseers to the alumni. This was accepted by the overseers, president, and fellows.

In reference to this movement, the Handlins note that "The agencies that administered academies and colleges, sustained by fees and endowments, broke away from state dominance and asserted their independence as private bodies." They note, for example, the break with Harvard; see Handlin and Handlin, *Commonwealth*, pp. 249–250 and p. 250, n. 17.

In 1871, on request from Yale, the General Assembly of Connecticut passed an act in accordance with Yale's suggestion that six alumni be elected in place of the six ex officio state senators.

For alumni movement at Yale, see also Ralph Henry Gabriel, *Religion and Learning at Yale: The Church of Christ in the College and University, 1757–1957*, pp. 158–159.

73. See Ranck, "Alumni Representation in College Government," pp. 108–109.

74. "Meeting of the New York Alumni," *Dartmouth*, January 1868, pp. 30–35.

75. Bartlett was a member of this committee. During his administration as president, he was considered a foe of alumni representation; his remarks and actions to block alumni representation except as an advisory body or with the stipulation that the board should "usually" elect the members nominated by the alumni, would seem to be reflective of a change of position. Bartlett noted, for example, "But as an alumnus and not as a trustee I frankly confess that the more I think of it the more it seems to me that in instituting a movement to change the charter in its fundamental trusteeship and in virtually inviting the body of alumni to join us, we have made the gravest mistake in the history of the college, as well as the greatest and most sudden change in the position of the board that has taken place" (ca. 1891); quoted in Richardson, *History of Dartmouth College*, 2:653.

But one should also note that aside from a change of heart due to the opposition of the alumni during his administration and to their positions which were opposed to his conception of the institution and his role in it, this may have been the type of alumni representation he perceived as appropriate. For example, during heated debates in 1870, after finding that their demands were not accepted, Bartlett talked of the pride the alumni would experience in seeing "their names printed in the annual catalogue" as part of the alumni examining committee. Quoted in Richardson, *History of Dartmouth College*, 2:580.

76. For a discussion of this, see "Dartmouth College and Its Alumni," *Dartmouth*, January 1872, pp. 1–11; Richardson, *History of Dartmouth College*, 2:578–281; Lord, *History of Dartmouth College*, pp. 378–379.

77. Quoted in Lord, *History of Dartmouth College*, p. 380.

78. "Old Dartmouth Crisis," "Scrapbook."

79. "Dr. Bartlett at Dartmouth," "Scrapbook."

80. "The Troubles at Dartmouth," *Springfield Republican*, 25 July 1881, "Scrapbook."

81. "Dartmouth and Her Alumni," *Springfield Republican*, 27 March 1882, "Scrapbook." A handwritten insertion indicates that C. B. Evans, class of 1873, wrote the article.

For an interpretation of the different courses institutions followed when confronted with financial pressures and demands for growth, and the development of alumni associations in these institutions, see W. Bruce Leslie, "A Comparative Study of Four Middle Atlantic Colleges, 1870–1915: Bucknell University, Franklin and Marshall College, Princeton University, and Swarthmore College" (Ph.D. diss., Johns Hopkins University, 1971), and Leslie, "Localism, Denominationalism, and Institutional Strategies in Urbanizing America: Three Pennsylvania Colleges, 1870–1915," *History of Education Quarterly* 17 (1977): 235–256.

82. Richardson, *History of Dartmouth College*, 2:659.

83. See George E. Peterson, *The New England College in the Age of the University* (Amherst, 1964), pp. 109, 118.

84. See Rudolph, *Mark Hopkins and the Log*, pp. 229–230, 206; Leslie, "Localism, Denominationalism, and Institutional Strategies," p. 242; Leslie, "Comparative Study of Four Middle Atlantic Colleges," pp. 49–50, 130–132; Thomas Jefferson Wertenbaker, *Princeton, 1746–1896* (Princeton, N.J., 1946), p. 376.

Alumni associations and clubs of various colleges and universities were frequently formed first in urban centers such as New York, Boston, and Chicago.

85. See Winton U. Solberg, *The University of Illinois 1867–1894: An Intellectual and Cultural History*, (Urbana, Ill., 1968), pp. 225–231.

86. In relation to this point, some of the university builders in the post–Civil War period noted that a college education was declining in favor with the populace and that the number of graduates was not keeping pace with the growth of the population. These types of remarks by university builders have generally been taken at face value without any critical analysis. See F. A. P. Barnard, Annual Report of the President of Columbia College Made to the Board of Trustees, 1866, p. 21. This is cited and critiqued in David Potts, "American Colleges in the Nineteenth Century: From Localism to Denominationalism," *History of Education Quarterly* 11 (1971): 376–377, n. 8.

For the growth of colleges from 1850 to 1890, see Comey, "The Growth of New England Colleges," pp. 200–219. Comey notes "that the proportional increase in the number of college students has far exceeded the increase in population." "Growth of New England Colleges," p. 200.

87. "Dartmouth College Troubles," *Boston Journal*, 18 May 1881 (Statement of a member of the Boston Alumni Association), "Scrapbook."

Chapter V
The Trustees

1. Report and Resolutions, Investigating Committee, Board of Trustees, 28 July 1881, in "Dartmouth College," *Boston Journal*, 30 July 1881, "Scrapbook."

2. Ibid.

3. Ibid.

4. Although they did not rescind all the measures seen as objectionable by the faculty and alumni of the Chandler Department, they did restore most of the entrance requirements—the point most strongly demanded by the alumni.

5. Records of the Board of Trustees, April 1882, Special Collections, Dartmouth College Library, Hanover, N.H. Governor Bell, an ex officio member of the board, was expected to cast a negative vote, but he was absent from the meeting.

6. See an Appeal by the Board of Trustees, Dartmouth College, September 1841, quoted in Lord, *History of Dartmouth College*, p. 265.

7. "President's Report," 1851, Lord Manuscript File, Special Collections, Dartmouth College Library, Hanover, N.H.

8. Resolutions of the Merrimack County Conference of Congregational Churches, 23–24 June 1863, quoted in Lord, *History of Dartmouth College*, pp. 322–323. Originally Lord was against slavery; he changed his position on religious grounds.

9. Resolution unanimously adopted by the Board of Trustees, Dartmouth College, 24 July 1863. Records of the Board of Trustees.

10. See Report of the Investigating Committee of the Board of Trustees, Records of the Board of Trustees.

The board indicated its opposition to Lord's views and directed that the report and resolutions of the board should be published and circulated among members of the conference.

Report adopted by the Board of Trustees by a vote of five to two.

11. For the development of President Lord's reasons for resigning in relation to his perception of his role as president, see pp. 109–110 of this study. Lord remained in Hanover until his death in 1870. When he resigned from his position as president, friends provided a $1,200 annuity for him. See Lord, *History of Dartmouth College*, p. 328.

12. Thorstein Veblen, *The Higher Learning in America* (New York, 1918).

13. Richard Hofstadter and Walter P. Metzger, *The Development of Academic Freedom in the United States* (New York, 1955).

14. For an example of a repudiation of this type of description, see David Potts, "American Colleges in the Nineteenth Century: From Localism to Denominationalism," *History of Education Quarterly* 11 (1971): 363–380. See also literature cited on pp. 189–190, note 5, of this study.

In a recent study, Allan Conway sheds much light on the nature and interests of trustees of two urban institutions. Conway illustrates how the differences in the composition of the boards of New York University and Columbia led to their choice of presidents and to the shaping of policies involving such questions as whom the universities would serve. He also illustrates the alliances between some of the clergy and businessmen on the boards. "Columbia and New York Universities Consolidation: A Study in Urban Social Consciousness" (Ph.D. diss., New York University, 1974).

15. In 1893, by act of the legislature, this was changed to seven out of twelve. This residency requirement was not unusual. For example, until 1880 members of the board of overseers of Harvard were required to be Massachusetts residents. See Samuel Eliot Morison, *Three Centuries of Harvard 1636–1936* (Cambridge, Mass., 1965), p. 359, n. 1.

16. One of the lawyers also was listed as a journalist.

The history of Amherst and Williams indicates that throughout the antebellum period the clergy did not dominate the boards of trustees.

See Thomas Le Duc, *Piety and Intellect at Amherst College, 1865–1912* (New York, 1946), p. 6, and Frederick Rudolph, *Mark Hopkins and the Log: Williams College, 1836–1872* (New Haven, 1956), p. 91.

17. See, for example, James Findlay, "The SPCTEW and Western Colleges: Religion and Higher Education in Mid-Nineteenth Century America," *History of Education Quarterly* 17 (1977): 47, and Natalie A. Naylor, "The Ante-Bellum College Movement: A Reappraisal of Tewksbury's Founding of American Colleges and Universities," ibid. 13 (1973): 269. For choice of clergymen-presidents and religious influence in the post–Civil War period, see J. David Hoeveler, Jr., "Higher Education in the Mid-West: Community and Culture," *History of Education Quarterly* 14 (1974): 395, and Winton A. Solberg, *The University of Illinois 1867–1894* (Urbana, Ill., 1968), p. 85.

18. Biographical information relating to the trustees was obtained from the following sources: *General Catalogue of Dartmouth College and the Associated Schools 1769–1910, 1769–1940* (Hanover, N.H., 1910, 1940); *Catalogue of the Officers and Students of Dartmouth College 1850–51, 1862–63, 1876–77, 1878–79* (Hanover, N.H., 1850, 1862, 1876, 1878); *Cat-*

*alogue of the Officers and Students of Dartmouth College and the Associated Institutions, 1878–79,
1880–81* (Hanover, N.H., 1879, 1880); *Appleton's Cyclopedia of American Biography*, rev. ed.
(New York, 1898); *National Cyclopedia of American Biography* (New York, 1907–44); *Dictionary
of American Biography* (New York, 1929–64); Perry Baxter Smith, *The History of Dartmouth
College* (Boston, 1879); Richardson, *History of Dartmouth College*; Lord, *History of Dartmouth
College*; Trustee Manuscript File, Special Collections, Dartmouth College Library, Hanover,
N.H.; Alumni Files, Special Collections, Dartmouth College Library, Hanover, N.H.

19. The orientation of the Dartmouth trustees seems to be in line with developments
in most colleges during the first half of the nineteenth century. The religious influence
was pervasive in most of these institutions. And while Protestant denominations seem
to have exhibited both cooperation and competition in their quest to permeate the country
with Christianity, as regards the founding and development of most antebellum institutions, the major features of these institutions were their Christian nature and local character—not the narrow sectarianism and denominational control portrayed in standard
accounts. For the religious character and evangelical aim see, for instance, Naylor, "Ante-
Bellum College Movement," pp. 261–274. The quotation in the text is on p. 270 of Naylor's
article. For an analysis of the local character and lack of denominational control (up to
mid-century), see David B. Potts, "American Colleges in the Nineteenth Century: From
Localism to Denominationalism," *History of Education Quarterly* 11 (1971): 363–380; Potts,
"'College Enthusiasm!' As Public Response," *Harvard Educational Review* 47 (1977): 28–43;
Potts, "Baptist Colleges in the Development of American Society, 1812–1861" (Ph.D. diss.,
Harvard University, 1967). See also Colin B. Burke, "The Quiet Influence: The American
Colleges and Their Students, 1800–1860" (Ph.D. diss., Washington University, 1973), p.
156.

For a varying interpretation regarding denominationalism and Presbyterian education,
see Howard Miller, *The Revolutionary College: American Presbyterian Education, 1707–1837*
(New York, 1976). A perceptive critique that questions some of the conclusions and assumptions of this important new study is provided by Phyllis Vine, in "Another Look at
Eighteenth Century Colleges," *History of Education Quarterly* 18 (1978); see especially pp.
65–66.

20. Quoted in Smith, *History of Dartmouth College*, pp. 386–87. The emphasis seems to
be on the purity of his actions emanating from the purity of his intentions. This seems
to be in line with the teaching of the moral philosophers and relates to Lord's resignation.
See p. 110 and p. 220, n. 65, of this study.

21. From Fletcher's will, quoted by his biographer in ibid., p. 387.

22. Rev. Nathaniel Bouton, *The History of Education in New Hampshire: An Address before
the New Hampshire Historical Society, June 12, 1833* (Concord, N.H., 1833).

23. William S. Tyler, *Colleges: Their Place Among American Institutions* (New York, 1856).
Address before the Society for the Promotion of Collegiate and Theological Education at
the West, cited in Daniel J. Boorstin, *The Americans: The National Experience* (New York,
1965), p. 160. Regarding community-college relationship see Wilson Smith, "Apologia pro
Alma Matre: The College as Community in Ante-Bellum America," in *The Hofstadter Aegis*,
ed. Stanley Elkins and Eric McKitrick (New York, 1974), pp. 125–153, Potts "American
Colleges," "Baptist Colleges," "'College Enthusiasm.'"

In a related context, see comments regarding the reciprocal relationship between Exeter
and the town and changes in 1880, in James McLachlan, *American Boarding Schools: A
Historical Study* (New York, 1970), pp. 232–233, 240–241, 345.

24. Records of the Trustees, Annual Meeting, 1834. This arrangement continued until
1866.

25. In addition to this provision, limited funds were available for needy students from
New Hampshire, and for those studying for the ministry, and tuition was kept low—
$31.50 in 1851.

For an analysis of the level of subsidization of students by colleges in this period see Burke, "Quiet Influence," pp. 77, 124, 126.

26. Lord, *History of Dartmouth College*, p. 245. For the popularity of this profession among Dartmouth graduates, see appendix 23 of this study and Paul H. Mattingly, *The Classless Profession: American Schoolmen in the Nineteenth Century* (New York, 1975), p. 175.

27. Allmendinger, in his study of the transformation of student life in the nineteenth century, suggests that the students indirectly pushed boards of trustees to adopt policies such as these. Although the students were in this sense agents of change, the policies of the board should also be seen within the context of the antebellum college as a community-oriented institution. See David F. Allmendinger, Jr., *Paupers and Scholars: The Transformation of Student Life in Nineteenth-Century New England* (New York, 1975), pp. 91–94.

28. Before coming to Dartmouth, Cogswell studied for the ministry, was pastor of a church, and then agent and secretary of the American Education Society.

29. From President's "Report," 1841, Lord Manuscript File, Special Collections, Dartmouth College Library, Hanover, N.H.

30. Ibid.

31. Ibid. As a great society of arts and sciences, as some of the members envisioned it, it failed; but it was successful as a literary society in the community. It declined in the 1850s and was revived in a different form in the 1870s as an association in which learned papers were read by the faculty. In the 1870s it included a scientific and literary and philosophical branch. See Lord, *History of Dartmouth College*, pp. 548–551.

32. Richardson, *History of Dartmouth College*, 1:397.

33. In the year 1832–33 they were free from debts, except to its own funds, which amounted to $4,668.

34. Richardson, *History of Dartmouth College*, 1:398.

35. Ibid.

36. Quoted in ibid.

37. Ibid., pp. 402, 404.

38. For the gifts and bequests, see Richardson, *History of Dartmouth College*, 2:400–403, 412, and Lord, *History of Dartmouth College*, pp. 261, 288, 604–605.

39. Although the number of students fluctuated, especially in the 1840s with a high of 331 students in 1841–42 and a low of 179 in 1845–46, there was a steady increase from 125 academical students in 1828 to 275 academical and 42 Chandler students in 1860. At times, Dartmouth led the colleges in numbers of students. In 1842, for example, during a period of very high student numbers, Dartmouth graduated 85 students, the highest number until 1894, while Harvard graduated 58 and Princeton 60. Yale with 105 exceeded Dartmouth. See Lord, *History of Dartmouth College*, p. 258, and Richardson, *History of Dartmouth College*, 1:393.

A great fluctuation in yearly income accompanied the fluctuation in student numbers. At times the college ran at a loss and at other times at a small surplus. From 1851–52 until the Civil War, the balance between income and expenditures was about even. From 1836 through the remaining years of Lord's administration, total deficits were $20,333 and total surpluses $11,948. See Richardson, *History of Dartmouth College*, 1:394–395.

40. Lord, *History of Dartmouth College*, pp. 225, 329.

41. See Potts, "American Colleges," p. 368; "'College Enthusiasm,'" pp. 33–36; Le Duc, *Piety and Intellect*, pp. 1–2.

42. To meet the expenses of the tour and the trip to Europe, Young acted as agent for the college and collected installments due on subscriptions to the college.

43. Lord, *History of Dartmouth College*, p. 288.

44. Thomas Bender, "Science and the Culture of American Communities: The Nineteenth Century," *History of Education Quarterly* 16 (1976):67–73. This analysis was very

helpful in furthering my understanding of the historical shifts involved in culture and science in nineteenth-century America. See also his essay, "The Cultures of Intellectual Life: The City and the Professions" in *New Directions in American Intellectual History*, ed. Paul K. Conkin and John Higham (Baltimore, 1979), pp. 181–195.

An interpretation of science and the changing nature of the professors of science at Dartmouth is provided by Sanborn C. Brown and Leonard M. Rieser in *Natural Philosophy at Dartmouth: From Surveyors' Claims to the Pressure of Light* (Hanover, N.H., 1974). Brown and Rieser provide some interesting information on professors of science in this period, but their interpretation is problematic, as they do not explore the possibility that there were structural shifts and shifts in the intellectual style of science during the nineteenth century. They note, for example, the role of Ira Young as a "popularizer" but fail to explore the possibility of a community-oriented science in this period as opposed to the more esoteric, professional science of the late nineteenth century.

45. "Practical" here means preparation for fields outside the traditional learned professions, for which most of the graduates up to mid-century prepared—the ministry, teaching, law, and medicine. The increase in interest in, and desire for, preparation for the fields of engineering, commerce, manufacturing, mechanics, and the scientific, notably the applied scientific, were within the rubric of these "practical" fields.

In line with this point, although nothing was done to facilitate this, in 1844 the trustees themselves discussed the possibility of establishing a scheme of education for students interested in commercial, mechanical, and engineering pursuits. Cited in Lord, *History of Dartmouth College*, p. 293.

During this period the Lawrence Scientific School at Harvard and the Sheffield Scientific School were established. Brown established a department of practical science in the early 1850s, and a few years later the University of Pennsylvania established a department of mines, arts, and manufacturers.

The use of the word "practical" here should not be interpreted to mean that the classical liberal arts curriculum did not prepare the students for secular success.

In relation to the character of the classical curriculum, including the place of science and the emphasis on secular success, see Douglas Sloan, "Harmony, Chaos, and Consensus: The American College Curriculum," *Teacher's College Record* 73 (1971): 221–51; Potts, "'College Enthusiasm,'" pp. 38–40; and Paul H. Mattingly, "The Meaning of Professional Culture," *The Review of Education* 3 (1977): 444.

46. To this point, Curti and Nash note that with the rise of a new elite of businessmen and manufacturers, men such as Lord "had to adapt" to these new demands or lose their share of the philanthropy designated for practical higher education. See Merle Curti and Roderick Nash, *Philanthropy in the Shaping of American Higher Education* (New Brunswick, N.J., 1965), p. 70.

47. From President Lord's discourse on 29 July 1852 representing the views of the trustees, as quoted in O[liver] P. Hubbard [Dartmouth Professor], *The Chandler Scientific Department of Dartmouth College* [copy from *Granite Monthly*, June 1880] pp. 356–357.

48. Ibid., p. 358.

49. Ibid.

50. Ibid.

51. Ibid.

52. As quoted in Lord, *History of Dartmouth College*, p. 265.

53. As quoted in ibid., p. 264.

54. For an illuminating treatment of this point in the development of Springfield, Massachusetts, from a town into a city, see Michael H. Frisch, *Town into City: Springfield, Massachusetts, and the Meaning of Community, 1840–1880* (Cambridge, Mass., 1972), pp. 48–49.

55. The board underwent some change by 1863. The 1851 trustees had served between nine and thirty-seven years—70% twenty years or more. But by 1863 a number had died or resigned. Of the seven present and voting regarding the resolutions and report, four were new members, three were New Hampshire residents, and one was a Vermont resident. For their ages and occupations, see appendixes 27 and 28.

56. Relative to this point regarding the board's sensitivity to the clergy as agents of support (in the sense of encouraging their parishioners in the community of northern New England to support the college), in 1849, at the time the board filled the chair for the Phillips Professorship of Theology, they passed a resolution probably in the hopes of pleasing these important supporters. The college charter contained no theological restrictions. The resolution they passed regarding the Phillips Professorship applied only to this professorship. It stated "that the Board have made the appointment of a Professor of Theology in the belief that his religious sentiments are in accordance with the compend of Christian doctrine set forth by the Westminster Assembly of Divines in their Shorter Catechism, and that any material departure from that platform is deemed by the Board a sufficient ground of removal from office." Quoted in Lord, History of Dartmouth College, p. 291.

57. This may be related to the informal, tangible relations within the organic notion of community, in contrast to the more formal segmented and abstract nature of relationships when community was defined with exclusive reference to one's peers.

58. Richardson, History of Dartmouth College, 2:508.

59. Resolutions passed by the Merrimack County Conference of Congregational Churches, 23–24 June 1863, in Records of the Board of Trustees, Annual Meeting, July 1863.

60. Report adopted by the board, in response to the Resolutions of the Merrimack County Conference of Congregational Churches, 24 July 1863, in Records of the Board of Trustees, Annual Meeting, July 1863.

61. See, for example, Wilson Smith, Professors & Public Ethics: Studies of Northern Moral Philosophers before the Civil War (Ithaca, N.Y., 1956), and D. H. Meyer, The Instructed Conscience (Philadelphia, 1972).

62. Lord to Trustees, 24 July 1863, Records of the Board of Trustees, Annual Meeting, July 1863.

63. Ibid.

64. Ibid.

65. Similar to the position taken by Lord is that noted by Wilson Smith in his study on the moral philosophers between 1830 and 1860. Smith notes that "the moral philosophers earnestly believed and taught that moral purity in a man's intentions determined the morality of his public actions." Professors & Public Ethics, p. 4. See also Meyer, Instructed Conscience, p. 77.

66. See pp. 216–217, note 18, of this study.

67. Along this vein, Paul Mattingly notes in his study of schoolmen in the nineteenth century that "bureaucratization" and "secularization" not only did not preclude but sustained certain new forms of religious fervor. See Mattingly, Classless Profession, p. xvii.

68. W. Bruce Leslie. "Localism, Denominationalism, and Institutional Strategies in Urbanizing America: Three Pennsylvania Colleges, 1870–1915," History of Education Quarterly 17 (1977): 242–43; see also Leslie, "A Comparative Study of Four Middle Atlantic Colleges, 1870–1915: Bucknell University, Franklin and Marshall College, Princeton University, and Swarthmore College" (Ph.D. diss., Johns Hopkins University, 1971), pp. 51–52.

69. For occupations of members of boards of trustees in the twentieth century, see Earl J. McGrath, "The Control of Higher Education in America," Educational Record 18 (1936): 259–272, and Hubert Park Beck, Men Who Control Our Universities: The Economic and Social

Composition of Thirty Leading American Universities, with a foreword by George S. Counts (New York, 1947). Beck provides an analysis of the social and economic characteristics of 30 members of the American Association of Universities for 1934–35. He does not study the actual function of these boards or their influence on the policies of these institutions.

70. This includes Hiram Hitchcock, who seemed to use his Hanover residence as a summer home.

71. See Richardson, *History of Dartmouth College*, 2:609.

72. Edwin B. Frost, *An Astronomer's Life* (Boston, 1933), pp. 14–15.

73. See Richardson, *History of Dartmouth College*, 2:601.

74. For his popularity, see Robert French Leavens and Arthur Hardy Lord, with a foreword by Earnest Martin Hopkins, *Dr. Tucker's Dartmouth* (Hanover, N.H., 1965), p. 14. For the nature of his congregation, see William Jewett Tucker, *My Generation: An Autobiographical Interpretation* (Boston, 1919), p. 78.

75. Tucker, *My Generation*, p. 86.

76. See proceedings of a meeting of the Boston alumni reported in "Dartmouth College Troubles," *Boston Journal*, 18 May 1881, "Scrapbook." Handwritten insertion indicates the name of the newspaper and the date.

77. For a development of these points, see pp. 137–139 of this study.

78. Quint, "N.Y. Alumni Assoc. v. Pres. Bartlett," 2:90–91.

79. Richardson, *History of Dartmouth College*, 2:611.

80. Ibid., p. 517.

81. The compensation for this position was set at $500, but the board noted that it hoped to raise it to a full salary. He seemed to be pleased by the new position. The trustees had thought it important to placate him for financial reasons. See Richardson, *History of Dartmouth College*, 2:528–529.

82. For an interesting treatment of this point, see Robert H. Wiebe, *The Search for Order 1877–1920*, with a foreword by David Donald (New York, 1967), p. 41.

83. See, for example, Leslie, "Localism, Denominationalism, and Institutional Strategies," pp. 246–247, regarding Franklin and Marshall College.

84. Lord, *History of Dartmouth College*, p. 245.

85. Richardson indicates only that excuses were granted to 73 students. He does not indicate if the Chandler students are included in this number. See Richardson, *History of Dartmouth College*, 2:550. If one includes only the academical students (265), the figure equals 27.5%. If one includes the academical and the Chandler (77) students, the figure equals 21.3%.

86. There were seventeen such temporary grants during the last year of Smith's administration; the number was considerably larger during the earlier part of his administration. See Richardson, *History of Dartmouth College*, 2:519.

87. The figures were derived from the aggregate amounts noted in the *Aegis*, July 1861, as cited in Lord, *History of Dartmouth College*, p. 245, n. 1.

88. See Charles F. Thwing, *American Colleges: Their Students and Work* (New York, 1879), pp. 36–37.

89. Smith himself noted that in 1874 almost one quarter of the students came from outside the New England region. Students came from twenty-three different states and territories. See A[sa] D. Smith, "Condition of the College in 1874," in *History of New Hampshire: From Its First Discovery to the Year 1830*, by Edwin David Sanborn (Manchester, N.H., 1875), p. 285.

90. Resolution of the board of trustees, August 1864, quoted in Lord, *History of Dartmouth College*, p. 341.

91. The president's salary was raised to $3,000.

92. For Harvard faculty salaries, see Samuel Eliot Morison, ed., *The Development of*

Harvard University Since the Inauguration of President Eliot 1869–1929 (Cambridge, Mass., 1930), p. xli.

93. Even in 1893 the average faculty salary of the most highly paid professor in 100 institutions on a national level was $2,015.50. The salary range of the highest paid professor was from $540 to $5,500. In 1890 the salary of the full professors at Dartmouth was $2,200. While the professors' salaries were much higher than many wage earners', only the most highly paid professors at the larger institutions received salaries comparable to the lower-grade officers of corporations. The lower-paid professors received salaries equal to highly skilled industrial workers. Thus, by the 1890s their salaries were not comparable with others in upper-middle-class professions.

See W. R. Harper, "The Pay of American College Professors," *Forum* 16 (September 1893):96–109.

94. In line with these developments, during the Smith administration the principal of nearby Kimball Union Academy criticized the trustees for not choosing faculty members from among schoolmen in the state. Cited by Richardson, *History of Dartmouth College*, 2:566.

95. See Lord, *History of Dartmouth College*, pp. 374–375.

96. Ibid., p. 409, and Richardson, *History of Dartmouth College*, 2:524.

97. The letter from the principal of the nearby academy criticized the faculty as well as the trustees. The faculty was criticized for such things as not having any interest in the common schools, not supporting state teacher associations, and not being friendly with ministers in the state, especially the ministers in smaller towns. Cited by Richardson, *History of Dartmouth College*, 2:566.

98. This fund was not completed until 1894.

99. See Richardson, *History of Dartmouth College*, 2:519.

100. *Catalogue of the Officers and Students of Dartmouth College 1877–78*, pp. 22–24. The second largest amount came from individuals in New Hampshire, 31.3%. Other individuals contributing scholarship funds were from Massachusetts, Iowa, Illinois, Maine, Vermont, Missouri, and England. There were financial awards for prizes in various areas obtained from individuals in New York City, Iowa, New Hampshire, and Texas. *Catalogue of Dartmouth College 1877–78*, p. 25.

101. See Richardson, *History of Dartmouth College*, 2:515, and Ralph Nading Hill, ed. *The College on the Hill: A Dartmouth Chronicle* (Hanover, N.H., 1964), p. 78.

102. For various gifts during this period, see Lord, *History of Dartmouth College*, pp. 345–346, 349, 359, 360, 361, 382, 404, 405. Some of the funds such as the Wentworth bequest could not be used until they reached a certain amount.

103. Quoted in ibid., p. 378.

104. Richardson, *History of Dartmouth College*, 2:525.

105. This amount was estimated at the current value of the gifts. Lord, *History of Dartmouth College*, p. 407.

106. The expenses of the Academical Department, for example, rose from $17,475 in 1859–60 to $49,745 in 1875–76. See Richardson, *History of Dartmouth College*, 2:526.

107. Ibid., 2:527. As during the Lord administration, the number of students fluctuated, but there was a general pattern of growth. From a low point during the Civil War period with only 161 students enrolled in the Academical Department in 1863–64, by 1870–71 the number of students in the Academical Department equaled 305. The number of students in this department fluctuated for the rest of his administration, averaging between 260 and 280, with 249 in 1875–76. The Chandler Department nearly doubled and then remained at a uniform rate, with an average of about 70 students. The numbers of students in the Medical School rose, and the combination of all these factors plus the advent of the new schools—the Thayer and agricultural—brought the number of students enrolled to

479 in 1875–76 (a number not equalled for nearly twenty years). See Lord, *History of Dartmouth College*, p. 409, and Richardson, *History of Dartmouth College*, 2:516, 518–519.

108. Lord, *History of Dartmouth College*, pp. 403–404. There was no evidence that the treasurer appropriated the funds for his own use.

109. Richardson, *History of Dartmouth College*, 2:524–525.

110. Bissell Hall was the gymnasium. When they approached Bissell for the funds, he was asked to allocate it for this building.

111. Culver Hall was to be used jointly by the college and the agricultural school. It was built at a cost of $40,000, with Dartmouth contributing $25,000; and because of its use for agricultural education also, they received a legislative appropriation of $15,000. It contained a chemistry laboratory and lecture rooms. The students seemed to appreciate the attempts to improve the appearance of the college. In March 1872, the *Dartmouth* stated, "spacious airy lecture room in Culver Hall, with its large and numerous windows and pleasant situation, as contrasted with the Cimmerian gloom of some of the recitation rooms of Dartmouth Hall." Quoted in Richardson, *History of Dartmouth College*, 2:539.

112. This was built through the efforts of the agricultural school and was to be used as a dormitory and dining hall for these students, although it was open to other students.

113. Joel Parker (former trustee) donated the trees and $1,000 for the purchase of land to improve the appearance of the college.

114. See Ernest Earnest, *Academic Procession: An Informal History of the American College 1636 to 1953* (New York, 1953), pp. 212–213.

115. By 1881 the board had five new members (including alumni trustees). Five of the 1877 board had died or retired. For age and occupation of this board, see appendixes 27 and 28.

Bartlett was not the first choice of the 1877 board, which approached Tucker in 1876. At thirty-seven, Tucker was presiding over (like Smith, before he came to Dartmouth) a leading church in New York City. But on balance, the 1877 board probably thought that Bartlett was a comparatively good choice for the $3,000 it was willing to pay. For a summary of his background, see pp. 2, 223n.116 of this study.

The changing nature of the faculty, alumni, and students and their growing assertiveness and self-consciousness as collegiate factions would be developed more fully by 1881. And they increasingly came into conflict with Bartlett's policies and style.

116. Bartlett served as a pastor in Monson, Massachusetts, in parts of New Hampshire, and in Chicago. He held professorial positions at Western Reserve in Ohio and in 1858 became a professor of biblical literature at the newly organized Chicago Theological Seminary. Bartlett was successful at raising funds for the seminary. He obtained $5,000 in Illinois and canvassed twenty-one towns in the East for more funds. He also had good connections with the American Board of Commissioners for Foreign Missions and the American Tract Society. He helped to organize the first Congregational Association of Churches in Ohio. He was active in the First National Council of Congregational Churches in 1871. See George Adams Boyd, *Three Stimsons and a Bartlett*, with family data compiled by Dorothy Stimson (Stonington, Conn., 1967), chap. 4.

117. The gifts included $60,000 donated by Henry Winkley, a crockery merchant from Philadelphia (the gift was unsolicited); $50,000 from B. P. Cheney, Boston, Massachusetts (the gift was unsolicited); $35,000 from Mrs. Valeria G. Stone of Malden, Massachusetts (the gift was secured through the efforts of Dr. Leeds of the College Church, a family friend, and President Bartlett); $10,000 from the Honorable Salmon P. Chase (unsolicited). See Lord, *History of Dartmouth College*, pp. 415–416. The report of the board noted that Bartlett had some influence in securing about $70,000 of the $170,000. This evidently includes the gift of Mrs. Stone plus some appeals for endowments for various chairs.

The report said: "Funds have come in from sources which had begun to flow prior to

Dr. Bartlett's administration, but of the $170,000 added to the permanent funds within the past four years, perhaps $70,000 came through the personal application of the President."

118. From the Report of the Investigating Committee, in "Dartmouth College," "Scrapbook."

119. The *Congregationalist* reported that Bartlett stated in a meeting before the General Association of Congregational Churches of New Hampshire that "the time would come when some things would be better understood. He proposed to keep silent however, feeling like the blacksmith who said he could pound out a better character for himself than all the lawyers in Christendom could give him." "The New Hampshire General Association," *Congregationalist*, 21 September 1881, "Scrapbook."

120. From the Report of the Investigating Committee, in "Dartmouth College," "Scrapbook."

121. Ibid.

122. Ibid. Within this context, the board also noted that "the attitude of the President should and must be in harmony with the policy of the board."

For the increasing distinction between public and private activities in the late nineteenth century, see Thomas Bender, *Community and Social Change in America* (New Brunswick, N.J., 1978), especially pp. 114–120.

123. The newspaper clippings are contained in the "Scrapbook" of the trial. The trial received the most publicity in New York City and Boston—leading urban centers where the alumni were well organized. The "Scrapbook" contains clippings from newspapers as far west as Cincinnati. The *Journal of Education* and other such publications also covered the trial. The newspapers advanced arguments for and against Bartlett from the pretrial period through its aftermath.

That the Bartlett controversy received so much coverage may have been due in part to the good connections some of the parties of the controversy had with the press. For example, Charles Miller, secretary of the New York Association of Alumni, was himself editor of the *New York Times*. Miller was able to use the *Times* as a forum for the views of the New York alumni. The general interest of the newspapers in this event also seems to fall within the rubric of a shift in emphasis away from governmental affairs to news of human interest and wider fields, as well as a new emphasis on "crusades" involving issues of social welfare. See Frank Luther Mott, *American Journalism: A History 1690–1960*, 3d ed. (Toronto, 1962), pp. 411–412, 414–415.

124. "Dartmouth Embarrassments," *Boston Evening Transcript*, 20 February 1882, "Scrapbook."

125. Ibid.

126. "Dissensions at Dartmouth," *New York Tribune*, 5 May 1881, "Scrapbook."

127. "The Dartmouth Discord," *Boston Post*, 29 May 1882, "Scrapbook."

128. *New York Times*, 24 April 1882, "Scrapbook."

129. "Dartmouth and Her Alumni," *Springfield Republican*, 27 March 1882, "Scrapbook."

130. "Dartmouth College," *Vermont Chronicle*, 28 April 1882, "Scrapbook."

131. "Dartmouth College," *Herald and News* (West Randolph, Vt.), September 1881, "Scrapbook."

132. Report of the General Association of New Hampshire (Congregational Churches), September 1882, "Scrapbook." As was noted previously, this should not be thought of as simply secular versus sectarian interests. William Jewett Tucker was no less imbued with religious fervor, although its form was different from that of Bartlett's.

133. "Dartmouth's Difficulty," *Congregationalist*, 3 August 1881, "Scrapbook."

134. Boston paper (n.t., n.d.), handwritten insert notes that the date was around September or October 1881, "Scrapbook."

135. "Old Dartmouth Crisis," *New York Times*, 3 May 1881, "Scrapbook."
136. "School and College," *Boston Transcript*, 30 May 1881, "Scrapbook."
137. "Old Dartmouth Crisis," *New York Times*, 3 May 1881, "Scrapbook."
138. "Are These the Facts?" [Letter to the Editor], *Boston Traveller*, 30 May 1881, "Scrapbook."
139. *Boston Transcript* (n.t.), 5 May 1881, "Scrapbook."
140. Ibid.
141. Along a similar vein, the trustees of Hamilton also seemed to look to an older form of harmony when they were confronted with a similar situation. See George E. Peterson, *The New England College in the Age of the University* (Amherst, 1964), p. 109.

Chapter VI
Conclusion

1. William Jewett Tucker, *The Historic College: Its Present Place in the Educational System. An Address Delivered by William Jewett Tucker upon his Inauguration as President of Dartmouth College, June 28, 1893, with the Exercises Attending the Inauguration* (Hanover, N.H., 1894), p. 34.
2. Robert French Leavens and Arthur Hardy Lord, with an introduction by Ernest Martin Hopkins, *Dr. Tucker's Dartmouth* (Hanover, N.H., 1965), p. 11.
3. Ibid. The specific reference here is to the dissatisfaction with Bartlett's ideas and policies among faculty, students, and alumni. But the same type of presentation regarding nineteenth-century conservatism is presented throughout.
4. This caveat is not meant to denigrate either the popularity of Tucker or his leadership in shaping the changes clamored for during the Bartlett controversy and accelerating changes already begun in previous administrations. He built upon such changes begun in the Smith and Bartlett administrations as an increase in electives, a more national constituency, alumni representaion in governance, an adjustment of the physical plant to a more "collegiate" setting, support of a faculty with more specialized training along specific disciplinary lines, and an expansion of course offerings in modern languages, social, and life sciences. In this way, Dartmouth evolved into a large and well-known eastern college in the Ivy League category.
5. Testimony of Judge William Fullerton, "N.Y. Alumni Assoc. v. Pres. Bartlett," 1:4.
6. Counsel for the prosecution included Asa W. Tenney, class of 1859, U. S. district attorney, Eastern District, New York, and later judge of the U.S. District Court, Eastern District; Sanford Steele, class of 1870, prominent lawyer and businessman, treasurer of the New York Association of Alumni, and organizer and president of the General Chemical Company of New York. The other member of the prosecution, Judge William Fullerton, served as counsel for many of the celebrated cases of the day and was considered one of the leaders of the New York bar.

Counsel for the defense included two prominent members of the New Hampshire bar, Hon. Harry Bingham of Littleton, class of 1843, and Judge William S. Ladd of Lancaster, class of 1855.
7. See George E. Peterson, *The New England College in the Age of the University* (Amherst, 1964), pp. 80–112.

I am grateful to Peterson for the suggestion in his book that the Bartlett controversy warrants further investigation by an educational historian. Peterson makes a beginning toward a reexamination of higher learning in nineteenth-century America, but he does not quite escape the tendency to view the changes in the New England colleges from the perspective of the ascendancy of the university.

8. For a description of the Andover trial from Tucker's perspective, see William Jewett Tucker, *My Generation: An Autobiographical Interpretation* (Boston, 1919), pp. 185–197.

9. James Willard Hurst, *Law and the Conditions of Freedom in the Nineteenth-Century United States* (Madison, Wis., 1955), p. 85. In developing this point in relation to the field of law, he notes that this period marked a renewed emphasis on the social environment and political organization and power that had been common in our constitution-making days. See *Law and the Conditions of Freedom*, pp. 71–108.

10. For varying approaches to and interpretations of these general themes, see Hurst, *Law and the Conditions of Freedom*; Michael H. Frisch, *Town into City: Springfield, Massachusetts, and the Meaning of Community, 1840–1880* (Cambridge, Mass., 1972); E. Digby Baltzell, *Philadelphia Gentlemen: The Making of a National Upper Class* (New York, 1958); E. Digby Baltzell, *The Protestant Establishment: Aristocracy & Caste in America* (New York, 1964); Robert H. Wiebe, *The Search for Order, 1877–1920*, with a foreword by David Donald (New York, 1967); Robert H. Wiebe, *The Segmented Society: An Historical Preface to the Meaning of America* (New York, 1967); Samuel P. Hays, "A Systematic Social History," in *American History: Retrospect and Prospect*, ed. George A. Bellias and Gerald Grob (New York, 1971), pp. 315–366; George M. Fredrickson, *The Inner Civil War: Northern Intellectuals and the Crisis of the Union* (New York, 1968); Gregory H. Singleton, "Protestant Voluntary Organizations and the Shaping of Victorian America," *American Quarterly* 27 (December 1975):47–58.

See especially Thomas Bender's recent seminal book, *Community and Social Change in America* (New Brunswick, N.J., 1978), which critiques the literature and calls for a major rethinking of community.

11. See Report of the Investigating Committee of the Board of Trustees, Dartmouth College, 28 July 1881, quoted in "Dartmouth College," *Boston Journal*, 30 July 1881, "Scrapbook."

12. "Dartmouth College," *Boston Advertiser*, 5 September 1881, "Scrapbook." A handwritten notation by the professor who compiled the "Scrapbook" indicates that the statement was made by one of Bartlett's supporters, Professor Emerson.

13. W. G. Veazey and W. J. Tucker, Committee of the Trustees, to the editor, "Dartmouth College—An Erroneous Impression Corrected," *Boston Advertiser*, 12 September 1881, "Scrapbook." A handwritten insertion indicates the date and the paper. The trustees had received letters from the faculty in reference to the September 5 article, noting the importance that the impression be corrected. See, for example, A. S. Hardy to W. G. Veazey, 7 September 1881, and D. J. Noyes to W. G. Veazey, 6 September 1881, Hardy, Noyes, and Veazey Manuscript Files, Special Collections, Dartmouth College Library, Hanover, N.H.

14. Records of the Board of Trustees, April 1882, Special Collections, Dartmouth College Library, Hanover, N.H. "Resolved. That we believe that the best interests of the college require that the members of the faculty should continue in their present positions and cordially co-operate in advancing the true interests of the college."

Bartlett had tried to pressure the trustees to dismiss some of the faculty members, especially Hardy, but the trustees did not dismiss any faculty members and passed the resolutions supporting the faculty.

For pressure exerted by Bartlett, see S. C. Bartlett to Judge Veazey, 28 September 1881, and S. C. Bartlett to Gov. Prescott, 5 December 1881 and 4 February 1882, Bartlett and Veazey Manuscript Files.

15. In 1890 the trustees received a petition from the Chandler faculty asking that the prohibition against the academical faculty teaching in the Chandler Department be rescinded. At the same time they received a petition from nine members of the academical

faculty in which they noted that while their request for an increase in salary was denied, the president was supplied with a rent-free house, and a supporter of Bartlett was able to supplement his earnings by teaching in one of the associated schools. The faculty members noted that the only way they could supplement their salary was to do the same in the Chandler Department. The trustees responded by raising their salaries to $2,200 with the proviso that if they taught in both departments, the compensation covered all services. See Richardson, *History of Dartmouth College*, 2: 626–627. The trustees may have been afraid of another conflict as Bartlett had written a pamphlet in reference to these memorials, and the head of the Chandler Department had asked to appear before the board. With the action of the board, the faculty did not voice any more complaints in reference to this issue.

16. For a description of the faculty, see Leavens and Lord, *Dr. Tucker's Dartmouth*, pp. 56–58, 143–148.

Evidencing his metropolitan orientation, Tucker noted, "It is far better that a faculty should be cosmopolitan than it should be provincial." William Jewett Tucker, "Administrative Problems of the Historic College," *Educational Review* 43 (May 1912):437.

In the field of science, see also comments regarding Professor Ernest Fox Nichols in Sanborn C. Brown and Leonard M. Rieser, *Natural Philosophy at Dartmouth: From Surveyors' Chains to the Pressure of Light* (Hanover, N.H., 1974), chap. 10.

17. Spaulding, "N.Y. Alumni Assoc. v. Pres. Bartlett," 2:93. As regards the custom of discussing appointments with the faculty see, for example, Noyes, "N.Y. Alumni Assoc. v. Pres. Bartlett," 2:59–61.

18. Ibid., p. 94.

19. See Richardson, *History of Dartmouth College*, 2:707–708. A faculty member was appointed to a position that could have been filled through the promotion of one of the members of the department involved. The department was not consulted regarding this appointment. The department concerned protested to the board and circulated a petition asking for a definition of the board's policy regarding appointments, promotions, and the function of departments in recommending new members. While the board did not modify its decision in this case, the board did indicate some recognition of peer evaluation in the case of new appointments.

20. "The Troubles at Dartmouth," *Springfield Republican*, 25 July 1881, "Scrapbook." The newspaper was responding to an assertion by one of Bartlett's supporters on the board that Hardy might be removed. No names are mentioned directly.

21. For New England colleges see, for example, Peterson, *New England College*. For Harvard faculty, see Robert A. McCaughey, "The Transformation of American Academic Life: Harvard University 1821–1892," *Perspectives in American History* 8(1974):239–332. See also chapter 2 of this study.

22. See, for example, W. Bruce Leslie. "A Comparative Study of Four Middle Atlantic Colleges, 1870–1915: Bucknell University, Franklin and Marshall College, Princeton University, and Swarthmore College" (Ph.D. diss., Johns Hopkins University, 1971). Franklin and Marshall College moved toward this direction much more slowly.

For the characteristics of the faculty at several New England colleges, see Peterson, *New England College*. For Harvard, see McGaughey, "Transformation of American Academic Life." At Harvard, during the 1880s and 1890s (rather than in the early part of his administration) President Eliot placed prime emphasis on hiring and rewarding faculty with original, specialized research. See McCaughey, "Transformation of American Academic Life," and Hugh Hawkins, *Between Harvard and America: The Educational Leadership of Charles W. Eliot* (New York, 1972); see also chapter 2 of this study.

23. See, for example, Leslie, "Comparative Study of Four Middle Atlantic Colleges" and W. Bruce Leslie, "Localism, Denominationalism, and Institutional Strategies in Ur-

banizing America," *History of Education Quarterly* 17 (1977):235–256, especially p. 247 regarding Swarthmore.

24. See McCaughey, "Transformation of American Academic Life," p. 337.

25. See Peterson, *New England College*, pp. 133–134. For influence of faculty in two women's colleges (Bryn Mawr and Wellesley), see Roberta Frankfort, *Collegiate Women: Domesticity and Career in Turn-of-the-Century America* (New York, 1977), pp. 52, 79, 82, 83.

26. See Howard Segal, "The Patton-Wilson Succession," *Princeton Alumni Weekly* 79 (November 6, 1978), p. 20. Some faculty and alumni who were trustees also seem to have pushed President Patton out of office. See Segal, "Patton-Wilson Succession."

In a related context, for instances in which alumni dissatisfaction with the president or with the extent of their voice in governance coincided with the faculty's interests and led to open conflict with the president, see Peterson, *New England College*.

27. Noting the importance of the alumni movement, Tucker said, "The opening of these college corporations to alumni representation had virtually put the colleges under alumni government. When the alumni representation is not numerically strong it is usually influential, and always by implication at least suggestive of authority in reserve." "Administrative Problems of the Historic College," p. 435.

28. See Lord, *History of Dartmouth College*, pp. 482–483.

29. Leavens and Lord, *Dr. Tucker's Dartmouth*, p. 134.

30. See Richardson, *History of Dartmouth College*, 2:688.

31. Leavens and Lord, *Dr. Tucker's Dartmouth*, p. 204.

32. This was not done on a formal basis until 1921, when the "Selective Process" was established whereby an alumni committee interviewed applicants. See Ernest Martin Hopkins, "The College and the Alumni," from an address delivered before the Seventeenth Annual Conference of the American Alumni Council, Amherst, Massachusetts, May 1930, in *This Our Purpose*, by Ernest Martin Hopkins (Hanover, N.H., 1950), pp. 211–212. Hopkins was president of Dartmouth.

For an important study analyzing changing admissions policies and problems of class discrimination and anti-Semitism in institutions of higher education, see Harold S. Wechsler, *The Qualified Student: A History of Selective Admission in America* (New York, 1977). See also Marcia G. Synnott, "The Admission and Assimilation of Minority Students at Harvard, Yale and Princeton, 1900–1950," *History of Education Quarterly* 19 (1979):285–304.

33. Tucker, "Administrative Problems of the Historic College," p. 435.

34. Leavens and Lord, *Dr. Tucker's Dartmouth*, pp. 199, 188.

35. See Richardson, *History of Dartmouth College*, 2:685, and Lord, *History of Dartmouth College*, pp. 496–497.

The effect of contributions such as Tuck's for business education helped to produce a trained group of leaders to steer the country's business concerns. For a development of gifts for business education and donations of alumni, see Merle Curti and Roderick Nash, *Philanthropy in the Shaping of American Higher Education* (New Brunswick, N.J., 1965), pp. 74–75, 186–211.

36. See chapter 4 of this study.

37. See Thomas Jefferson Whitenbaker, *Princeton 1746–1896* (Princeton, N.J., 1946), p. 376, and Leslie, "Comparative Study of Four Middle Atlantic Colleges," pp. 130–132.

38. See *Alumni Weekly*, April 1900, cited in Whitenbaker, *Princeton*, p. 376.

39. See pp. 132–133 of this study.

40. Leslie, "Comparative Study of Four Middle Atlantic Colleges," p. 145, and Leslie, "Localism, Denominationalism, and Institutional Strategies" pp. 248–249.

Once the alumni received their power, they carefully protected their rights. See, for example, Peterson, *New England College*, regarding President Carter's attempt to influence an alumni election (p. 126).

41. Leslie, "Localism, Denominationalism, and Institutional Strategies," pp. 246–247, 251.

42. See, for example, Thomas Le Duc, *Piety and Intellect at Amherst College* (New York, 1946), p. 133. Leslie, "The Response of Four Colleges to the Rise of Intercollegiate Athletics, 1865–1915," *Journal of Sports History*, 3 (1976):213–222, and references regarding students in this chapter. See also interpretation by Christopher Lasch, "The Corruption of Sports," *New York Review of Books*, 24 (April 28, 1977), p. 29.

43. See Frankfort, *Collegiate Women*, chap. 6.

44. H. C. Pearson '93, "Clarkson, Right Guard," in *Echoes from Dartmouth: A Collection of Poems, Stories, and Historical Sketches by the Graduate and Undergraduate Writers of Dartmouth College*, ed. H. J. Hapgood and Craven Laycock (Hanover, N.H., 1895), pp. 19–20.

45. See Richardson, *History of Dartmouth College*, 2:710–712, and Lord, *History of Dartmouth College*, p. 501.

Women college students during the nineteenth century were primarily upper middle class or middle class. By the first decade of the century, however, they seem to have had an influx of more wealthy students (similar to the students at the exclusive men's colleges). See Frankfort, *Collegiate Women*, pp. 30, 38, and David F. Allmendinger, Jr., "History and the Usefulness of Women's Education," *History of Education Quarterly* 19 (1979):119.

46. Students enrolled in 1908–9, all classes and all schools, cited in Richardson, *History of Dartmouth College*, 2:711.

The trend is an acceleration of that noted by Smith back in 1874. He indicated that nearly one quarter of the students came from outside the northern New England area and the students represented 23 states. It is also in line, not only with the class of 1881, but with the student body in 1879–80. Of the academical students, 18.9% were from places outside New England, and of the Chandler students, 26.5% were from places outside New England. And 57.9% of the academical students and 55.1% of the Chandler students resided in northern New England, while 16.7% of the academical students and 12.2% of the Chandler students resided in Massachusetts. In addition to the decline of students coming from northern New England in 1908–9, the increase in students coming from Massachusetts that began in the Smith administration increased greatly, so that by 1908–9, 42.9% came from Massachusetts and 25.1% came from outside New England. For Smith administration, see A[sa] D. Smith, "Condition of the College in 1874," in *History of New Hampshire from Its First Discovery to the Year 1830* by Edwin David Sanborn (Manchester, N.H., 1875), p. 285. For 1879–80, see *Catalogue of Dartmouth College and the Associated Institutions 1879–80* (Hanover, N.H., 1879).

47. President's Report to the Trustees, 1900–1901, cited by Leavens and Lord, *Dr. Tucker's Dartmouth*, p. 142. The other occupations listed were 23.5% from professional backgrounds, 24% from wage-earning backgrounds. No specific subdivision is given for the wage-earning groups, so it is difficult to determine what this means. It could include those who worked in an office and were salaried, or those who were skilled craftsmen, or both. I have been unable to locate the original document to see if Tucker himself provided any subdivision for this category. While it is not possible to make any definitive statement without correlating the occupational index to the wealth and status index during this period (see Michael B. Katz, "Occupational Classification in History," *Journal of Interdisciplinary History* 3 [1972] : 63–68), the writings from the period, the histories, the move to a more metropolitan constituency, their expenses, their decreased age, along with the occupational index indicate a shift in the upper middle class noted in the Smith and Bartlett administrations.

48. See Richardson, *History of Dartmouth College*, 2:712. The minimum being spent was $483 a year.

49. Ibid., p. 711. In 1895 scholarships started with a flat rate of $50 and went up to $75 and $85, depending upon the grades earned.

50. William Jewett Tucker, "The Part Which Our Colleges Must Henceforth Be Expected to Take in the Training of the Gentleman" [Convocation Address of 1905], *Dartmouth Bi-Monthly* 1 (October 1905):14.

Medical students also organized a fraternity—Alpha Kappa Kappa—and it became the parent organization of thirty-six chapters; see Lord, *History of Dartmouth College*, p. 537.

As in the 1880s, cribbing remained a problem during this period. See Leavens and Lord, *Dr. Tucker's Dartmouth*, pp. 114–115. In addition to the fraternities, numerous other student organizations were in existence during this period. These included a glee club, band, mandolin club, orchestra, dramatic club, debating club, and literary magazines. Carnival Week (1899) with athletics, parades, fireworks, dances, concerts, a minstrel show, and a baseball game with Williams also evolved during this period. It became known as Prom Week and continued in this form.

Palaeopitus, a student organization, also was formed at this time. Secret at first, two years later, in 1902, it became open. It included the captains and managers of the teams, the editor of the *Dartmouth*, the president of the debating club, and other officers, plus some members elected by the junior class. According to one source, some alumni encouraged the formation of this organization.

See Richardson, *History of Dartmouth College*, 2:731–732; Lord, *History of Dartmouth College*, pp. 537, 501; Leavens and Lord, *Dr. Tucker's Dartmouth*, p. 222.

51. See Richardson, *History of Dartmouth College*, 2:732.

52. For reference to the number of students without fraternity affiliations, see ibid.

53. Owen Johnson, *Stover at Yale*, with an introduction by Kingman Brewster, Jr. (New York, 1968), p. 20.

54. For developments at Harvard, see Samuel Eliot Morison, *Three Centuries of Harvard 1636–1936* (Cambridge, Mass., 1965), chap. 16, and Owen Wister, *Philosophy Four* (New York, 1903). For developments at Yale, see Johnson, *Stover at Yale*.

55. For further development of this point, see pp. 140–142 of this study. They also built new dormitories and a college commons with dining facilities. See Richardson, *History of Dartmouth College*, 2:732, and Lord, *History of Dartmouth College*, pp. 486–488.

56. Quoted in Leavens and Lord, *Dr. Tucker's Dartmouth*, p. 228.

57. H. C. Pearson, '93, "In Senior Days," in *Echoes from Dartmouth*, pp. 37–38.

58. See Richardson, *History of Dartmouth College*, 2:728–731, and Leavens and Lord, *Dr. Tucker's Dartmouth*, pp. 228–236.

59. Henry Seidel Canby, *Alma Matre: The Gothic Age of the American College* (New York, 1936), p. 58.

For interpretations of student life in the late nineteenth and early twentieth centuries see, for example, Leslie, "Comparative Study of Four Middle Atlantic Colleges," Peterson, *New England College in the Age of the University;* Ralph Henry Gabriel, *Religion and Learning at Yale: The Church of Christ in the College and University, 1757–1957*, especially pp. 187–189; Ernest Earnest, *Academic Procession: An Informal History of the American College* (Indianapolis, 1953); Thomas Le Duc, *Piety and Intellect at Amherst College, 1865–1912* (New York, 1946), pp. 125, 139–140.

For student life at Wellesley and Bryn Mawr, see Frankfort, *Collegiate Women*, especially pp. 53, 63, 68, 81–82.

60. Woodrow Wilson, "What Is a College For?" *Scribner's* 46 (November 1909):572–575.

61. See, for example, Leslie, "Comparative Study of Four Middle Atlantic Colleges, p. 208.

62. Earnest, *Academic Procession*, p. 213. See also James McLachlan, *American Boarding Schools: A Historical Study* (New York, 1970).

63. See Le Duc, *Piety and Intellect*, p. 125.

64. See, for example, Winton U. Solberg, *The University of Illinois 1867–1894: An Intellectual and Cultural History* (Urbana, Ill., 1968), p. 192.

65. Merle Curti and Vernon Carstensen, *The University of Wisconsin: A History. 1848–1925*, 1:659–665.

66. Cited in George Wilson Pierson, *Yale College: An Educational History, 1871–1921* (New Haven, 1952), p. 232. See also Howard Savage, *American College Athletics* (New York, 1929), pp. 13–20; Leslie, "Response of Four Colleges to the Rise of Intercollegiate Athletics"; Leslie, "Comparative Study of Four Middle Atlantic Colleges," p. 99; Peterson, *New England College*, pp. 83–84.

67. Curti and Carstensen, *University of Wisconsin* 1:693.

68. Ernest Martin Hopkins, "The College of the Future," Address Delivered at his Inauguration as President of Dartmouth College, 6 October 1916, in *This Our Purpose*, p. 117. For insights into the careers of women college graduates, see Frankfort, *Collegiate Women*.

69. In line with the trend of the class of 1881, in the distribution of graduates through 1910, New York City (including Brooklyn) ranked first for graduates and Boston ranked second. See *General Catalogue of Dartmouth College and the Associated Schools 1769–1910*, pp. 836–837.

70. Baltzell, *Protestant Establishment*, p. 135. See also Oscar Handlin and Mary F. Handlin, *The American College and American Culture: Socialization as a Function of Higher Education* (New York, 1970), p. 47; Earnest, *Academic Procession*, pp. 217–218.

71. For the development of this point in the making of a national metropolitan upper class, see Baltzell, *Philadelphia Gentlemen*.

For the development of the metropolitan men's club, see Dixon Wecter, *Saga of American Society*, chap. 7.

For important insights into the changing structure and experience of community, see Bender, *Community and Social Change in America*.

72. For development of these points, see Tucker, "The Historic College: Its Present Place in the Educational System."

73. Quoted in "Baccalaureate," *Daily Dartmouth*, 27 June 1898.

74. President's Report to the Trustees, 1900–1901, quoted in Leavens and Lord, *Dr. Tucker's Dartmouth*, p. 166.

75. See Tucker, "The Historic College: Its Present Place in the Education System."

76. Tucker, as quoted in Peterson, *New England College in the Age of the University*, p. 176.

77. William Jewett Tucker, *Public Mindedness: An Aspect of Citizenship Considered in Various Addresses, Given While President of Dartmouth College* (Concord, 1910), p. 39.

78. William Jewett Tucker, "The Mind of the Wage Earner," Address before the Twentieth Annual Convention of the Officials of Labor Bureaus of America, in ibid., pp. 171, 172.

79. Woodrow Wilson, "Princeton for the Nation's Service," *Science* 16 (1902):724, quoted in Laurence R. Veysey, *The Emergence of the American University* (Chicago, 1965), p. 245.

For an interesting interpretation of the development of the social thought of men such as Wilson and academics in the 1880s, see Dorothy Ross, "Socialism and American Liberalism: Academic Social Thought in the 1880s," *Perspectives in American History* 11 (1977–78):7–79.

80. Tucker pushed for the introduction of sociology into the curriculum. Professor D. C. Wells, appointed to the chair of sociology, noted: "The demand for training to fit the student to understand . . . [social problems] is so general as to justify the new movement in higher education." The course at Dartmouth included such topics as race, the envi-

ronment, social institutions, and the faculty. Quoted in Peterson, *New England College in the Age of the University*, p. 236, n. 7.

As regards the development of the doctrine of service, see also Le Duc, *Piety and Intellect*, chap. 8, and Peterson, *New England College*, chap. 7 and Epilogue.

For an international perspective on the development of Christian colleges and the concept of Christian education as service, see Ruth Soulé Arnon, "The Christian College," *History of Education Quarterly* 14 (1974):235–249.

As regards the promotion and development of institutions such as settlement houses (e.g. Andover House) as a means of resolving larger social problems, Douglas Sloan provides insights into a related, although somewhat different development in the case of the promotion of cultural institutions. (In this case, the idea that social problems were cultural problems that could be resolved through the promotion of cultural institutions and through the leadership of the "cultivated elite.") See Sloan, "Cultural Uplift and Social Reform in Nineteenth Century Urban America," *History of Education Quarterly* 19 (1979):361–372.

For important insights into institutionalization and education and questions of authority, see also Thomas Bender, Peter Hall, Thomas Haskell, and Paul H, Mattingly, "Institutionalization and Education in the Nineteenth and Twentieth Centuries," *History of Education Quarterly* 20 (1980): 449–472.

81. Tucker, *My Generation*, p. 38.

82. Ibid.

83. For a more general development of this point in relation to the qualities of intelligence that were now emphasized, see Daniel H. Calhoun, *The Intelligence of a People* (Princeton, N.J., 1973). In 1882 Dartmouth Professor John Wright noted that the stress centered on skills to "balance, weigh, and discriminate." See "The Place of Original Research in College Education," *Journal of Addresses and Proceedings of the National Educational Association* (1882), p. 113.

For insights into the changing intellectual style as well as the changing structural base, see also Thomas Bender, "The Cultures of Intellectual Life: The City and the Professions," in *New Directions in American Intellectual History*, ed. Paul K. Conkin and John Higham (Baltimore, 1979), pp. 181–195.

84. For an illuminating treatment of a more general development of this point, see Gladys Bryson, "The Comparable Interests of the Old Moral Philosophy and the Modern Social Sciences," *Social Forces* 11 (October 1932):19–27. Gladys Bryson, "The Emergence of the Social Sciences from Moral Philosophy," *International Journal of Ethics* 42 (April 1932):304–323; Gladys Bryson, "Sociology Considered as Moral Philosophy," *Sociological Review* 24 (January 1932):26–36.

85. For a development of the range of courses, see Leavens and Lord, *Dr. Tucker's Dartmouth*, chaps. 3, 7.

86. Tucker, "The Historic College: Its Present Place in the Educational System," p. 20.

87. To this effect, Tucker noted, "The Sunday vesper service in Rollins Chapel at Dartmouth gave me while president of the college the unusual opportunity of attempting to supply to some degree what I have called the moral supports of instruction. . . . The service allowed a very wide range of subjects and an entirely informal habit of speech." William Jewett Tucker, *Personal Power, Counsels to College Men* (Boston, 1910), pp. vii, viii.

88. Tucker, *My Generation*, p. 297–298.

89. Cited in Leavens and Lord, *Dr. Tucker's Dartmouth*, p. 261. In reference to the tremendous preoccupation with growth in several universities, see also Veysey, *Emergence of the American University*.

90. Tucker, "Administrative Problems of the Historic College," p. 435.

91. The *Denver Republican* (February 1891), cited in Hugh Hawkins, *Between Harvard and America: The Educational Leadership of Charles W. Eliot* (New York, 1972), p. 215.

92. It should be noted that in his inaugural address, Eliot had distinguished the presidency of a university from that of a business position: "A university cannot be managed like a railroad or a cotton-mill." Quoted in Hawkins, *Between Harvard and America*. For changing developments in his administrative policy see Hawkins, *Between Harvard and America*. See also comments by Charles Biebel, "Higher Education and Old Professionalism," *History of Education Quarterly* 17 (1977):319–325.

93. Leslie, "Localism, Denominationalism, and Institutional Strategies," p. 250.

94. See, for example, Alfred D. Chandler, Jr., *The Visible Hand: The Managerial Revolution in American Business* (Cambridge, 1977). See also comments by Peter Hall, in Bender et al., "Institutionalization and Education," pp. 456–457.

95. Tucker, *My Generation* p. 270.

96. Ibid., pp. 269–270.

97. Tucker to the editor of the *Dartmouth*, quoted in Leavens and Lord, *Dr. Tucker's Dartmouth*, p. 107.

98. Tucker, *My Generation*, p. 325.

99. Richardson, *History of Dartmouth College*, 2:722.

100. Tucker, as quoted in Wilder D. Quint, *The Story of Dartmouth* (Boston, 1914), p. 278.

101. Tucker, Convocation Address, 1902, as quoted in Leavens and Lord, *Dr. Tucker's Dartmouth*, p. 216.

BIBLIOGRAPHIC NOTES

The Introduction, the Conclusion, and the beginning of the chapters on the faculty, students, alumni, and trustees describe current problems involved in the study of the history of American higher education, particularly the serious limitations of standard accounts and the slim analytical literature available on nineteenth-century colleges. The Notes and the text provide a bibliographic guide to the secondary literature pertinent to the issues raised in this study. Highlighting questions such as institutionalization, communal development, professionalization, and developments in the larger society as well as educational and cultural change, the literature should be of interest to students of educational, cultural, social, and religious history. While I have not attempted to cite all the literature on nineteenth-century higher education, where relevant, I have tried to include some of the better of the older studies as well as the new historical literature that has followed in the wake of Bernard Bailyn's reconceptualization of the history of education and Wilson Smith's call for a "new historian of education."

A few words should be said about the extensive primary sources and biographical material that I used in this study. References to many of these sources can be found in the Appendixes, the Notes, and the text. An earlier version of this study as a Ph.D. dissertation contains some additional bibliographic citations (see University Microfilms International, publication #7803036). Rather than repeating the references cited, in this section I will try to use some of the Dartmouth sources to illustrate the range of materials that should be helpful to other scholars interested in undertaking an in-depth analysis of the transformation of academic community in comparable nineteenth-century institutions.

The Special Collections, Dartmouth College Library, contains much of the manuscript material and other archival records I consulted on the students, alumni, trustees, and the Dartmouth College presidents. The Alumni/Student Files contain biographical data, newspaper clippings,

235

obituaries, correspondence, and other assorted materials on individual students, faculty members, alumni, and trustees. They are arranged by class—class of 1881, for example—and then alphabetically under the individual's name. In general, the file folders are much more extensive for the post–Civil War period than for the antebellum period. The Records of the Board of Trustees from the 1830s through the 1890s and the Records of the Faculty from the 1840s through the 1890s provide detailed minutes of the various meetings. They contain discussions of various concerns such as governance, discipline, and courses of study. When combined with other sources and looked at during various historical periods, they can be helpful in providing insights into historical shifts. The Manuscript Files contain numerous papers, diaries, and the like relating to the individual faculty members, students, alumni, and trustees during the periods under question. The files for Presidents Samuel Colcord Bartlett, Nathan Lord, Asa Dodge Smith, and William Jewett Tucker also contain the presidents' reports.

When I was using the material at Dartmouth, the ten volumes of trial testimony (the typewritten notes of the official stenographer) and the "Scrapbook" containing the newspaper and magazine clippings of the trial were housed in the safe of the Special Collections Division. These sources were helpful in illuminating some of the issues involved in the Bartlett controversy and developments in the larger society. I also used the seventh census, 1850, and the tenth census, 1880 (Population Schedules, Manuscript Records of the Census), for locating the occupations of the fathers of the members of the classes of 1851 and 1881. These records are on microfilm. They can be found at a variety of locations, including the special divisions of the New York Public Library, particularly the Schomburg Center. (I also found some of the old City Directories helpful in ascertaining the occupations of the fathers.)

The numerous printed primary sources were also very helpful in providing biographical data and illuminating changing notions of community and other historical shifts. I found these sources in the Special Collections of the Dartmouth College Library and in the New York Public Library (especially the Main Division, the Education/History/Social Science Division, and the branch on Forty-third Street and Tenth Avenue). The various classes often printed booklets on their freshman year, sophomore year, and so on. As alumni, classes, such as the class of 1881, produced histories of their classes, including biographical sketches. Student newspapers and magazines also provide insights into the students of the period, as do the various announcements printed by students and alumni. Printed addresses by various faculty members, alumni, trustees, and the Dartmouth College presidents before Dartmouth groups and other organizations outside the college highlight changing perceptions of the various groups in the college community. The printed catalogues also contain useful information including residences of the students during college, course of study, costs, scholarships, prizes, changing occupations of the alumni, and so forth. I also found the general biographical dictionaries and encyclopedias located in most libraries helpful in supplying additional biographical information. Autobiographies and biographies of individual faculty members, alumni, and Dartmouth College presidents provided insights into the various groups and the periods under question. This material was supplemented by the histories of the college; by materials on the town, New Hampshire, and the region; and by miscellaneous educational publications and general sources from the period.

Index